SCORELESS

Omaha Central,
Creighton Prep,
and Nebraska's Greatest
High School Football Game

JOHN DECHANT

Foreword by
GALE SAYERS

UNIVERSITY OF NEBRASKA PRESS | LINCOLN AND LONDON

Library of Congress Cataloging-in-Publication Data
Names: Dechant, John, 1983– author.
Title: Scoreless: Omaha Central, Creighton Prep, and Nebraska's greatest
high school football game / John Dechant; foreword by Gale Sayers.
Description: Lincoln: University of Nebraska Press, 2016. |
Includes bibliographical references.
Identifiers: LCCN 2015044538
ISBN 9780803285729 (pbk.: alk. paper)
ISBN 9780803295100 (epub)
ISBN 9780803295117 (mobi)
ISBN 9780803295124 (pdf)
Subjects: LCSH: Football—Nebraska—Omaha—History. | Omaha Central
High School (Omaha, Neb.)—Football—History. | Creighton Preparatory
School—Football—History.
Classification: LCC GV959.53.063 D44 2016 | DDC 796.332/6209782254—dc23 LC
record available at http://lccn.loc.gov/2015044538

Set in Sabon Next LT Pro by M. Scheer.

CONTENTS

List of Illustrations . . vii

Foreword . . ix

Prologue . . 1

Part 1. The Fundamentalists

Chapter 1 . . 5

Chapter 2 . . 25

Chapter 3 . . 49

Part 2. Fall 1960

Chapter 4 . . 63

Chapter 5 . . 84

Chapter 6 . . 100

Chapter 7 . . 135

Part 3. Scoreless

Chapter 8 . . 163

Chapter 9 . . 181

Part 4. As Good As It Gets

Chapter 10 . . 211

Chapter 11 . . 224

Epilogue . . 233

Acknowledgments . . 241

Bibliographic Essay . . 245

ILLUSTRATIONS

1. Central football coaches Frank Smagacz
and Jim Karabatsos . . 23

2. The "new" Creighton Prep, pictured around the time
of its 1958 opening . . 27

3. Assistant Principal C. T. Shinners, S.J. . . 30

4. Creighton Prep history teachers . . 46

5. Assistant Coach Tom Brosnihan . . 53

6. The consummate All-American boy Gale Sayers . . 66

7. Senior class vice president Maris Vinovskis . . 80

8. Fred Scarpello . . 82

9. Prep quarterback Mike McKim . . 87

10. Size matters: Prep's powerful linemen . . 99

11. Don Leahy demanded respect and execution . . 103

12. Prep runner Rich Cacioppo . . 107

13. Gale Sayers running the hurdles . . 117

14. Huddled up—the 1960 Omaha Central Eagles . . 120

15. Don Lee, perfect beat writer for high school sports . . 122

16. The Central High cheerleaders . . 132

17. Don Leahy's sideline communication . . 148

18. Vernon Breakfield finds running room . . 152

19. Don Leahy rallies his team during halftime . . 156

20. Bill Pycha . . 159

21. Howard Fouts . . 170

22. Central quarterback Jim Capellupo . . 178

23. Omaha Central coach Frank Smagacz . . 191

24. John Bjelland snags runner Ardell Gunn . . 193

25. Creighton Prep supporters at a postseason banquet . . 226

26. Prep and Central at Rosenblatt Stadium in 2010 . . 234
27. Tom Jaworski . . 235
28. Participants from the 1960 game met again in 2010 . . 236
29. The demolition of Rosenblatt Stadium . . 239

FOREWORD

THE LONGER I'M RETIRED from football, the larger the legends of those old games seem to grow. I'm sure most former football players are guilty of this sort of thinking. Fans, too. I suppose that's okay. But in the case of the 1960 game between Omaha Central and Creighton Prep, let me tell you . . . the legend isn't far off from the facts.

Some call that Central versus Prep game the greatest high school game ever played, in Nebraska at least. Are they right? Some say yes. I say maybe. I'm sure of one thing, though: it's the best high school game I ever played in.

That whole season on the football field was a great escape for me. For four quarters every Friday night, I could take my mind off the college recruiters, the schoolwork I needed to finish, and the uncertainty of my future. It was just football, and it was pure. Much has changed about football in general since 1960, and the effects have trickled down to the high school game. Passing is more prevalent. Athletes today are bigger and faster. Coaches are now more prepared than ever before. And the kids spend nearly every day in the offseason playing seven-on-seven, lifting weights, and looking for advantages once the season starts. Sometimes I wonder what it would be like playing today. I'm sure retired coaches wonder whether they could still call a game today, with all that's changed.

Central High meant a lot to me and to my older brother, Roger. We made great friends there, students and teachers alike. And we had the sort of coach, Frank Smagacz, whom every parent wishes for their child. All these people played an important part in our lives, and we're both so grateful to this day.

That season came down to one very important game. It was our offense against their great defense, and boy what a show we put on that night. My teammates and I had a great deal of respect for Creighton Prep and their coach, Don Leahy, so we knew what was in store. I doubt anyone in the crowd would have guessed what was about to happen, but I don't think you'll find too many complaints.

For a game that was played mostly in the trenches, it came down to a Central touchdown and a penalty flag that's still argued about today. You can guess what I think, so I won't waste any ink here writing about it. I'll let you make up your own mind about that play.

I'd like to give my best to the coaches, the late Frank Smagacz and Jim Karabatsos of my own team and Don Leahy of Prep. Cheers to my former teammates and to the guys on the other sideline. Finally, I cheer this effort to record the story of the 1960 football season for all time.

Enjoy this volume, which I'm hoping will make you feel like a member of the huge crowd that night. I have to say, had either team won, the story would be greatly diminished. It's all here, and I'm happy to say those of us in the book lived it.

Gale Sayers
Central High School, class of 1961

SCORELESS

PROLOGUE

ON THIS DAY IN 1957, it seemed every Jesuit priest at Creighton Prep High School wanted Tom Brosnihan by his neck. Even the Jesuit superior general (sometimes called the Black Pope), had he not been in Rome, might have lined up to tongue lash him. Why, they wondered, did Creighton Prep's frosh football coach elect to play his squad on such a hideous afternoon? A persistent fog had crawled into Omaha at midday on this cooler-than-normal Friday in September, and a light drizzle soon followed. The drizzle had turned to rain by the time the game kicked off, and now the football turf at Creighton University Stadium was under attack from a swarm of cleat-wearing fourteen- and fifteen-year-old boys with little regard for the playing surface beneath them. By game's end, the field would be turned to mud, and there would hardly be a playable surface for the varsity game later that night. The frosh game meant little, really—just an opportunity to gain some experience and settle neighborhood bragging rights. What was Broz thinking?

The kids didn't seem to mind. They sloshed around in the rain, which amounted to a third of an inch, wearing mismatched hand-me-down uniforms and barely adequate helmets with facemasks they assembled themselves. It was the first freshman game of the season, and they were eager to play. One player from Omaha Central, Prep's opponent, was so excited to don football gear for the first time, he borrowed his sister's white shoe polish to cover up all the old scuffs and dirt marks on his helmet. It might have glistened like a pearl the night before, but after two hours of exposure to the rain, his teammates looked over and saw white streaks of shoe polish running down his black face.

The action started fast. Central running back Vernon Breakfield ripped off a 40-yard touchdown run late in the first quarter to give Central a 6–0 lead. The extra point missed. Breakfield was part of a promising young backfield that Central rooters expected to be a handful for opponents during the next four years. Freshman coach George Andrews was trying to surround the speedy runners with better line play, and he hoped to find the answer from "several husky frosh."

Creighton Prep runner Rich Cacioppo ran the third-quarter kickoff all the way back to the Central 1-yard line, and Prep scored a play later to tie the game at 6. Again, the extra point missed. The rest of the game was dominated by defense, and when it ended, the score remained tied, 6–6. There was no overtime, so the tie would stand. That night, the Creighton Prep varsity squad "splashed" its way to a 44–6 win over Thomas Jefferson High School on the same field, "covered in goo" that made it nearly impossible to decipher jersey numbers from the sidelines. Another Omaha high school game that Friday night was postponed to spare the field from damage caused by the rain.

This rainy outing was the first Prep-Central game for these young men. There would be more, but only one would be remembered as *the* game—the one they would argue about in retirement; the one they'd tell their grandkids about; the one that would earn them honor in their respective alumni bases. Three cold Nebraska winters would come and go before that game, a game that would decide more than neighborhood bragging rights among freshmen.

Some would consider it the greatest high school football game in Nebraska history.

1

The Fundamentalists

CHAPTER 1

FRANK SMAGACZ KNEW BETTER. So did a few of his upper-classmen. What seemed like 130 young men, each with aspirations of joining Omaha Central's football program, had turned up for the squad's first formal practice at seven o'clock that sultry August morning in 1960. The sight of that many teenaged boys on the cocklebur-infested practice field must have been eyepopping, at least to the untrained eye. Not so for Smagacz, nor his assistant, Jim Karabatsos.

The numbers wouldn't last, and they knew it.

The coaches had seen this sort of first-day turnout before. Central's two previous squads each numbered thirty-three players, and both underwent attrition during the first week of practice. To say attrition was the coaches' goal would have been an overstatement; it was simply a natural outcome of sweat and fatigue, the realities of high school football practice.

"By tomorrow afternoon," Smagacz assured Karabatsos, "we'll have our team."

Half of the estimated 130 wouldn't even make it to the three o'clock practice that first day. A few more stragglers brave enough to show up the next morning would find any number of reasons not to come out again for the second afternoon session: no water breaks, for one; heat exhaustion; too much running; cold showers; no grass on the practice field; even a mouth full of dirt-covered teeth. These were valid excuses in the minds of those who'd had enough of Omaha Central football. They would have to find another activity for the fall.

As third-year cornerback and backup running back Gayle Carey put it, "They cut themselves."

In 1960, Principal J. Arthur Nelson was responsible for "piloting Central High School's missile of knowledge," according to the school's annual *O-Book*, its yearbook. By the *O-Book*'s account, Nelson was a proficient administrator who had "manned the controls for 16 prosperous years" at Central High. His rise to Central's top administrative office included stops at nearby Midland College, where he earned a bachelor's degree; the University of Nebraska, where he earned a master's degree; Monroe School, where he served as principal; and Omaha North High School, where he served as assistant principal. His genuine dealings kept him on good terms with the student body, and caring for his prize-winning irises kept his disposition amiable away from the job.

The space race theme was sprinkled throughout the 1961 *O-Book*'s 156 pages. The yearbook's slogan, "Launching pad to the future," was as aptly coined as the following student-written epiphany: "There is a sadness in leaving Central behind. It is the same sadness you always feel in relinquishing any part of your life to which you can never return. But this is not the end; you are about to be launched on another phase of your flight."

As for the actual space race, America's seven Mercury astronauts, not yet household names, played the waiting game until the day when one of them would be the first man launched into space. Astronaut Scott Carpenter suspected that moment would come in early 1961. Others—with last names such as Grissom, Glenn, Shepard, and Slayton—projected confidence and dedication to the mission of their newfound profession. In 1961, Carpenter's prediction was proven prophetic when Alan Shepard became the first American in space.

Located at 124 North 20th Street in Omaha, Central High

School seemed as far away from Cape Canaveral as any student cared to imagine. Perched atop a hill on the north side of Dodge Street, Omaha's main east-west artery, Central's façade stood stalwart against even its most notable neighbors, the Joslyn Art Museum and Creighton University. If the stately building on the hilltop seemed to passersby more like a house of justice and government affairs than a high school, it's probably because the Nebraska Territory's capitol once sat there in the days before Nebraska became a state. That structure was eventually removed so Central High could be constructed on the prime piece of property. Inside Central, separate stairways surrounded the school's courtyard and segregated the sexes. Boys used one stairway, girls the other, since separate bathrooms were located on the landings between floors. The 1960 ninth-grade class, numbering 370 students, promised to be the "last large freshman class" to enter Central, due to the opening of Lewis and Clark Junior High, which the following year would start accepting ninth-graders.

Students could choose from a host of activities and clubs to pursue their extracurricular interests, including theater, choir, orchestra, concert band, journalism, debate, student council, math team, National Honor Society, Junior Classical League, Inter-American club, Latin club, German club, Russian club, French club, science club, library club, audio-visual club, Red Cross, cheerleading, Road Show (a two-act variety show that celebrated its forty-seventh year in the spring of 1961), Future Teachers of America, Future Nurses of America, homemaking club, chess club, outdoorsmen, Reserve Officers' Training Corps (ROTC), and the Greenwich Villagers, a group dedicated to exploring art mediums and vocations.

And, of course, Central offered athletics.

Academically, Central had earned a reputation as one of the city's finest schools. Some even considered it *the* finest. That fall, the *Central High Register* dubbed it "the Harvard of high schools." In 1955, Central began an experimental Advanced Placement program, offering students college-style classes in subjects such as English literature, physics, and Latin. Principal Nelson was hopeful that foreign languages, including French and Spanish, would soon join the AP offerings. The school even invested $8,500 in new equipment for the language laboratory, mostly special soundproof recording booths that allowed eleven different languages to be taught at once. (Not to the same student, of course.) In 1957, *Newsweek* named Central one of the top thirty-eight high schools in the country.

That same year, the Soviet Union launched Sputnik, the first artificial satellite to orbit Earth. The launch accelerated the United States' space race with the Soviets and triggered a trickle-down effect in education, to Central's benefit. Sputnik was the first perceived threat to the sense of invincibility that Americans had enjoyed since the end of World War II, and it signaled to educators the need to up the ante. At Central, that meant physics teachers were granted more funding and access to better materials, and students could learn Russian so as to be better equipped to handle the Cold War. Admission to a first-rate college, even an Ivy League school, was attainable with a Central diploma. "The kids were very aggressive academically," said assistant football coach Jim Karabatsos. "Athletically, we were kind of limited."

Those limitations occasionally allowed for a talented ballplayer every few years, but the coaches felt that Central lacked the athleticism and depth to compete with rival public high schools such as Omaha South, Omaha North, and Omaha Technical High, whose hallways seemed to be full of more well-built young men. "We just never had the numbers," said Karabatsos. "In a given year we might have twelve or thirteen good football players and then it really fell off. Whenever we had any injuries, we suffered through makeshift patches."

The blame for the talent drop-off could hardly fall on the coaches. Smagacz coached the track team and developed a good rapport with his spring athletes, recruiting some of them to come out for football. Karabatsos coached baseball, and many of his players also went out for football. Lack of recruiting wasn't the problem.

Facilities were even more limited than the supply of athletic young men. The football team practiced on a fenced-in patch of earth on the west side of the school that *Omaha World-Herald* sports columnist Wally Provost once deemed "the skimpiest football practice facility of any large school in the state." Measuring 60 yards long and 45 yards wide, the surface was mostly clay, full of broken glass and brick fragments that poked out of the ground and waited to catch exposed shins and forearms as players were taken to the ground. The only green the players ever saw was the cocklebur patches that grew around the field's outer edges. They were so prickly that players feared landing on them more than getting tackled. During stretches of particularly dry Omaha weather, two-a-day practices turned into dust cloud skirmishes only a Laundromat owner would have enjoyed.

Sometimes during two-a-days, the team would practice at Kellom Elementary, north of 24th and Cuming Streets. The team would rent a flatbed truck from a rental center close to Central, pile players into the back, and drive up to Kellom, their steel football cleats sliding on the slick surface of the flatbed the whole way there. Sometimes they went even farther north, to Adams Park. During the season, they would take a truck on Tuesday nights all the way out to Boys Town, located at 144th Street and West Dodge Road, to scrimmage "Skip" Palrang's team. The players loved it because it was the best field they practiced on, but the switch from hardpan to soft grass became the cause of frequent leg cramps.

In the cold winter months, Central coaches would sometimes take their athletes up to the school's third floor and run laps on the old wooden floorboards to build endurance. Smagacz would have a student manager or an assistant hold open the doors so the athletes could keep running without breaking stride.

The hardscrabble practice environment fostered a blue-collar sense of toughness in Central's football teams, but even the most workmanlike of attitudes can only take a team so far. Eventually it needs athleticism and talent to achieve a higher level of performance.

That's just what Central got when speedy Roger Sayers burst onto its sports scene by winning Nebraska state championships in the 100-yard and 220-yard dashes in 1958. Sayers also played football, and his blazing speed earned him the nickname "Rocket," along with all-city and all-state honors. As one former teammate remembered, "Roger's uniform and pads didn't slow him down at all." It seemed the only thing he did slowly was talk, but it didn't reflect a lack of intelligence. He was a fine student who appreciated the value of a well-constructed, well-spoken sentence. Roger Sayers represented the potential of Central High athletics. He was just one player, but suddenly it seemed that Central was capable of producing the type of athletes necessary to compete with its inner-city rivals.

The Rocket had a younger brother coming up through the ranks who had just as much talent. As a tenth-grader, he was slotted on the 1958 varsity roster as a running back. One '58 game day program transposed the letters of his surname, which may have caused readers to wonder whether the "Sayres" kid was related to the speedy Sayers boy. He put on fifteen pounds the following year, and a few people around the city started taking notice. By 1960, it seemed that everybody had heard of him.

His name was Gale.

The Omaha Central football program was "miserable" before Frank Smagacz arrived, according to one former coach. The team managed just 2 wins combined in the falls of 1948 and 1949, the two seasons before Smagacz's arrival. A 2-4-1 record in the '48 season helped claim a fourth-place finish in the Omaha Intercity League, Central's highest finish in four years. The team's best effort in the winless 1949 campaign was a hard-fought 14–12 loss to Omaha North, where, as the school's annual *O-Book* stated, the kids "played their hearts out." During one twelve-season stretch, Central failed to score even a single point against Lincoln High School, a key rival.

Victories over Benson, Omaha Tech, and Abraham Lincoln High Schools in the 1950 season, Smagacz's first at Central, quickly injected life into the football program and the student body. As Assistant Coach Jim Karabatsos remembered, "Frank came in and won a few games and they were ready to crown him king of Omaha."

Nail-biting 2-point defeats to crosstown rivals, no matter how hard-played, would no longer be the standard that Omaha Central would use to measure football success.

Smagacz's path upward through the coaching ranks to one of the state's largest and most competitive institutions began in his hometown of Columbus, Nebraska. Located about eighty miles west and north of Omaha, Columbus is situated along the north banks of the Platte River and its much smaller tributary, the Loup River. There his love of sports took root. The youngest of ten children, Frank grew up in a house of Polish immigrants, and Polish was often the language of choice around the Smagacz house. His father was a police officer, and at least one of Frank's older brothers joined their father in the profession.

Athletics became part of young Frank's persona during a successful sports career at Columbus Kramer High School in 1929–1933. He was a tremendous all-around athlete, garnering all-state football honors as a tight end and leading the basketball team to the 1933 Class A state championship. He earned three letters in football and basketball and two in track.

His success continued at the college level. After briefly considering Omaha's Creighton University—even enrolling, by at least one report—Smagacz matriculated at Midland College in nearby Fremont in the fall of 1934. Competing in football, basketball, and track, he earned ten varsity letters at Midland and was valuable enough that when he missed a basketball game due to a bout with the flu, as he did in January 1937, his absence was reported in the *Omaha World-Herald*. He was named a Little All-American tight end and years later became a charter member of Midland's athletic hall of fame.

Smagacz kept busy in the summer by playing catcher on the Fremont baseball team that played in the Elkhorn Valley League. He was no slouch on the baseball diamond, even considering his prowess in other sports. In 1939, after graduating from Midland, he joined the Duluth Dukes ball club of the Northern League in Duluth, Minnesota. The Dukes were affiliated with the St. Louis Cardinals organization, and Smagacz again donned a chest protector and facemask to play catcher. Nothing if not self-aware, he decided his thirty-five-dollar-per-game stipend was insufficient compensation for having to squat behind the plate for nine innings covered in protective gear, and Smagacz bolted from professional baseball to become a coach in his native Nebraska. It was a choice that shaped the rest of his life.

Offered a job at tiny Silver Creek High School located along Highway 30 about twenty miles southwest of Columbus, Smagacz decided to accept the offer for a yearly salary of $990. Shortly after taking the job, he received a better offer from the school district in Arlington, Nebraska, also located along Highway 30, nine miles east of Fremont. The

Arlington job paid $1,150, and Smagacz could little afford to turn down the money. He presented his case to the Silver Creek school board and politely asked for a release from his contract. The school board granted the release, provided Smagacz serve his first week on the job, presumably to allow the school district time to find a suitable replacement.

The Arlington stint lasted two years before a more lucrative offer came his way from Tekamah, Nebraska. Almost an hour's drive nearly due north of Omaha, the Tekamah school district wanted Frank Smagacz for more than just his coaching talents. The town's baseball team needed a catcher. He was paid a salary of $1,400 per year to coach football, basketball, track, and summer baseball. The $5 bonuses he received for each game he caught for the baseball team were icing on the cake. Competition in the Pioneer Night League was fierce and drew sizeable crowds to small-town ballparks scattered across the Nebraska prairie. Tekamah's town team was used to winning, and their ball club's newest member fit in well. The Tekamah sports fans took a shine to Frank Smagacz, and family members would hear of his baseball exploits from townspeople for years.

Tekamah was an essential stop in Smagacz's life, where in addition to gaining valuable coaching experience he also cut his teeth in the classroom where he taught math and science. He also found a life partner. Shortly into his tenure, he was introduced to Frances Tobin, the daughter of an Irish farmer, by a matchmaking Tekamah sports booster named Gordon Bryant who thought the pair would make a cute couple. It turned out Bryant was right. She went by "Fran" and had grown up on her family's farm, three miles north of town. Fran was a working girl, holding down employment as a secretary at the county courthouse. Frank and Fran were married in 1940.

Just like the job at Arlington, the Tekamah job, at least initially, lasted two years. This stint was interrupted—not by a more lucrative offer, but by World War II. In 1942 Frank Smagacz began a four-year hitch in the U.S. Navy. He and Fran also welcomed their first child, Mike, that same year.

Smagacz completed his basic training at Great Lakes Naval Base north of Chicago before being sent to his duty station at Fort Pierce, Florida. Though his naval service never sent him overseas, he spent considerable time and effort dodging the likes of John Polanski, Hampton Poole, Bill Daley, and other football stars, some of them professionals, who joined him during his two seasons playing tight end and defensive end for Fort Pierce's Famous Amphibs football team. Smagacz liked to joke that nobody knew his identity among the high-profile stars in the Amphibs team picture. Poole, a four-year veteran of the NFL's Chicago Bears, served as the team's player-coach, and Smagacz soaked up as much of the Bears' system as Poole cared to dispense, perhaps knowing it would one day become a staple of his own coaching toolkit. "The competition is plenty keen," Ensign Smagacz wrote to the *Omaha World-Herald* in 1944. "But it keeps a fellow in good shape."

Smagacz didn't make the trip to Florida alone. Fran and baby Mike came too, and the family grew when Fran gave birth to their second child, Mary. They found a house on the beach, but oceanfront living lost some of its luster after hurricane-force severe weather swept through Fort Pierce during their stay. Thankfully, they survived unscathed.

Aided by his four-year degree, Smagacz attained the rank of chief petty officer, but he was no career navy man, and when his hitch ended in 1946, he returned to Nebraska and resumed coaching, this time for the University of Nebraska baseball team. His tenure as the head of Husker baseball, while successful, lasted just one season (1946) while he earned a master's degree at the university on the GI Bill. His team posted an overall record of 9 wins and 7 losses, with 7 of the wins and 5 of the losses coming in conference play, good enough for third-place honors in the Big Six Conference. The Smagaczs lived in Tekamah, and Frank commuted nearly ninety miles by car to Lincoln every day.

One season of Husker baseball was enough, and Smagacz returned to coaching Tekamah athletics the following year. Tekamah was a good fit for Frank and Fran and their young family. They lived in a small house three blocks north of the high school and grade school, close enough that Mike could walk back and forth to school by himself. Frank's likable personality made him a hard man to turn down when called upon for a favor; at least that's what a few of his baseball players found out when he asked them to help dig out a basement for his house. The team pitched in, making the project an underground success.

In the summer of 1949, Smagacz took his American Legion baseball team to Omaha to play in what was deemed the "biggest midget baseball push in Omaha history." A total of 161 teams descended on Omaha that June and July to compete in twenty-three leagues on twelve ball diamonds over the course of a month. Smagacz decided a heavy dose of city competition was just what his small-town boys needed, and he brought his "lads" to Omaha twice a week to play in the Fontenelle League. "We need such competition to build ball players," he told the *Omaha World-Herald*. "Tekamah Legionnaires believe it will be more than worth the cost."

When Frank wasn't teaching or coaching—or playing, for that matter—he could usually be found near a sporting event. He officiated area basketball games for many years until his aging knees, sore and overused from years of hard contact and lots of squatting behind the plate, made it too painful for him to run up and down the court. In the summers, if he wasn't coaching, he could be found umpiring baseball games.

"He was always hustling to make extra money," remembered his son Mike.

He was a well-liked official, at least by one man, Frank Knapple, dean of boys at Omaha Central High School. So impressed was Knapple by the up-and-coming coach from Tekamah—who boasted a record of 45 wins and just 7 losses in six football seasons, including a 34-game winning streak—that he asked Smagacz to come teach and coach at Central High.

Smagacz took the job.

It's unknown how heavily the decision to leave Tekamah for Omaha weighed on Frank. Or Fran. Whether they spent a series of restless nights mulling over the offer or gave Knapple a "yes" right on the spot, in the fall of 1950, Frank Smagacz became a math teacher and the head football coach at Omaha Central High.

Frank and Fran found a house at 2876 Newport Street in Omaha's Miller Park neighborhood and kept a small vegetable garden along the railroad tracks nearby. Later, they moved to 1015 Mercer Boulevard, in the Cathedral neighborhood. Their kids, at least the ones old enough for formal education, attended elementary and grade school at Blessed Sacrament, a Catholic school in close proximity to the family's first Omaha home. The Smagacz family, growing at an almost alarming rate, would ultimately number ten children: Mike, Mary, Ann, Pat, Pete, Jean, Tracy, Tony, Rose, and Suzi. The ever-expanding number of Smagacz progeny became a friendly running joke among Frank's friends at Central. The school's student newspaper, the *Central High Register*, even placed a column after Jean's birth, noting that their beloved coach had become "indifferent to the whole procedure" of fatherhood after he fell asleep while waiting for Jean's 5:30 a.m. delivery. "Well, only eight more boys for a football team," the article's author quipped.

There was tremendous competition among the children, especially the boys, but the Smagacz kids all looked out for each other. "We just kind of looked at the older ones as role models," said Rose, the second youngest. "My older sisters were like my second mom. They were fifteen years older than I was.

"It was a good Catholic family. Hard-working. Everybody just pulled together and got things done. Mom was very organized. She had to be because Dad was not home, always working. But when he did come home, we knew he was in control. We respected him."

"Dad wouldn't let us get by with anything," echoed Mike. "Mom was pretty docile. She was a typical mother, making meals and stuff like that, making sure the house was clean. Dad was pretty domineering with us. We never wanted to buck him. None of us smoked or drank or did anything like that."

With his short hair and sturdy build, wearing the look of a man full of energy, Frank Smagacz looks like one of the guys in Central's 1950 football team photo. His presence seemed to breathe life into even the photo, the most mundane of team rituals. Wearing white jerseys, padded pants, and black high-top cleats, the players stood erect, each with his hands clasped behind his waist, chest sticking out. They look like a group that had something, or someone, to play for. Mel Hansen, one of the team leaders from the previous season, excelled in 1950, earning all-city and all-state recognition. He duplicated the all-state feat that spring as a member of Coach Tom Murphy's baseball team. Other football team leaders included Jack Lee, Bassie Johnson and Joe Prucka, each winning all-city honorable mention.

A year after Smagacz's arrival, fate walked through the door to the coach's office in the form of Jim Karabatsos. With no prior relationship—Karabatsos had only read about Smagacz in the newspapers—the pair struck up an easy friendship that first summer.

Karabatsos was full-blooded Greek and had been raised near 15th and William Streets in South Omaha, near Saint

Wenceslaus Church. A student at Omaha South High School, Jim knew that his parents John and Georgia relied on him to bring home a few dollars each week to help make ends meet, so he delivered newspapers instead of going out for sports. "My paper route brought home important money for the family," he said. "I was a kid when the Depression hit. My dad had lost his job with the railroad. He was a gandy dancer. He put the ties and rails down and kept the switches clean. He got laid off from the railroad and went down and washed dishes at some restaurant. I was twelve and old enough to carry papers, so I got a route and carried them my freshman, sophomore, and junior years."

Entering his last year of high school, Karabatsos couldn't take standing on the sidelines any longer. "I just *got* to have a chance to play," he begged his parents. They relented, and he joined the South High basketball team. He turned out to be a natural athlete. That spring he played baseball, and he continued playing that summer with an American Legion team. He grew up poor, but Jim Karabatsos and others like him in South Omaha were determined to make something of their lives. Success in athletics felt like progress toward that objective.

"I grew up right down there in the middle of town with Bohemian people and Italians. A big mix," he said.

"Surprisingly a great many of those kids went on to become lawyers and dentists and pharmacists and what-have-you. So it proves that psychologically you don't always have to have all the advantages. They worked hard and made something of their lives. I was always proud of that."

Karabatsos hoped to make something of his own life directly out of high school by joining the navy. He was just seventeen. With another son already in the army, his parents refused to sign the papers to allow his enlistment, so he chose to enroll in college at Omaha University. That lasted only a semester, and he was drafted in May. Like Smagacz, he completed basic training at Great Lakes. A superior officer was reviewing his test scores and noticed he had a semester of chemistry and biology under his belt from Omaha U. and told Karabatsos he was going into the hospital corps.

Karabatsos was sent to San Diego, California, for a six-week training course before his transfer to a naval hospital in New Orleans. Karabatsos joined a baseball and basketball team at the New Orleans base, and a sports-crazed commander froze him and his teammates on the base for nearly a year while they watched all their buddies ship out for overseas duty. The commander eventually let them go, and Karabatsos headed for Okinawa, a series of small islands that compose the southernmost prefecture in Japan. While Karabatsos was en route, the Americans flexed their military muscle by dropping the second atomic bomb, and by the time he arrived in Okinawa the war had all but come to an end and peace accords had begun.

A points system had been established for discharging soldiers, but it was dramatically skewed in the favor of older, married soldiers rather than young, single guys like Karabatsos. With his discharge date uncertain, he joined a group of seamen headed to North China to operate a sick bay that cared for a Marines unit and a Navy Seabees outfit. Working as a medic, he serviced American troops in the area, many of whom were responsible for aiding a large contingent of Japanese settlers who had been living in North China since the 1930s. The settlers had established schools, hospitals, and other essential community services, and the American troops were loading them onto boats and helping them return to Japan. Karabatsos spent close to ten months in North China before returning to the United States the following June.

Back on native soil, he enrolled at Creighton University in Omaha and completed a degree in English. He also played basketball and baseball for Creighton as an undergraduate. He decided to pursue a master's degree, and during his time as a graduate student at Creighton he became part of a memorable day in Omaha sports history: October 17, 1948. It was that Sunday—with a temperature of just forty-seven degrees, better suited for football than baseball—that Karabatsos took the field, the baseball field to be precise, in front of ten thousand paid fans to play on the opening day of Omaha's brand-new million-dollar Municipal Stadium (later known as Rosenblatt Stadium). The exhibition pitted a team of Major Leaguers, including starting pitcher Rex Barney, who had pitched a no-hitter the previous summer for the Brooklyn Dodgers, against the Johnny Monaghan Storz team. Karabatsos's role in the game came rather suddenly: "The pro team didn't have enough players, so I got a call that day asking if I wanted to play," he told the *Omaha World-Herald* years later. He made the most of his opportunity, delivering a pinch-hit single in his only at-bat on a chilly afternoon that left many players with numb fingers and cleared out the stands long before the game was decided.

It was also during his time as a graduate student that Karabatsos decided he wanted to be a coach. It was clear he had a passion for athletics, but he lacked a coaching pedigree. Having played just one year of high school sports, a few years of college athletics, and no organized football, he knew he had much to learn.

He found it in the library.

Karabatsos noticed an emerging trend in the coaching profession: successful, big-time college and professional coaches had turned to the publishing world. Books were becoming the latest coaching megaphone, capable of reaching a much wider audience than coaches could reach on the field or in the gymnasium. One of his favorites was George Allen's *Complete Book of Winning Football Drills*, which Karabatsos remembers as a delightful "little paperback." It was 570 pages. Allen's other notable titles include *How to Scout Foot-*

ball and *George Allen's Guide to Special Teams*. Jack Mitchell's book on defense also became required reading for Karabatsos, and in it he learned about the most popular defenses being used by college and professional teams. He absorbed the lessons, learning each position's responsibilities for every kind of in-game play call imaginable. His favorite defensive alignment was the 5-4, predicated on sound fundamentals and little stunting.

"Every successful coach was producing a book to make a little money," Karabatsos said. "If any of those guys wrote a book I'd grab it right away and read the whole damn thing. There's wonderful stuff in those books."

His approach worked. He was hired as assistant football and basketball coach at Shenandoah High School in Shenandoah, Iowa. A year later he was hired at Omaha Central to coach the football and basketball reserve teams and teach English.

He made an impression on Smagacz immediately. All it required was a simple observation and a little gall. And his encyclopedic knowledge of George Allen's *Complete Book of Winning Football Drills*. "The thing I really learned from that book, and he wrote it right in the front of the book, was to incorporate into your drills things that you actually do in the game," Karabatsos recalled matter-of-factly. "He said it was silly to do something that didn't somehow pertain to the game.

"I told Frank, 'You know, we start practice warming up and we have two lines of guys go out for passes. It's kind of stupid, Frank, to have tackles and centers and guards running out for short little passes. They'd be better off spending their time doing something else that was more closely adaptable to the blocking and tackling they were called on to do in a game.'"

Smagacz agreed, and he appreciated his assistant's candid observation. Central changed its practice routine right there on the spot. From then on, every practice drill had a game-specific purpose.

After two years on the job, Karabatsos was promoted to varsity football assistant coach. He also became Central's head baseball coach, a post he would hold for nine years. Given his lack of coaching pedigree, he must have felt satisfied, especially considering his first few years at Central were something of a coaching jigsaw puzzle. Tom Murphy was a member of the Central coaching staff when Karabatsos arrived, serving as head baseball coach and Smagacz's varsity football assistant. Murphy also taught physical education, and Karabatsos would sometimes voluntarily give him a hand during baseball practice. They became good friends—so good, in fact, that Karabatsos asked Murphy to be a groomsman in his 1952 wedding. Two seasons after Karabatsos arrived, Murphy left Central to take a job at Omaha Technical High School. The move was complicated and stemmed from Tech's coach, Ken Kennedy, requesting dismissal from the Tech job. Kennedy was sent to Central to assist Smagacz, and Murphy went to Tech to coach the reserve squad. Murphy and Karabatsos remained friends, and eventually Murphy left coaching to join the insurance business, where his polite manner and likable personality served him well.

At Central, Kennedy coached the Eagles' line play, but ultimately the experiment of having two head coaches on the same team didn't last. Kennedy left coaching for a job at Russell Sporting Goods, and Karabatsos was named assistant to Smagacz.

Karabatsos and Smagacz got along well together, both on and off the athletic field. Karabatsos and his wife, Lucy, welcomed their first child in 1954, and three others followed in '55, '59, and '61. All were girls: Kathy, Lynn, Kristine, and Mary. Frank's kids were older, and if the Karabatsos family ever needed a babysitter they could choose a member of the capable Smagacz brigade.

Fig. 1. Whistles in hand—Central football coaches Frank Smagacz, *left*, and Jim Karabatsos, *right*. Photo courtesy of the Central High Foundation.

At football practice, Karabatsos primarily coached the defense and Smagacz the offense. When the squad broke into units, Smagacz worked with the linemen and Karabatsos taught the offensive backfield. Smagacz trusted his assistant completely and let him put his own stamp on the defense. That meant implementing his favorite aspects of Jack Mitchell's 5-4 scheme. Inspiration came from other places, too.

"You pick up things from everyone," said Karabatsos. "We used to go to coaching clinics. We broke down into small units. A coach like Ara Parsehigan from Notre Dame or somebody from the University of California or Tennessee would come and explain their overall philosophy. Then they'd break down the kicking game, defensive schemes, and offensive football. So we picked up information that way.

"And I read damn near everything I could find. I had to learn the game. I hadn't played college ball because Creighton had dropped the football program. Some of my buddies went to other schools and played, but I decided I wanted to get a good education. I knew I might have a chance to coach, so I had to get a major and be capable of teaching a subject, because that's what schools hired you for. Coaching was kind of an aside. They paid about one hundred dollars and let you go."

Karabatsos also had contact with his coaching icons in writing. Fishing around one offseason for an offensive advantage, he became enamored with the unbalanced-T formation being used by Michigan State coaches Duffy Daugherty and Clarence Lester "Biggie" Munn. Karabatsos wrote to the Michigan State coaches asking for more information about the unbalanced-T. When the letter arrived in East Lansing, Michigan, it was funneled down the command chain to a young assistant coach, likely with instructions to answer in as much detail as necessary. Perhaps the Michigan State coaches were public relations-conscious and hopeful that open communication with high school coaches would pave the way for a recruiting pipeline if capable prospects ever became available. Or maybe they were just being polite.

A few weeks later a three-page response arrived at Central explaining the Spartans' offensive system and the necessary steps the Central coaching staff would need to follow to implement the T formation's many variations. Karabatsos and Smagacz put the information to use, trying out different T hybrids such as the split-T, wing-T, and unbalanced-T.

Karabatsos kept the letter, and it sat in a drawer in his home for the rest of his life. The young coach who wrote him, a graduate of Alma College who got his feet wet coaching Michigan high school football before joining the Michigan State staff, personally signed the letter.

He was none other than future Nebraska coaching legend Bob Devaney.

CHAPTER 2

IT SEEMED EVERYBODY AT Creighton Prep High School was conscious of Don Leahy. As a teacher, coach, and eventually athletic director, he was the consummate authority figure. When he spoke, there was little doubt he knew what he was talking about, whether he was lecturing students on history and political science or addressing a group of boosters about Prep's football program. When he walked down a hallway, there was no question who was in command. There was a certain absoluteness about Leahy, and it started with his flattop haircut, which looked as neat and tidy as the always-buttoned sport coats and skinny neckties he wore in the classroom and on the sidelines. Leahy, who also coached Prep's baseball team, even posed for the team photo wearing a tie and jacket; so did his assistant coach, George Kocsis, likely at Leahy's suggestion. Prep's students—if they wanted to stay in his good graces—were expected to show Leahy and his fellow faculty members respect. Those who did were treated in kind. Those who didn't were shown the quickest route toward the exit, care of the Rev. Charles Thomas Shinners, Prep's bulldog-like assistant principal and chief disciplinarian.

Such was the nature of Omaha's most prominent parochial high school.

"There's a little bit of God in Don Leahy," one of his former quarterbacks once said. "Like John Wooden. A very quiet person, but people respected him."

When Leahy stood in front of the student body in the Prep

gymnasium in the early fall of 1960 and told the assembled mass of Prepsters that his football team was adopting the slogan "Third Straight State" as its mantra for the upcoming season, there was little reason to doubt him. After all, Leahy said it, so it must be so.

Creighton Prep was going to win its third-straight Nebraska state football championship.

To say anything else could have caused panic. Everyone at the school was used to winning. Prep's 1958 and 1959 title runs had set the bar, and anything less than a state championship would have been disappointing to players, fans, and students—but most of all to Leahy. As Leahy scanned his list of players returning from the previous year's team, there was no question in his mind that his squad had the talent and leadership necessary to vie for the title he fully expected to win. Success on the football field was nothing new to Creighton Prep's all-male student body. Nor was a quest for three straight state championships, their having accomplished that feat in the 1932–34 and 1953–55 seasons.

Creighton Prep High School was a single, long, blond-brick building located at 7400 Western Avenue in Omaha. "Way out in the country back then," remembered one former student.

The student's memory is correct. When Prep students looked west from the school's parking lot they saw nothing but farmhouses and cornfields as far as their eyes could wander. It would be years before the urban sprawl would transform the mostly untouched landscape into shopping malls and housing developments, gas stations and office complexes, golf courses and soccer fields. Even the landmark John A. Gentleman Mortuary at 72nd and Western Avenue, which for years greeted members of the Prep community on their way to school each day, wouldn't be built for another eight years.

Prep students came from all over the city. Three to four

FIG. 2. The "new" Creighton Prep, pictured around the time of its 1958 opening, was a state-of-the-art center for carrying on the Jesuit model of education. Photo courtesy of Paxton & Vierling Steel.

Prep-bound city-run buses picked up students along Omaha's busy Dodge Street from downtown all the way out to 72nd Street before heading north toward the school's parking lot. By the time the buses reached Prep they were nearly full of freshmen, sophomores, and upperclassmen who were either too young to drive or had no access to a car. This was the new Creighton Prep, built in 1958, full of creature comforts that Don Leahy and his fellow faculty members had previously only dreamt about. Modern classrooms. Lockers for every student. Pleasing vistas.

"We thought that was the Taj Mahal," Leahy recalled later. "We had so much space. That was the west end of Omaha back then. Crossroads Shopping Center hadn't even been built yet."

Only the Jesuit priests, whose permanent residence wouldn't be built until 1961, had reason to complain. Some of the "Jebbies," as they were known, found lodging in two houses southwest of the school while others took refuge in unused classrooms. The Rev. J. J. Labaj, S.J., principal of Creighton Prep, established residence in a narrow utility closet in the school's gymnasium. The closet's door was plain-looking, the type students expected to open up to racks of inflated basketballs or tennis racquets. Instead, it housed a cot and Labaj's modest collection of personal belongings.

Prep, since its formation in 1878, had operated under the auspices of Creighton University until it had become evident in the middle part of the twentieth century that each school would stand a better chance for success by operating autonomously. Land west of Western Avenue, once owned by Mr. Matt Scanlon, was purchased in 1953 for $50,000, and fundraising for a new school began in earnest in 1956. The new, 105,000-square-foot building was finished two years later, free of debt, at a cost of $1.6 million.

Considered "the Jesuit high school of Omaha," according to the 1961 *Jay Junior* yearbook, Prep was one of forty-three Jesuit high schools in the United States and one of hundreds in the world "teaching eloquent, well-rounded young men how to live and work as Catholic gentlemen." Two of those young men, Francisco Cifuentes and Wilfried Arzt, added an international flavor to the student body. Both were exchange students. Cifuentes, "a small, black-haired, lively boy," was from Santiago, Chile. At Prep, he was often seen lugging a suitcase through the halls. It held his textbooks from various fields of study: Spanish, French, physics, even philosophy. With a "flashing smile" and "ready wit," the German-born Arzt fit in well at Prep, even organizing the school's chess club. There were few classmates who could keep pace with Arzt on the chess board. Together, the two exchange students conducted a panel discussion with the Senior Sodality Council, where they spoke about Catholics in their native countries.

The Very Reverend John J. Foley, S.J., celebrating in 1960 his Silver Sacerdotal Jubilee to commemorate twenty-five years of priesthood, was Prep's president. Born and raised in Whittemore, Iowa, Father Foley had spent much of his life in the Midwest. His administrative career included stops at Marquette High School in Milwaukee, Wisconsin, where he spent thirteen years as principal; Creighton University, where he worked one year as assistant dean; and the Creighton University School of Medicine, where he spent six years as a regent.

"The Jesuits, Prep's hearty band of educators, are Prep's prime movers," the *Jay Junior* noted. "They are the sculptors who, with skilled and versatile hands, mold the men that Prep produces. But they only guide and instruct; the student must educate himself."

Among the mostly Jesuit faculty, the Rev. C. T. Shinners, S.J., assistant principal, figured most prominently in the lives of students. In his role as chief disciplinarian, the youthful-looking Father Shinners was a perfect fit. Students respected him, or at least feigned reverence, fearful of getting rammed headfirst through a locker door. He was the John Wayne of 72nd and Western Avenue. A smoker, he had little tolerance for the habit in his students, and he owned what seemed like the world's strongest pair of binoculars, which he used to spot students hiding out to sneak a few puffs over their lunch break.

The Jesuits at Creighton Prep ruled by discipline, and their primary method of enforcement—aside from occasional physical confrontation—was known as JUG, or Judgment Under God. Each student was allowed a maximum of forty demerits per semester. About the size of a driver's license, demerit cards were inscribed with verbiage that cut right to the point: "After acquiring five demerits for one offense (or if teacher keeps card), report to JUG the same day." Demerits were handed out like floss at the dentist's office, and any

FIG. 3. Assistant Principal C. T. Shinners, S.J., commanded respect from Creighton Prep's all-male student body. Reprinted with permission of the 1961 *Jay Junior*.

time a Jesuit or lay faculty member saw a student fall out of step with the school's conduct policy, the student was given a demerit. A student could even be given a demerit for failing to carry the card on his person. Machiavellian students somehow found access to extra cards, thus hedging against serious punishment. Five demerits resulted in an automatic JUG, an hour-long after-school session of academic exercise or physical equivalent, and forty demerits meant expulsion. "To be reinstated," the demerit cards read, "bring your parents for a conference with the school's authorities."

If a Jesuit was feeling ornery, a JUG session could last upward of ninety minutes. Parents rarely complained to the school if their sons arrived home late for chores or dinner because of JUG, and coaches rarely accepted JUG as an excuse for missing practice. If nothing else, Prep taught its students time management. The Jesuit models of education and discipline worked, at least at 7400 Western Avenue. Generations of doctors, lawyers, community leaders, and successful Omaha businessmen got their high school diplomas from Creighton Prep.

The lines between Jesuits and civilians were sometimes blurred, and the hierarchy was even more confusing for outsiders. Certain members of Prep's faculty, usually younger than administrators such as Fathers Foley or Labaj, wore clerical clothing but were addressed as "Mister" instead of "Father." These men had not completed the process of Jesuit formation and therefore were not yet priests. One of them was P. J. Connelly, S.J., and civilians unfamiliar with Prep would become noticeably confused when they overheard students addressing the Roman-collar-wearing scholastic as "Mr. Connelly."

The results of an eighth-grade admission exam determined who became part of Prep's student body—and who didn't. The test also laid the groundwork for a homogenous, competitive ranking system that grouped students according to academic performance. There was an A class, a B class, a C class, and so on. Freshman rankings were determined by the entrance exam, and students could move into a different class during their four-year careers if classroom performance trumped their test scores.

Prep was competitive in the classroom and equally competitive on the athletic field. Decades of proud football tradition began in 1932 with Prep's first Nebraska state championship and continued right on through Don Leahy's playing days in the 1940s. From 1932 to 1959, the school amassed a staggering thirteen football state championships.

Eighteen lettermen returned in 1960 from the most recent state championship squad, including two-time letterwinners John Bozak, Rich Cacioppo, and Tom Jaworski. The 1959 team won 7 games and lost only 1, and an undefeated season seemed well within the realm of possibility in 1960. Most observers considered Prep one of four favorites to vie for the intercity and state titles, along with Omaha Tech, which boasted as much raw talent as any team in Omaha; Lincoln High, led by fleet-footed running back Bobby Williams; and Omaha Central, whose roster included a talented triumvirate in the backfield consisting of Vernon Breakfield, Ardell Gunn, and 1959's intercity scoring champion and only junior selected to the *Omaha World-Herald*'s all-intercity league team in 1959, Gale Sayers.

Leahy surmised the path to the title would go through Sayers and the Central Eagles. "He had such a great junior year, I knew he was going to be a handful to stop. I had watched him play, and he was just amazing."

Years of coaching experience had taught Leahy not to address a future opponent with his own team, at least not until the week of the game. It was a new season and a new team, and he and his staff would be starting over from scratch, just like always, on a hot sunny day in August.

Don Leahy never thought of himself as a farm kid, although he had reason to. Raised on a family farm about sixty-five miles south of Omaha in Peru, Nebraska, he, like future coaching counterpart Frank Smagacz, was the youngest of ten children. Don was five years old when his parents divorced and his mother moved him to Omaha. Soon Don began moving around frequently, living with older brothers and sisters off and on while his family situation got settled. Omaha became one stop among many. Farm life drifted away in the rear view mirror.

Some of his older siblings attended Peru State College. Three of his four older brothers played high school football, and his brothers John and Bill went on to play collegiately at Creighton University. Because of the age difference and the divorce, Don attended very few of his brothers' football games, but he saw enough at a young age to develop an appetite for the sport.

When Leahy arrived as a freshman at Creighton Prep in the fall of 1943, few, if any, could have imagined the titanic imprint he would leave on the school and the city of Omaha over the course of his life. Athletics was the first place he left his mark. He earned two varsity letters in football, two in basketball, and three in baseball. He became a permanent fixture in the starting lineups of all three sports during his junior and senior years at Prep, even serving as captain of the baseball team. He played summer baseball, too, filling spots in the outfield, on the pitching mound, and at third base for an Omaha American Legion team.

As quarterback of Prep's football team, which played its games in the double-decker Creighton Stadium that stood in the shadows of Prep and its parent university, Leahy earned all-metro honors while leading his team to a city championship. As a senior, Leahy threw 14 touchdown passes and kicked 13 consecutive extra points.

Leahy's playing days at Prep laid the foundation for his

own coaching career, and the exposure he received to different styles of teaching football proved invaluable. Before the final game of Leahy's junior year, Prep coach Morrie Pratt invited a visitor, a young-looking man in a military uniform, into the Prep locker room. He was Don Fleming, a former player at Creighton University, who would become Prep's coach the following season. Fleming believed passionately in keeping football simple, and he hated complicated terminology. It drove him nuts to see grown men invent complicated concepts just for the sake of looking good on the football field.

Fleming's no-nonsense approach made sense to his young quarterback.

"You're a coach," Fleming told Leahy years later while explaining his philosophy. "You have to remember that you've been doing this for years. But this is the first time around for these young people, and you've got to make it simple so they can understand it and accept it and put it into operation."

Fleming knew what he was talking about. He was a state champion coach in Wisconsin, Iowa, and Nebraska. When he coached the football team at Omaha's Holy Name High School, his offense once used the same starting signal on every down of football they played for an entire season. His team would huddle up and then hurry to the line of scrimmage, get set, and snap the ball quickly, almost on the run, before the defense could get set in proper alignment.

Set and go. Set and go. Over and over again.

Fleming's prototype hurry-up offense gave his team a tremendous advantage. Once or twice a game, he told his players not to snap the ball. The team would break the huddle, hurry to the line of scrimmage with the same gusto they'd been using all game, and then lock into their stances and wait for the other team's defensive line to jump offsides trying to anticipate the snap of the ball. The tactic drew a penalty flag nearly every time. Fleming believed not so much in *what* was being executed as in *how well* it was carried out.

Leahy's successful high school career presented the opportunity to play collegiately, and he chose Marquette University in Milwaukee, Wisconsin, at the recommendation of Bob Pazderka, a standout center from Creighton Prep who entered Marquette a year ahead of Leahy. Pazderka subsequently transferred to West Point to join the army, but his absence did little to change Leahy's mind about Marquette. Creighton University had dropped its football program in 1942, so following his brothers' path to his hometown university was no longer an option. Leahy stayed at Marquette, and no doubt his familiarity with Jesuit education made the decision an easy one. So did the presence of two other members of Prep's 1947 graduating class, Richard Peters and Jim Green, who joined Leahy at Marquette on football scholarships.

Standing 6' tall and weighing 180 pounds, Green packed a lot of punch on the football field. He played tackle at Prep and specialized in knocking defenders on their backs. Marquette head coach Frank Murray noticed Green's enthusiasm for the gridiron immediately. "He lives for football," Murray told a newspaper reporter. "It's all he can do to keep still when he is not in a scrimmage."

Leahy and Green, in addition to working on the same railroad gang over the summer, became roommates at Marquette and developed a close friendship, like "two peas in a pod," claimed an article in the *Milwaukee Journal*.

Coach Murray had Green pegged as a pass rusher, but Leahy's future was under center. At 6' tall and weighing about 170 pounds, Leahy had a strong arm and a smiling disposition that all quarterbacks were supposed to have. Freshmen were prohibited from playing varsity football in those days, so Leahy had a year to learn Marquette's offense under Murray's tutelage. His offensive education took place among

130 other aspiring players on Coach Art Krueger's freshmen team. The frosh squad's primary duty to Marquette football was preparing Coach Murray's varsity unit by running the plays of upcoming opponents during the weeks of practice leading up to games. Murray specialized in running the single wing and T formations, and a plaque commemorating his 1959 induction into the Wisconsin Sports Hall of Fame credited him as "an early exponent of spread formations and flanker plays." Leahy learned enough of the offense that when Marquette took the field against the Iowa Hawkeyes for a season-opening road contest in his sophomore season, he found himself on the field, starting at quarterback.

His first taste of college football was bitter. One play ended his season and nearly ended his career.

As Leahy took his stance under center, the Iowa defensive line shifted, leaving an open space over Marquette's right guard. Leahy noticed the shift and changed the play to a quarterback sneak. The ball was snapped, and Leahy darted past the defensive line and moved quickly into the Iowa secondary. The play was wide open, and Leahy knew it meant big yards. Iowa's safety came up to make an open-field tackle, and Leahy twisted around to avoid contact. As he spun to the ground, another player's knee smacked him in the head, directly above his right eye. Like all players in those days, he wore a leather helmet with no face mask.

The punishing hit resulted in a skull fracture and a brain concussion, and Leahy spent a week in an Iowa City hospital, abruptly ending his first eligible season of college football. His teammates' prospects were only slightly better. They dropped a hard-fought battle to the Hawkeyes in the game's final minutes, 14–12. Marquette compiled a record of 2 wins and 8 losses that season, the worst record in Frank Murray's nineteen seasons at the university.

No right-minded person would have blamed Leahy if he had put an end to his football career right there in his hospital bed in Iowa City. He could have retreated to a more relaxed college life, his head buried in a textbook and his mind on an upcoming fraternity party. But he was no quitter, and he was tough.

Leahy's return to the field was aided by a reunion of sorts when Don Fleming, his former coach at Creighton Prep, joined the Marquette staff as backfield coach after an assistant coaching stint at the University of Washington. Leahy was ecstatic when he heard the news and knew what was in store for his Marquette mates in the backfield. The Marquette offense seemed to hit full stride when line coach Lisle Blackbourn was promoted to head coach after Frank Murray's 1949 retirement, likely spurred by a series of health problems.

Dubbed "plain spoken" and "rugged" by Marquette's annual *Hilltop*, Blackbourn was an energetic coach, "perpetually working." His inaugural season (1950) at the helm of Golden Avalanche football ended with a record of 4 wins, 4 losses and 1 tie. Leahy's emergence as an offensive threat came late in the season against Holy Cross. Trailing 19–14 in the homecoming game's deciding minutes, Leahy and teammate Jim Tobias came off the bench together to connect on a key fourth down conversion. Tobias snatched Leahy's pass from the grasp of two defensive players in the end zone for the go-ahead touchdown, and Marquette held on for the 21–19 win. "LEAHY TO TOBIAS" was the homecoming headline.

As a senior, Leahy quarterbacked the Golden Avalanche through an eleven-game schedule, the longest in fifty-nine years of Marquette football. It was also one of the toughest. The team's 4-6-1 record wasn't indicative of its grit, nor did it cause the enthusiasm of the student body to wane. Highlights included a hard-fought loss to the University of Wisconsin in front of forty-six thousand fans in Madison's Camp Randall Stadium and a near upset of top-ranked Michigan State, 20–14. So impressed with the Marquette team was Michigan State coach Biggie Munn that he proclaimed them the Spartans' "toughest opponent." Leahy shone that season, finishing third nationally in passing average and gaining 1,543 yards rushing, good enough for seventeenth-best nationally. His standout senior year even earned him the right to play quarterback for the North squad in the annual Blue-Gray College All-Star game. A caption beneath a photo of Leahy stepping up in the pocket to deliver a pass that ran in the 1952 *Hilltop* declared what Marquette fans thought of their beloved quarterback: "Leahy + blocking = touchdown."

Don Leahy, at least on the campus of Marquette University, had become a star.

Leahy's prolific Marquette career left him with a choice to make about his future. His options included an offer from Marquette to stay in Milwaukee and coach the 1952 freshman team—a job that could possibly have led to an ascent up the Marquette coaching ladder—and the chance to pursue various "pro offers" he was receiving because of his passing prowess. A third and seemingly less attractive proposition also emerged: return to Creighton Prep to coach and teach. A job had opened at his alma mater to teach social studies and work as an assistant football coach under Head Coach L. G. Friedrichs. Leahy decided to take it.

Friedrichs, a player-friendly coach whom Leahy described as an "extremely good motivator" and "efficient classroom teacher in mathematics," had a project for his new assistant. Friedrichs wanted to switch from a single-wing offense to the T formation, and Leahy—familiar with the T from his Marquette days—was just the man for the job.

"He wanted to switch totally to the T, so we took the entire offense I brought from Marquette and installed it 100 percent that first year," Leahy said. "I appreciated him giving me that kind of leeway."

One of the reasons for the switch was a desire for offensive balance. If Creighton Prep could become equally proficient at running and passing the ball, Friedrichs and his offensive-minded assistant figured, it would become less predictable and more difficult for opposing defenses to stop. Friedrichs and Leahy set a goal of 150 yards passing and 150 yards rushing every game. Leahy called the statistical benchmark an "ideal balance." Opposing coaches probably thought the concept was bunk. High school football in the 1950s consisted of running, running, and more running. Capable passing quarterbacks were rare. Receivers who could run routes and consistently catch passes were just as hard to find. Leahy disagreed and eventually changed the stereotype.

"We threw the ball much more than other high school teams in my early years," he said. "Everybody thought you shouldn't pass until it's third down and 12 yards to go, and we changed that. We thought the best passing down in high school football was first down. It's the best passing down at any level. Defensively, you just didn't know what we were going to do. It created opportunities on each play."

Leahy's utopian offensive vision was aided by "Magic" Mike Dugan, a dazzling high school quarterback capable of making all the throws necessary to make a passing offense flourish. Other Omaha-area high school coaches could only dream about calling plays for such a talent.

Praised by the *Omaha World-Herald* for his "now-you-see-it, now-you-don't football wizardry," the 6'1", 175-pound T formation prodigy led Prep to undefeated seasons in 1953 and 1954, earning spots on two all-intercity and all-state *World-Herald* teams. Dugan excelled in other arenas, too, including baseball, basketball, and the classroom, where he made the honor roll all four years. But football was his sanctuary. His season total of 57 points won the 1953 intercity scoring title, a feat equaled a year later by teammate Bob Varley, who scored 54 points.

In Dugan's 1954 Prep finale against Omaha Benson he completed 8 of 13 passes for 118 yards, recovered 2 fumbles, intercepted a pass, made numerous tackles and even knocked down 2 pass attempts late in the game to preserve a 32–13 win and extend Prep's winning streak to 18 games.

Dugan was a winner, every time out.

He finished his senior season at Prep completing 64 of 113 pass attempts for a 15-yard average, totaling 989 yards for the season. Dugan's fantastic high school career would lead him to the University of Notre Dame, where he played behind eventual Heisman Trophy winner Paul Hornung. "Modest" and "scholarly," Dugan was tailor-made for Don Leahy's offensive system. His understanding of football was so complete that "Magic" Mike even earned Leahy's trust to call his own plays in the huddle.

Leahy's stature as an assistant coach rose on the heels of Prep's mastery of the T formation. He was young and talented, and, by virtue of his recent participation in major college football, he possessed cutting-edge knowledge of the sport's most recent innovations. It was no surprise that he would be linked, as reported by the *Omaha World-Herald*, to other coaching jobs. One rumor making the rounds in Omaha in 1956 pegged Leahy as the top candidate for the coaching job at Iowa State University following Vince DiFrancesca's resignation, but the gossip was quickly put to rest when Leahy and Iowa State athletic director Louis Menze issued public denials. Leahy was flattered to be thought of so highly but had not even applied for the job. When his college coach, Lisle Blackbourn, left Marquette to become head coach of the NFL's Green Bay Packers in 1954, Leahy was offered the chance to reunite with Blackbourn, apparently as a player and a coach. His boss L. G. Friedrichs's aspirations to coach college football were well known around Creighton Prep, and sensing a chance to become Prep's head coach in the future, Leahy passed on the NFL. Blackbourn's tenure with the Packers lasted only a few seasons, and he would return to coach Marquette in 1959, becoming party to a sudden, sad episode in Marquette athletics when the university dropped its football program on December 9, 1960, because, as the Rev. Edward J. O'Donnell, S.J., reported to the Marquette fan base, the school was no longer able to support its cost. For Blackbourn, who had a framed photo of Leahy from his playing days displayed with pride next to portraits of other football stars on a bookshelf behind his desk, the news was surprising.

For Don Leahy, the future at Creighton Prep came sooner than expected. In 1955, L. G. Friedrichs took a job coaching St. Ambrose University in Davenport, Iowa, where he was offered a three-year contract. Leahy was named Creighton Prep's head football coach. At twenty-six, he became the first alumnus to return to Prep as its head football coach and the youngest head boss in the intercity league.

"It's a little early to refer to this as a lifetime ambition, but I've had it in my mind ever since I played ball at Prep," he told sportswriter Don Lee of the *Omaha World-Herald*.

An underwhelming start to his head coaching career would have been forgiven in light of the standards set during Prep's dominant run before he took the program's reins. L. G. Friedrichs had won twenty games in a row to finish his tenure, with an overall high school record of 78-15-1, establishing Prep's foothold atop intercity football. Leahy was unburdened by the lofty expectations and guided his team to a third-consecutive undefeated season in his inaugural campaign. Prep posted a 15-1-1 combined record during Leahy's first two seasons on the job, a mark that quickly defused any speculation that Prep had erred in its coaching hire.

One of the secrets to Leahy's success was the capable band of assistant coaches in his stable. They included Dudley Allen, a product of the U.S. Military Academy who joined Prep in 1955, the same year Leahy became head coach. Allen—who was given the nickname "Dud," a moniker that for obvious reasons he never grew to appreciate—filled L. G. Friedrichs's teaching slot on the math faculty and served as Prep's defensive coordinator and offensive line coach. He also agreed to become Prep's head track coach. Allen was the same age as Leahy, and their relationship dated back to their high school playing days. Allen had attended Abraham Lincoln High School in Council Bluffs, Iowa, across the Missouri River from Omaha, where he played fullback and multiple positions on the defensive line. His exposure to first-rate coaching was unmatched. During his time at West Point, Vince Lombardi was in the midst of a five-year assistant coaching stint; also on the army staff was Murray Warmath, who in 1960 would lead the University of Minnesota to a Rose Bowl appearance and national championship season.

Allen and Leahy got along well for many reasons. For one, their wives—Don's wife, Carmen, and Dud's wife, Kay—worked together. Their love of football formed another bond. Allen admired Leahy's organization and efficient use of practice time. He also appreciated a coach who was willing to throw the football.

When Allen accepted the job at Creighton Prep, he received a bottom-line piece of advice from his predecessor as math teacher, L. G. Friedrichs. Allen had come up through the coaching ranks in Valley, Nebraska, a much smaller school than Prep with fewer, and likely less talented, athletes. Friedrichs knew that Allen would be amazed by the potential he saw in his new crop of players. "Potential makes no difference," Friedrichs told him. "Here you're going to see a lot of kids that can play, and the only thing that's going to count is what they actually do. Performance is the only thing that counts."

Allen took the advice to heart.

Bernie Berigan, a 1948 Prep alumnus and close friend of Don Leahy, worked as a volunteer assistant for Prep, first under L. G. Friedrichs and then under Leahy. Berigan, a year younger than Leahy, had followed his pal's path to Marquette University, and the two were roommates for a few years until Berigan got married or, as he put it, "changed roommates." Berigan and Leahy got along well together. Berigan admired Leahy's dedication to his faith—he prayed a rosary every night at bedtime—and to helping others.

After graduating from Marquette, Berigan took a job teaching and coaching at St. Cecilia Parochial School in Hastings, Nebraska, 160 miles southwest of Omaha. The next year he left Hastings to join his family business, the Berigan Brothers Livestock Commission Company, in Omaha. His workdays in the stockyards began at 5:00 a.m. and ended in the early afternoon, which freed him up to work at Prep as a volunteer coach specializing in line play. His players liked him, except when he brought his favorite coaching utensil to practice, a fraternity paddle he used to whack players on the rear end if he didn't like the look of their stance. Berigan and his paddle got results.

Leahy trusted Berigan completely and admired his knack for teaching the game's fundamentals. Together the pair installed the Marquette offense and added a few new wrinkles to make it unique to Creighton Prep. Berigan earned more notoriety after his days at Prep when he started the Omaha Mustangs, a semiprofessional team that was a strange but highly successful mix of barbers, construction workers, players from Canada, and former college stars who never made it in the NFL. Berigan coached the Mustangs for five seasons, and Leahy served as his offensive coordinator. Proving his resourcefulness, Berigan, with little money and nowhere to practice, approached Monsignor Nicholas Wegner and Coach Skip Palrang at Boys Town about using the school's fieldhouse to practice, and they agreed.

The Professional Football League of America was formed, and the Mustangs, boasting the league's finest practice complex, competed against teams from Lincoln, Grand Rapids, and the Quad Cities.

Over the years, other, younger assistants, usually Prep graduates, joined Leahy's staff, often in a volunteer capacity. Jack Jackson, a 1954 Prep alumnus, helped coach line play while he was still a college student and employee of the Union Pacific Railroad. Jackson did a little bit of everything for Union Pacific—switch tender, brakeman, switchman—and worked at the railroad's headquarters at the time of his college graduation. He became a jack-of-all-trades for Prep, too, when he was hired full-time in 1960 as a typing teacher, football assistant, and swimming coach. He barely knew how to type, but he learned from typists that you were supposed to keep your eyes looking up at what you were typing. He sat at his desk, instructing his students to start typing out of their books, and he threw chalk-covered erasers at anybody he caught looking down at their hands. He later taught economics and speech and worked as a counselor.

Jackson became friendly with Tom Brosnihan, another young assistant who coached football and basketball. Sturdily built, with a round face and sometimes wearing glasses, Brosnihan—called "Broz" by students and faculty alike—was well liked by everybody at Creighton Prep. Broz's round face helped him earn the nickname "Piggy," but few students ever said it to his face. During the 1961 basketball season, his first as head coach at Prep, Broz's team reeled off an improbable string of wins in the state tournament that led to a runner-up finish. It was a result that impressed some and annoyed others, but it shocked them all.

Leahy recognized in Brosnihan an impressive ability to motivate young people. It helped that the students admired him and responded well to his teaching methods. As a physical education instructor, Brosnihan continually invented unusual games to play during class, often taking a traditional activity like dodgeball and mixing in elements of basketball or baseball to come up with an off-the-wall hybrid with difficult-to-follow rules of play. The students loved it as long as they avoided injury. Although Brosnihan lacked the polish and command of language evident in his boss Leahy, his dedication to helping students reach their full potential made him a frequent (and rousing) speaker at Junior Jay pep rallies.

The success of the Creighton Prep football program continued to fuel speculation that Leahy would soon be headed for a higher-profile coaching job. The speculation quickly became reality in April 1957 when Leahy decided to accept a job at the University of California as varsity football assistant under Head Coach Pete Elliott. Elliott's ties to Nebraska stemmed from his employment in 1956 as the University of Nebraska head coach. Just twenty-nine years old, he guided the Huskers to a record of 4 wins and 6 losses before Bill Jennings replaced him the following season. During that time he met and apparently developed a professional relationship with Leahy.

Several days of phone negotiations between Leahy and Elliott reached a crescendo when Cal athletic director Greg Engelhard called Leahy one evening to inform him the job was his if he wanted it. The *Omaha World-Herald* reported that Leahy, just twenty-seven years old, would receive a starting salary of at least $7,000, and he was scheduled to fly to California on April 10, one week after the announcement was reported in Omaha, to begin the job. Leahy's closest friends organized a farewell get-together before he left town, and everybody at the party presented him with a goodbye gift. Leahy planned to leave for Cal, where spring practice was set to start on April 23, and his wife, Carmen, would stay behind in Omaha until he returned over the summer to settle his business affairs.

FIG. 4. Creighton Prep history teachers: (*left to right*) Tom Brosnihan; Rev. R. P. Neenan, S.J.; Don Leahy; Rev. R. B. Bargen, S.J.; Mr. J. S. Amrhein, S.J. Reprinted with permission of the 1961 *Jay Junior*.

Publicly, Leahy said all the right things about leaving. "Becoming associated with the University of California is a tremendous opportunity which cannot be by-passed," he told the *World-Herald*. "I shall consider it a privilege to work under the direction of a man the caliber of Pete Elliott.

"Naturally I regret leaving surroundings which have been so favorable in all aspects. I shall always be indebted to the Jesuit fathers, particularly Father Sullivan (the Rev. Henry L. Sullivan, S.J., principal) and Father Shinners."

Privately, the opportunity had developed so fast that he had failed to thoroughly research the job (and Elliott) to the extent one would expect from a man as exacting as Leahy. His first task when he arrived in Berkeley was recruiting. Elliott handed him a list of junior college and high school players he wanted recruited, and Leahy was floored when he saw the list included players as young as high school sophomores, just fifteen and sixteen years old.

The idea of preying on young athletes made Leahy uncomfortable, and he voiced his displeasure to Elliott: "Pete, I wouldn't even *allow* a college coach to talk to my players at this age. I don't feel right about it."

Leahy felt the same way about junior college players, believing that they should only be recruited after their final season of junior college eligibility.

Elliott didn't care for Leahy's opinion and was in no mood to parley with his new assistant.

The philosophical stalemate with his boss put Leahy in a bind. He realized he had made a mistake by not visiting Cal to check out the program before committing to the job. His wanderlust had momentarily gotten the better of him. It seemed he was stuck in an impossible situation, but then the phone rang. It was Bernie Berigan, calling to check in from Omaha.

When it became clear over the phone that Leahy wanted out of the Cal job, Berigan said, "Well, why don't you just come back to Prep?"

If only it could be that easy, Leahy thought.

"I don't know if they'll take me," he said.

Berigan told his friend he would call him back in an hour. He headed to Creighton Prep to find Father Shinners who, as part of his duties as assistant principal, served as athletic director. Prep had taken steps toward promoting Dudley Allen to replace Leahy as head coach, but the school had not yet made a formal announcement.

"Well, gosh, if you can get Leahy back, you'll sure take him, won't you?" Berigan asked Shinners.

"Well . . ."

Berigan knew he was putting Shinners on the spot. He also thought the school would be foolish to pass up an opportunity to bring back their beloved and highly successful coach. Shinners ran the idea up Prep's chain of command and informed Berigan once a consensus was reached.

Leahy could return. Berigan called to give Leahy the verdict.

"I spoke with Father Shinners," Berigan began.

Leahy held the receiver up to his ear and swallowed hard.

"And we decided you can keep the gifts from your going-away party if you come back to coach Prep, so come on home."

The relief in Leahy's voice came through the phone. In total, his dalliance with Cal lasted just nine days. It occurred during Prep's Easter vacation, so he failed to miss a single day of school as he remembers it. He told the *Milwaukee Sentinel* that he regretted leaving Cal but "my major interests are at Creighton Prep." From that point forward, Leahy committed himself totally to Creighton Prep and to Omaha.

"Everything kind of worked out," Berigan said. "Prep was happy to get Leahy back. And anybody would. What an outstanding gentleman. He was a great classroom teacher and an excellent disciplinarian. The kids all loved him. He was extremely successful.

"You know, I've never even heard him swear. He wouldn't say 'shit' if he had a mouthful. He's that kind of guy. I'm Irish, and if I hit my thumb with a hammer, I'll cut loose, but he might just say, 'Oh, gosh, that hurts!' I'm not the only one who will say that, either, I'm sure. I think an awful lot of him."

The power brokers at Creighton Prep thought an awful lot of him too. Don Leahy was headed home.

CHAPTER 3

THE SMELL OF BACKYARD barbecue at the annual Russell Sporting Goods coaches' party became as familiar to inter-city league coaches as checking out equipment or calling quarterback sneaks. There was hot food—lots of it—and cold beer, or soda pop if that was your preference. Many coaches brought their wives along to socialize. This yearly rite of passage signaled to coaches such as Frank Smagacz and Don Leahy that their favorite time of year, football season, was fast approaching.

Located at 1816 Farnam Street in Omaha, Russell Sporting Goods Company, having in 1960 been in business for more than eighty years, was one of two prominent Omaha sporting goods stores that supplied equipment to area high schools. The other was Hauff's, located nearby at 13th and Farnam. Russell's satellite operations in Lincoln, Grand Island, North Platte, and Scottsbluff—the latter located nearly five hundred miles due west of Omaha—were a clear indicator that the sporting goods business in 1960 was no sucker's racket. A guaranteed constituency of high school athletes aided business. Russell and Hauff's were the go-to suppliers of varsity letter sweaters, which cost a shade under $14.00 each. For another $2.25, a student could purchase the letter itself. Chevrons cost $0.45 apiece, the same amount customers paid for an All-American Meal at McDonald's, "the drive-in with the arches."

The Russell store's proprietor's annual gathering of the coaching fraternity gave coaches a chance to get acquainted off the field. Central's Jim Karabatsos struck up a close connection with Prep's Dudley Allen at a previous iteration of the Russell party, and they "became friendly," said Karabatsos. That friendship continued to grow as time passed. They'd bump into each other, sometimes at the grocery store or other spots across Omaha, and always took time to chat with each other, sometimes about football, other times about family. Allen was also close with Frank Smagacz, whom he had first met while coaching Valley, whose league rival was Tekamah, where Smagacz had coached.

"He was a hard-working guy," Allen said of Smagacz. "A fundamentalist."

Jim Karabatsos knew Don Leahy from his days as a student at Creighton University, where he had shared a campus with Prep student and football star Leahy. Karabatsos in those days attended most Prep games played at Creighton Stadium and had seen Leahy's playing career blossom before his own eyes. Now they were *both* coaches: competitors on equal footing.

"We had a high level of respect for Prep because we knew the quality of work that they did coaching their team. We knew we had to do a hell of a job to try and even keep up," Karabatsos said.

That level of respect wasn't reserved exclusively for Leahy and Prep. Clearly Leahy's nearly unbeatable teams in his first five years at Prep had established his place among the statewide coaching hierarchy, but in 1960 there were others with lengthier résumés. Smagacz, for one, was entering his eleventh season at the helm of Omaha Central. Of Nebraska's 208 high school football coaches, the longest-tenured was Ed Colleran of Spalding Academy, who in 1960 began his twenty-seventh season on the job. Ed Haenfler's twenty-two seasons coaching Grant placed him second. Legendary coach Maurice "Skip" Palrang in 1960 began his eighteenth season at Boys Town. According to at least one account, Palrang's tenure at

Boys Town didn't begin until Father Edward Flanagan was able to meet the coach's salary demands, a figure that Palrang thought was beyond the means of the humble community for homeless boys. Flanagan called his bluff and asked him to start immediately. Under Palrang's direction, Boys Town played a national schedule for many years that would have made many college coaches jealous, and the visibility earned the coach well-deserved recognition. Flanagan, a visionary in so many ways, appreciated the visibility the football team provided his orphanage. He also believed strongly in racial equality, and his football teams, with players of many races and colors, became symbolic of his own principles.

These long-tenured coaches proved to be the exception, not the rule. Turnover came with the territory. In 1960, eighty-five Nebraska high school football coaches were in their first seasons at their respective schools; forty-four were in their second years; and twenty-three were in their third years. The high school coaching fraternity wasn't one of means, either. The pay was barely sufficient, and most coaches taught classes ranging from history to physical education. Many coached multiple sports, and others officiated games to bring home extra money. Some, including Frank Smagacz in his later years at Omaha Central, taught driver's education during the summer. A group of Creighton Prep coaches including Jack Jackson, Tom Brosnihan, and Don Leahy did the same. Jackson recalls that he was the only one of the three properly certified with a driver's education certificate. Brosnihan, who often chewed tobacco, marked his territory with tobacco spit stains inside the doors of most of his driver's ed cars over the years. One particular night certainly could have brought his credentials under scrutiny, and the story, in one form or another, has survived in Creighton Prep lore ever since.

Brosnihan was supervising a group of student drivers one night when the phone rang at Prep for Father Labaj.

"Father, it's Broz," Brosnihan said. "Father, I'm in Carter Lake, and I'll be back a little late tonight."

"Well, that's all right, Tom," Labaj said, confused. "Just come on back."

"No, Father . . . see, I'm *in* Carter Lake."

Brosnihan's student drivers had driven toward Eppley Airfield, a couple of miles north of downtown Omaha, bordering on the town of Carter Lake, Iowa. The student-operated car started to swerve, and Brosnihan slammed on the emergency brake, causing the student to lose control of the vehicle completely and drive toward the 320-acre lake.

This is the point at which legend diverts from fact. Generations of Creighton Prep men have heard the story culminate with a sunken driver's ed car in the middle of Carter Lake. One of the students in the vehicle that night says the car never made it into the lake, yet its fate was nearly as catastrophic. Brosnihan was apparently fanatical about jets and loved driving by the airport to watch them take off and land. In the early days of jet travel into and out of Omaha, their presence was still a novelty. On this rainy spring night, the '61 Ford was driving along a frontage road that bordered Abbott Drive, which was still under construction. Brosnihan was scanning the sky, looking for jets, when the student driver encountered an uneven patch of road, which had by then turned to mud from the rain. The student momentarily lost control of the vehicle, and as Brosnihan felt the car start to swerve, he panicked and punched his foot on the instructor's emergency brake. The driver, attempting to correct the swerve, then totally lost control of the vehicle and it slid into a muddy ditch bordering Carter Lake. The passenger-side doors were jammed against an embankment, so everyone in the car had to crawl out through the driver's-side window. As Brosnihan tried to squeeze his bulky frame through the window, he split his pants. The incident left him unnerved.

FIG. 5. Assistant Coach Tom Brosnihan, pictured, moonlighted as a driver's education instructor. Reprinted with permission of the 1961 *Jay Junior*.

Brosnihan sent the student walking to the nearest pay telephone to call Father Labaj and explain the peculiar ordeal. Labaj told them he would send a tow truck, but what arrived was just a man driving a large pickup with a chain to extricate the car. Things went from bad to worse when that vehicle got stuck, splattering Brosnihan and his students head to toe in mud, so Labaj had to send for another tow truck, this time an actual wrecker, to pull out both vehicles.

The story, in its many versions, illustrates the wide-ranging duties thrust onto high school coaches and the diverse skill set needed to handle the job. Being a coach took more than just the ability to blow a whistle.

These sorts of shenanigans fostered a sense of togetherness among high school coaches. So did other parts of the job, like finding game officials, arranging transportation and securing fields to practice and play on. When Creighton Stadium was torn down, Prep's football team became a vagabond squad, playing games at Municipal Stadium, Benson High School, and other local venues. So competitive was the search for stadiums in Omaha that some athletic directors began scheduling varsity football games on Thursday nights instead of Fridays. Don Leahy was one coach who liked the arrangement because it afforded him the chance to personally scout upcoming opponents on the off night. Prior to Prep's 1958 move to the "new" Creighton Prep campus on 72nd Street, the school was located within earshot of two other inner-city schools, Omaha Tech and Omaha Central. In those days, when Prep played Tech at Tech, the Prep players would dress in their locker room at Prep and walk up the street to Tech for the game, then walk back to Prep when it finished. During track season, Frank Smagacz sometimes took his runners a few blocks up the street to the track at Creighton Stadium to practice baton handoffs and techniques for using starting blocks. In a competitive environment, a community-first spirit emerged.

Although coaching circles in 1960 may have seemed small, these coaches were part of something much bigger. America was embracing football at all levels. A report from the National Football Federation indicated that football, with more than six hundred thousand players, had the most participants of any sport in the nation's secondary schools. The majority of them played eleven-man ball (including a reported 185 eleven-man teams in Nebraska), while some in rural areas played on eight-man or six-man squads. Basketball was close behind in the participation race, track and field third, and baseball, the national pastime, was fourth.

Being a coach's wife was as demanding as coaching and

was often a more thankless job. For starters, your Friday nights during the fall were usually spent bundled up in the bleachers of a high school stadium surrounded by parents and other coaches' spouses while watching your husband's team play. You could forget about dinner and a drive-in movie or a night on the town. And if your husband coached other sports, those nights spilled into the rest of the school year. You reveled in the wins and suffered right along with your spouse during the losses, and you were responsible for a number of behind-the-scenes tasks that nobody ever knew about. During the first few years at the "new" Creighton Prep on 72nd Street, before the school had outfitted its athletic department with washing machines, Don Leahy and a student manager would show up at Leahy's house after practices and games with large containers full of sweaty practice jerseys, socks, and jockstraps for his wife Carmen to wash and dry. Don may have taught his players how to block and tackle, but Carmen was the person responsible for making sure her husband's squad looked—and smelled— like a winning team.

One likely topic of conversation at the Russell Sporting Goods party that evening was the ongoing 1960 Rome Olympics. Omahan Bob Boozer joined his college basketball rivals Oscar Robertson and Jerry West to help lead his countrymen to a gold-medal victory over Russia. Just weeks later, Boozer and the "Big O" would sign professional contracts with the Cincinnati Royals—contracts that were negotiated in Rome immediately after the games. Boxer Cassius Clay became the Olympic light-heavyweight champion in Rome, which began his sudden ascent into the national consciousness. In late October, Clay dominantly won his professional debut over small-town police chief Tunney Hunsaker in Louisville, Kentucky. The *Omaha-World Herald*'s coverage of the bout, likely borrowed from a national news service, carried the headline "CASSIUS BATTERS CHIEF OF POLICE," failing to mention that the police chief was off duty, the pummeling was sanctioned, and the fight occurred inside the boxing ring.

Other chatter between inner-city coaches likely included the upcoming football season. As *Omaha World-Herald* sportswriter Gregg McBride pointed out in an early September column, the 1960 Nebraska high school football season was scheduled to be one of the state's shortest on record. Teams were allowed to begin practice on August 22, and nearly all games were scheduled to be played by November 4, a noticeable contrast from previous seasons that sometimes stretched through Thanksgiving Day. There were no playoffs and no scheduled state championship game; at the time, no such postseason structure existed. The sprint through prep football contrasted with the marathon that was basketball season, a full four-and-a-half-month campaign in the middle of the cold Nebraska winter. "It is little wonder tempers flare during late February and early March games," McBride wrote.

McBride was also aware of the intensity Nebraskans reserved for football. Sensing the impending backlash over his weekly prep rankings, he wrote, "Fans can do well to start loading their pens and laying in supplies of asbestos writing paper."

McBride's prep rankings were his own creation, and football fans went nuts for them. No other Nebraska sportswriter had ever rated high school teams, or at least not in as much detail as McBride. He was an icon around Lincoln and out-state Nebraska. In a golden era of sportswriting, he was king. "Everybody knew Gregg McBride," said veteran Nebraska sportswriter Larry Porter. "He was revered. When I was in the seventh grade I became a *World-Herald* newspaper carrier. I would get two bundles because I had quite a big route. I would snap the wires off of one bundle and sit on the other pile to read the sports section before I ever made my deliveries. Gregg McBride was my hero, as he was everybody's. I said to myself, 'Boy, one day I would like to be Gregg McBride.'

"He liked to take trains when he traveled out-state. He would go out to Grant or Ogallala by train, and when the train came into town, the people knew that Gregg McBride was coming to cover their football game. The whole high school band would be at the train station to meet him and break into song for him. This was in a time when newsmen were revered. Out in the little towns, Gregg McBride was the man. He was the deliverer, the guy that gave everybody what they wanted to read. They were all enamored with Gregg just as much as any high school coach or player. If Gregg came to cover your game, you were special. A town's pride and manhood was wrapped up in its high school athletic program. Back then, that was all they had. There was no TV to turn on the NFL game. Life was funneled through the high school athletic programs."

McBride was described as a good journalist by other sportswriters, a man who would tenaciously pursue his craft. Those closest to him knew of his love for trapshooting, and he covered the state contest every year in Doniphan, Nebraska. His friends also knew him as a devoted practical joker. Once while eating in a restaurant with Tom Allen, another Nebraska sportswriting darling, and their wives, McBride pulled the maître d' aside and quietly passed him a few one-dollar bills. "This should cover what my wife's about to steal from you," McBride told the man.

"Well, what does she steal?" the maître d' asked.

"Toilet paper. She'll go to the restroom and steal a roll of your toilet paper. She always does it."

Halfway through the meal, McBride's wife and Allen's wife stood up and excused themselves to use the ladies room. McBride looked over at the maître d' and winked, as if to formalize their arrangement. When the wives returned, the maître d' kept staring at Mrs. McBride, trying to figure out where she had hidden the stolen roll of toilet paper. He was perplexed. He couldn't see it anywhere. Of course, she had never stolen a roll of toilet paper, and McBride was simply trying to get a laugh. Finally, McBride's wife, annoyed by the host's glances, stood up and said, "Gregg, make that man stop looking at me like that!" McBride smiled and winked casually to the maître d', signifying that everything would be all right. He had gotten his laugh.

Once, McBride was invited to an athletic banquet in Grant, Nebraska, a small community out-state, directly south of Ogallala. He had recently picked against the Grant team in one of his columns, and Grant had gone on to win the game in question. So the fine citizens of Grant served for their honored guest a plate of baked crow. McBride played along with the gag with great enthusiasm, even posing for a photo with a napkin tucked into the neck of his shirt and his knife and fork ready to attack the crow.

McBride was the out-state man, based out of the *World-Herald*'s Lincoln bureau. Don Lee, a prolific journalist in his own right who became famous for his coverage of Omaha's Ak-Sar-Ben racetrack, covered sports in metropolitan Omaha. Devoted readers who thought they noticed a touch of provincialism in the editorial stances of Lee and McBride were not imagining things. McBride, by virtue of his duty, knew more about athletes out-state than Lee, and Lee, by the same token, had the details for all the metro teams. Readers got a kick out of seeing Lee or McBride make a mistake in their rankings and didn't hesitate to let them know about it. Students at Creighton Prep thought McBride was sometimes unfair in his assessment of the Junior Jays, and his columns rarely escaped the attention of Don Leahy, who sometimes used them to motivate students at pep rallies. Leahy would hold up a copy of a newspaper and say, "Well, it seems our old friend Gregg McBride doesn't think we can win this week."

But make no mistake—any recognition Leahy and his team received was due in no small way to the sportswriting of McBride and Lee. They stirred the drink, and readers took note.

Nebraska, a state with just two legitimate metropolitan areas and countless small towns, used a class system to organize high school athletics. Class A comprised the largest schools, Class B the next largest, and so on. Class A included Creighton Prep, Omaha Central, and other inner-city schools. The only two schools from outside the metropolitan areas of Omaha and Lincoln to finish in Gregg McBride's 1959 top ten were Scottsbluff and Beatrice.

As a city, Omaha was—and has remained—a great sports town. If you didn't like sports, particularly amateur sports, there was a good chance you would be spending a lot of time by yourself. Talking sports was more than a way to pass time around the coffee pot. It was like flashing a membership card for the in-group, only everybody had one. The absence of a top-flight professional franchise in the city may have fueled the ethos. It seemed that everybody in Omaha, men and women alike, had at least a passive interest in athletics, whether it was University of Nebraska football or the local high school scene.

"Grade school girls in Omaha knew more about sports than most men in other cities," said a former Omaha resident. "The Dallas–Fort Worth area is a close second, but not with the intensity of Omaha. The girls I knew weren't going to get a date unless they knew all three sports seasons and knew facts from high school all the way through the pros. I don't care if she was the valedictorian and was going to major in physics."

In the fall of 1960, Omaha and its rabid sports fans would be treated to one of the more exciting seasons—and the best game—they had ever seen.

2

Fall 1960

CHAPTER 4

GALE SAYERS'S LETTER SWEATER was covered with so many stars and chevrons that it looked like the night sky. That's the way teammate Tim Nelson describes it. When Sayers wore the sweater into a high school gymnasium in 1960, he was impossible to overlook. If he was flanked by teammates Ardell Gunn and Vernon Breakfield, action around them virtually came to a stop so everyone could sneak a glance, half-expecting the seas to part in their very presence. Wearing the sweater, Gale resembled General Omar Bradley, festooned in regalia from neck to waist. One look at the thing, clad with reminders of his many athletic accolades, and you knew you were watching a shooting star. To go with it, he had a bright smile and a clean cut, all-American appearance. Sayers was the perfect star athlete: running back on the football team, a blur in track and field, decent in the classroom, and well-liked by his fellow students at Omaha Central. Even his opponents on the football field struggled to find anything negative to say about him. His name was on the tip of the tongue of anyone familiar with Omaha sports in 1959 and 1960.

Sayers was a shooting star, certainly, but that was his public persona. Those who knew him best thought he was fun but quiet, not a "rah-rah" type. He once confessed to the student newspaper that his most embarrassing moment was getting stopped by police for speeding while coming home from a track meet. Readers familiar with his athletic gifts were probably shocked to learn he was driving a car and not on foot at the time of the encounter. Gale seemed to care more about his friends than about the attention he received as an athlete, a personality trait that made him the consummate teammate. His coaches swore they had never seen a more coachable kid. But that's what you'd expect from a young man who once listed football as one of his favorite hobbies. Gale worked hard at practice, usually one of the first players onto the field and one of the last to leave. "He was just outstanding," Tim Nelson said. "And sometimes he got inundated with press and so forth, but internally he was basically one of the guys. He mixed very well with everybody on the team."

Public attention for exploits on the football field was nothing new to Gale Sayers. He had been exposed to that sort of celebrity through his older brother, Roger, who had taken the Omaha sports scene by storm at Central High. Roger was a state champion sprinter, an all-city football player, and a fine student. Surprisingly, Roger decided against playing football his senior year (1959) and instead focused his attention on track and field. The decision was aided in part by his mother's suggestion that he avoid the hard contact of football and bear down on his studies to win a college scholarship for track. It was a decision he later regretted, he said, especially after a pulled muscle in the spring that derailed his track season and limited his scholarship offers. He enrolled at Omaha University and ran track with great success, and eventually football coach Al Caniglia convinced him to join the team, even offering him a partial scholarship.

Gale was different. There was no keeping him off the football field. And there was no stopping him on it. He shared his brother's competitiveness and disdain for losing, but physically he was a different specimen. He was bigger, thicker, a more physical runner. Terry Mollner, who competed in track and field for Creighton Prep, said Sayers was a different class of athlete, altogether exceeding the normal physical traits of a typical teenager. "You know that crease that runs between your butt and your thigh? Well, Gale didn't have one. They were one continuous piece of muscle."

Roger could run past defenders with his blazing speed. Gale would run past most people, but he could also make them miss or simply run them over. Opposing coaches were terrified by his ability to reverse his field and turn potential losses into positive gains. And he was a terrorizing linebacker on defense, capable of disrupting entire offensive schemes. He could intercept passes, recover from over-pursuit by tracking down plays from the backside, and chase down ball carriers before they even made it through the line of scrimmage. According to the *Central High Register*, he averaged nearly 8 tackles per game.

"He had good speed and instincts for football," said Central assistant coach Jim Karabatsos. "I don't know how you teach that. I don't know how you teach how or when to cut. You can teach certain things, but he was like an animal chasing down another animal. An animal will dart and swerve and cut, and you can never predict how it will move. Gale would do those things automatically. He had that natural ability. Gale played within the system, but at times he could also break out of the system and do something special.

"He did everything we told him. He had the speed. He could hit. We knew we had a jewel there, something in the making."

"Heck of a player, even then, as a high schooler," said James Brown, a Central teammate. "He had the speed. Very fast. His second step, he was gone."

Terry Stickels, a former quarterback who played high school football during the tail end of the Sayers era in nearby Council Bluffs, Iowa, and played college football for the University of Nebraska at Omaha—and later for the semi-professional Omaha Mustangs—said that Omahans got to

Fig. 6. The consummate All-American boy—nobody could catch Central running back Gale Sayers in 1960. Reprinted with permission of the *Omaha World-Herald*.

see some of the best high school football talent around during the late 1950s and early 1960s, thanks in part to the Sayers brothers. "You can't name another backfield in America during that time that had the quality of talent as Gale and Roger Sayers," Stickels said. "The amazing thing was that everybody was aware of it. It wasn't like we all looked back twenty years later and said, 'Well I guess we didn't know what we had.'

"No, we knew. *Everybody* knew. There was something special going on. Everybody wondered, 'Is Roger Sayers really that fast, and is Gale really that good?' It was unheard of. If you could broad jump 19 or 20 feet in 1960, you were a hero. Here comes Gale and he nails a 24-foot jump. I saw that in the newspaper and thought it was a misprint."

During Gale's junior-year football campaign of 1959, he led the Omaha Intercity League in scoring, notching 68 points in intercity contests and totaling 79 points in all games. The scoring title was a Sayers family repeat, as Roger had won it in 1958 with the same 68-point total. Equally impressive was Gale's ability to land scoring strikes from anywhere on the field—long runs, short runs, kickoff returns. Field position didn't seem to matter to Gale Sayers. He could score, period.

Sayers was unquestionably a hot college football prospect, and his recruitment also made the news. University of Nebraska football coach Bill Jennings probably wished it hadn't, thanks to at least one particularly unflattering incident. Jennings was fielding questions at a Chamber of Commerce Gridiron Luncheon when a fan asked him why the Nebraska coaching staff had not visited the star runner from Central. The fan, claiming to have been informed by Central coach Frank Smagacz, also said he had heard that Big Ten Conference coaches were hot on the Sayers recruiting trail and he was most likely headed up north. The question put Jennings on the spot in a public setting. He did his best to diffuse controversy within this faction of Nebraska's success-starved fan base, telling the crowd that it was his policy not to contact players until the completion of the football season and that his staff, in fact, had written to Sayers and talked to him over the phone, even inviting him to a Cornhusker football game. Clearly, the fan was representative of most Cornhusker supporters who were anxious to see the state's homegrown talent play college football in scarlet and cream. Nebraska coaches and their fans would ultimately lament their relaxed attitude toward Gale's recruitment; coaches from other schools would wisely take a more aggressive approach.

By the time Gale was a senior, more than seventy-five college programs were offering him scholarships. That number is staggering enough to make any reasonable person wonder how he ever settled on one college. Gale visited some of these schools on recruiting trips—Iowa State, Nebraska, Notre Dame, and others—before making a decision. Ultimately, he chose to attend the University of Kansas, where he earned the nickname "The Kansas Comet."

Given his ability as an open-field runner, likening him to a comet seemed appropriate. He streaked across the Big Eight landscape like a celestial body. Gale seemed to know where the holes in a defense were going to be before they appeared, and when none were available, he'd run over whoever was in his way. Gale's 99-yard touchdown run against Nebraska in 1963 was a classic example of his running style. Kansas was backed up on its own 1-yard line when Sayers took a pitch 4 yards deep in his own end zone. He ran around the left end, slipped through two potential tacklers at the goal line, two more 10 yards downfield, and outran his remaining pursuers by midfield before covering the remaining half of the field untouched.

There was only one Gale Sayers.

Central High and Kansas were just the beginning for Sayers. The accolades that awaited him were unimaginable, even to his biggest fans. He became an All-American, a first-round NFL draft pick, the inspiration for the 1971 movie *Brian's Song*—which has a way of moving even the toughest men to tears—and a Pro Football Hall of Fame member.

A local fast food proprietor who operated Otoe's Drive-In, perhaps in an effort to scare up business on Friday nights, began a promotion during the football season of 1960 that awarded a gift certificate for the restaurant's Pookie Snack'n Burger to any player who scored a touchdown in a prep contest. A former Otoe's employee remembers the Pookie Burger as a double-decker hamburger with all the necessary accoutrements that we today associate with any value meal hamburger. For Gale Sayers, the Otoe's promotion was a license to eat himself silly. In three different games that season he scored 3 touchdowns, good enough for six patties' worth of Pookie Burgers. He ate so many Pookie Burgers that friends gave him the nickname "Pookie." Such are the sacrifices one has to make as a high school football star.

Life at home presented a stark contrast to the glitz and glamour of high school athletics for the Sayers boys. Their father, Roger Sayers, once a semiprofessional baseball player, polished cars for a living, earning between fifty-five and seventy-five dollars per week. A lot of that money went toward paying rent wherever the family was living. Originally from Nicodemus, Kansas, Roger moved to Wichita, Kansas, where the boys were born and where he worked as a mechanic for the Goodyear Tire and Rubber Company. Son Roger was born in 1942 and Gale came along thirteen months later, on Memorial Day 1943. A third son, Ronny, was born in 1948. Roger was eight and Gale was seven when the family lived for a short stint near Phillipsburg, Kansas, close to the Nebraska border. From there they moved to Omaha in 1951. A relative put them up for a few months until Roger Sr. found steady employment, and then the family moved into its own house, which began a vagabondish series of unsettling moves during the boys' adolescent years.

"We were all over," said Roger Sayers. "Our family was struggling from month to month."

"All over" generally meant around 30th and Lake Streets in north Omaha. Other stops included 27th and Lake, 24th and Pinkney, 27th and Grant, and 24th and Spencer. Money was tight. Sometimes the family had to go for weeks in the winter without coal for their furnace. In his autobiography, Gale recalled times when he and Roger became so hungry that they took their BB guns outside and shot catbirds, then fried one and ate it. "He didn't taste bad, either. When you're hungry, they all taste good," Gale wrote.

Gale also recalled relations between his mother and father souring—arguments, fighting, even temporary separations.

They weren't unlike other families in their predominantly black section of north Omaha. Most of the adult men in the neighborhood worked in the meat packinghouses of South Omaha. If the boys ever had money in their pockets, that meant they had a choice to make: use it to pay bus fare to school in the morning or use it to buy lunch. Lunch usually won out. As youngsters, they mostly walked to and from Howard Kennedy School. Same thing at Central High. Sometimes Roger Sayers Sr. would give them a ride on his way to work. In the winter they hitchhiked. Shift changes at the packinghouses coincided with the time kids walked to school, and the extra cars on the road provided more opportunities to hitch. If a police officer drove by and noticed a group of teenagers hitching, he'd stop and tell them to knock it off, which they did, at least until his cruiser was out of sight—but the second he was gone, they'd start thumbing rides again.

Like most younger brothers, Gale followed Roger around everywhere he went and did whatever his big brother did. After school they played football, sometimes tackle, in nearby Kountze Park, often until dark. When they were old enough, they played for Coach Bob Rose in Omaha's midget football program, which had a weight limit of 110 pounds.

"Both of us had the same general initiation into football and track, and that was in grade school, running track, playing flag football, and playing midget football for Roberts Dairy," Roger Sayers said. "One of the reasons we enjoyed doing this is that we enjoyed being around the people who were coaching. All the coaches that we had—and we were fortunate—were, for us, excellent people. For those who are still living, to this day, we still feel like we have relationships with them. Our earliest coaches recognized whatever talent might have been there and encouraged us to go ahead and make the most of it. They put us in positions where we could utilize our talent."

Talent indeed. The Sayers brothers' exploits, even at a young age, garnered nearly as much ink in the sports section of the *Omaha World-Herald* as those of college and professional stars. In one midget contest in 1955, the Sayers brothers combined for 7 touchdowns in a 45–0 Roberts romp. The lengths of the touchdown runs were even more staggering than the volume: 95, 75, 75, 72, 45, 40, and 6 yards. To clinch the performance, the Sayers boys scored all three of the team's point-after conversions, too.

The strong ties with Bob Rose extended beyond the football field. Recognizing the sort of talents he was coaching, Rose tried to expose the Sayers boys to greatness, taking them down to nearby Creighton University to watch future Major League Baseball Hall of Famer Bob Gibson play basketball for the Bluejays. These outings meant a lot to Gale and Roger, who otherwise wouldn't have had the money for such luxuries.

When it came time to choose a high school, the choice for the Sayers brothers, like most blacks in their north Omaha neighborhood, was between Omaha Tech and Omaha Central. Had they not enrolled at Central, they almost certainly would have wound up at Tech. "Central was a school that better black students were supposed to go to—or were *expected* to go to," said Roger Sayers. "As opposed to going to Tech. There were very few blacks who went to North; there were some. There were very few who went to Benson. So it was Tech and Central at that time. Most of the black athletes went to Tech. Teachers would encourage us to attend Central. They'd say, 'Hey, you have the academic skills and prerequisites, so I'd think about going to Central if I were you.'"

When Central and Tech met on the athletic field, some less-than-stellar members of Omaha society called the contest "the niggers against the blacks." The disgusting sentiment was representative of tenuous race relations in the city and indicative of the need for nationwide civil rights reform that would peak in the 1960s.

The examples set by Omahans Gibson and Bob Boozer, who both parlayed successful high school careers into college scholarships, and, eventually, successful professional sports careers, were important for Gale and Roger. Boozer, who had his heart set on attending the University of Iowa, was disappointed to learn that Iowa coach Bucky O'Connor had "already met his quota of negro ballplayers" and had no need for the promising power forward from Omaha. So Boozer went to Kansas State, where he played for Tex Winter, became a two-time All American, and helped lead the Wildcats to the Final Four. But Gibson and Boozer both went to Tech. At Central, the Sayers brothers were blazing their own trail.

When they attended Central, the black student population, Roger Sayers estimates, was somewhere between 10 and 12 percent. Most of their classmates were white. Many were Jewish. And nearly all had more money than they did. Roger played freshman football for Coach George Andrews, but it was varsity coach—and track coach—Frank Smagacz to whom Roger, and later Gale, became close. In those days, when there was a track meet outside of Omaha in towns such as Fremont or Lincoln, Smagacz would pile his tracksters into his own car and drive them to the meet. The windshield time gave the Sayers brothers a chance to get to know their coach on a personal level. Sometimes they would plot strategy or discuss other sports, while other times they just talked about life.

"It was an intimate relationship," said Roger Sayers. "He'd tell stories, and we all had a great deal of interaction at that time. Smagacz was really, *really* a family man. You could tell. He treated his players like family. With all of his own kids, you could tell he enjoyed being around young people. He was a disciplinarian in his own way, but you would never know it. He didn't come across that way. He was really easy-going and mild-mannered."

On some weekends, Smagacz would invite the Sayers brothers and other athletes over to his house for cookouts. The many large houses on Mercer Boulevard where the Smagaczs lived were a far cry from the struggling north Omaha neighborhood where Gale and Roger grew up. "Being invited there felt like we were going to an upscale place," Roger said. "Smagacz probably didn't have much more money than most folks, but we thought we had died and gone to heaven."

That's probably how Smagacz felt when he got a look at his young gridiron prodigies on the first day of football practice.

But one player does not a team make. Gale had team-mates who were quite capable. It started in the backfield with Vernon Breakfield and Ardell Gunn, a pair of speed-sters who, when lined up next to Gale, made for the most dynamic, most feared backfield in Nebraska high school football. The *Central High Register* went so far as to call it the most explosive backfield in intercity history. It was a hard point to argue. They were explosive in track and field, too. As a member of the 4x100 relay team, Sayers often ran in the third slot, usually reserved for the slowest runner. The track facilities, Sayers recalled, were just as limited as those for football. "We could never set up more than three hurdles in a row and the distance runners had to take to the streets."

Those who liked to lump the three backs together into one great triumvirate did so with cause. In the fall of 1959, they were called "The Junior Jets" by the Central *O-Book*; they even lined up together in the front left row of the '59 team photo. They ran together, blocked for each other, and wrecked the hopes of opposing teams with each sudden scoring play. One particular play, known to the players as the "butcher play," called for a Sayers/Breakfield double-team block on the defensive end lined up over the right or left tackle. Shoulder to shoulder, Sayers and Breakfield would plow through the end, who by that point was more defense-*less* than defensive, to clear a path for Ardell Gunn, who would receive the handoff and look for daylight. He usually found it. If a rivalry existed between the talented runners, nobody noticed. They were competitive, certainly, but remained great friends and encouraging teammates. However, the speedy Eagles were not immune to defeat, especially in 1959, when they struggled to a 4-5 record en route to a fourth-place finish in the intercity league. A year later, it seemed the speedy had gotten speedier and the strong had gotten stronger.

Breakfield, whom many teammates called "Break," was, like Sayers, a track star. One of his pet sayings was "be cool," and he was. Break possessed elite speed that was uncommon in 1960. As a straightaway runner, he was hard to match. Many remembered he ran even faster than Sayers. And he had a slashing ability that the coaches raved about. Breakfield became even faster once Frank Smagacz got a hold of him and applied some of his homespun sports psychology. Smagacz had a knack for maximizing an athlete's abilities, sometimes by resorting to motivational tricks such as shaving a few tenths of a second off a player's 40-yard dash time to convince him of his own potential. "When Smagacz had the guy convinced that he had run, say a 4.8 forty, before you knew it, with the added confidence in himself, the guy did start running that fast," Breakfield explained to a *Central High Register* writer, years after his playing days.

Breakfield lived near Sayers, and they were involved in many of the same activities growing up. These included playing ping pong and shooting pool. Like Gale, Break came from a family of little means. They hung around together, listened to music, played sports, and even tried talking to girls. In this department, it seems Breakfield had the edge. "He was outgoing and I was quiet then, very shy," Sayers wrote.

Ardell "Charlie" Gunn, according to teammate Howard Fouts, was probably the toughest guy on the team, pound for pound. In actual pounds he weighed a shade under 140. He was called both Ardell and Charlie, depending on who was doing the calling. He was friends with Sayers and Breakfield, but not as close. Sayers remembered him as a bit of a loner with a penchant for mischief. Sometimes all three got in on the mischief, including the time when the entire crowd on hand at Norris Junior High School for a Central basketball game suspected them of igniting a cherry bomb and dropping it beneath the bleachers while the game was being played. The loud "pop" caused a stir. Everyone in their section of the stands turned around and looked for the culprit, but Sayers, Breakfield, and Gunn kept their eyes straight ahead, hoping to avoid suspicion. On the athletic field, and sometimes off it, they always had a way of attracting attention.

Fouts shared the quarterback duties with Jim Capellupo. Their backup was junior Don Buresh, whom *Central High Register* reporter Jeff Wohlner predicted would be taking over the quarterback job for the Eagles in the fall of 1961. Fouts, according to the *Register*, was a natural athlete, a quality that helped earn him the team's punting job. He possessed good foot speed, but his arm strength was limited due to a dislocated shoulder he suffered in practice after a particularly hard tackle. The injury reared its ugly head on many occasions throughout his high school sports career, including one notable flare-up during a sliding drill at baseball practice. The shoulder popped out, and Fouts, a four-year base-ball player, screamed, "Coach! Pop it back in."

"Fouts, what the hell's the matter?" asked baseball coach Jim Karabatsos, who was on the scene. With little knowledge of human anatomy, he performed admirably to relieve his star player.

"I didn't know what he was talking about when he screamed, but when I got over there I could see that shoulder was out of place, and I jammed it back in. I don't know what the hell I was doing—but I fixed it, and he finished practice."

"Thanks, Coach," Fouts said.

Fouts grew up near 52nd and Leavenworth Streets, which was a long way from Omaha Central, especially in 1960. He thought about attending Omaha Tech, but when he learned his friends were headed for Central, Howard followed, and it was an experience he never forgot. "I've heard many younger guys say, 'Oh, you grew up in the '50s and '60s, that had to be a fun time,'" he said. "I thought about it, and it really was. Sock hops, drive-in movies. It was a fun place to go to school. Central had a lot of Jewish kids and South Omaha stockyards kids and Polish kids and black kids. It was a big melting pot."

Capellupo, according to the *Central High Register*, was a defensive convert from the previous year's team. He sometimes went by the nickname "Cappy." Cappy grew up in South Omaha, sandwiched around a crowd of future Creighton Prepsters, including five starters on the 1960 Junior Jays football team. He almost went to Prep himself, even taking the admissions test. Like Fouts, he suffered from an aversion to throwing the football. It didn't stop him from playing third base on the Central baseball team, but it did limit Central's play calling.

"No question it made us a little one-dimensional," Howard Fouts said.

The linemen who protected Fouts and Capellupo and cleared running paths for Sayers and others had both size and athleticism. They were players such as James Brown, a thick-chested junior guard who tipped the scales between 235 and 245 pounds, depending on the season; Maris Vinovskis, a lanky Latvian-born end who was vice president of the senior class and towered over the rest of his teammates in the team photo; and Don Fiedler, a hustling 207-pound tackle who played with great energy and carried himself with a free spirit.

Brown anchored Coach Norman Sorensen's wrestling team and lost just one match his junior year in the heavyweight division en route to capturing the state championship. He was well liked by the coaches and had a good sense of humor. Despite his massive size, he was remembered for his teddy bear–soft personality and jolly attitude. Brown also played in the Central band and was vice president of the orchestra. One day he was late for football practice due to his band commitments. Jim Karabatsos pulled him aside and jokingly said, "Brown, if you're ever late again, I'm going to take that piccolo and jam it up your you-know-what." What Karabatsos either didn't know or had forgotten was that Brown played the oboe, which he had taken up after years of clarinet lessons at the suggestion of his band instructor. After high school, Brown would play football for Bob Devaney at the University of Nebraska, where he was a two-year letterman and earned a starting position as a senior.

Vinovskis's life story was worth its own book. Born in Riga, Latvia, during World War II, the Vinovskis family (Maris, father Arveds, mother Lucija, sister Daila) fled the country in 1943 to escape the Soviet occupation. They eventually landed in an American zone in Munich, Germany, and when the United States passed legislation that allowed hundreds of thousands of displaced people to enter the country, the Vinovskis family emigrated to Blair, Nebraska, a small community of five thousand near Omaha. The Blair newspaper ran a profile of the family, and Arveds was able to tell his life story. The publicity prompted a fundraising effort from the community that provided the family money to live in a motel until they got settled. Maris and his sister, neither of whom knew English, began school, and by the second grade they had a decent command of the language. To better support his family, Arveds took a job at Omaha's Cudahy meat packinghouse, moving his family to the city with him.

In his homeland, Arveds had a law degree and worked a government job. In the United States, facing a language barrier and an unfamiliar legal system, he was relegated to the Cudahy job. It paid his wages and took care of his family, but it was a far cry from the white-collar world he occupied in Latvia before the occupation. And there never seemed to be enough money. The family's first Omaha home fell victim to freeway construction, and they had to move. When the Cudahy plant closed, Arveds found another minimum-wage job at an Omaha printing house. When Lucija took Maris and Daila to buy their clothes at Goodwill, their social position hit Maris like a slap in the face.

"I was ashamed when we came to this country," he said. "When you're a kid, you don't want to buy your clothes at Goodwill. My father used to clean up the areas where they killed animals, and he never complained. He never discussed this with me or talked about it, he just did it. That makes you want to work hard."

Despite their financial challenges, the Vinovskis family persevered. Maris, to his credit, became a fine student and a standout athlete. But in the Vinovskis household, excellence in sports mattered little; academics were king. His parents never made it to any of his football or basketball games, but they did care about his studies. Their thinking was partly shaped by an association with a group of Latvian emigrants who, just like the Vinovskis family, had been smart and ambitious enough to escape the Soviets. Maris was up to the challenge, earning high marks in the classroom and a National Merit scholarship that would pay for college. Amazingly, Central High students accounted for twenty of Nebraska's ninety-five National Merit semifinalists. There were just ten thousand such recipients nationwide. Just to prove that he was more than a jock, Maris joined the Central chess club in order to compete in the citywide chess tournament, where he finished second. He also ran for senior class vice president and won, thanks to his notoriety as an athlete and an underdog campaign where he carried a briefcase to school and wore a beanie with a flashing light on it to attract attention. And when a horrific car accident took the lives of six Omaha teenagers in Elmwood Park that fall, Vinovskis personally surveyed the student body about their attitudes toward car safety and traffic laws. The results of his survey were compiled and made front-page news in the *Central High Register*.

For Maris Vinovskis, football was just another activity he did, not his sole purpose in life. However, it provided him an identity among his fellow students.

"I had never even heard of football before coming to this country," he said. "I was a relatively big kid and in pretty good shape, and when they formed the Blair junior football group when I was in sixth or seventh grade, I was asked to play. It was one of those things that I fell into because somebody asked me to do it. At Central, once I made the ninth-grade team, people just expected me to keep doing it. I practiced seriously and paid attention, but it wasn't like I started out thinking this was a big deal. I don't feel I actually ever fit into a group at Central. I interpreted my whole life, early on, as an emigrant. I was kind of a loner. But I was loyal to Central. I had friends, and I think I was, in a sense, popular. So sports absolutely gave me an identity."

Fɪɢ. 7. Senior class vice president Maris Vinovskis was a success in the classroom and on the football field. Reprinted with permission of the 1961 Omaha Central High School *O-Book*.

A photo of Don Fiedler in the 1961 *O-Book* looked like an audition for the lead role in TV's *Adventures of Superman*. Wearing every part of his football uniform except his helmet, Fiedler leapt off the ground—and seemingly off the page of the yearbook—with both arms extended above his head like the man of steel. It seems apt, given his thespian persuasion. According to his teammates, the photo captured his untamed exuberance. Fiedler was a ferocious competitor, well respected by his teammates and opposing players. In adulthood, he became a lawyer who lived in a condo above the French Café in Omaha's Old Market district. He was active in local stage productions, once portraying Yossarian in an Old Market adaptation of Joseph Heller's *Catch-22*. His fellow attorneys remembered him for his strong criminal work but mostly for his public stance in favor of legalizing marijuana. One night, after hours, he came into the Omaha Police Station and told the guard on duty he was there to drop off some cigarettes for a client. The guard bought his story and took the package from Fiedler to deliver to his client. The cigarettes, which of course looked like a normal package of tobacco cigarettes, had been doctored and contained reefer.

One player absent from the Central offensive and defensive lines in 1960 was Fred Scarpello, a senior with a likable smile and a stocky build. As a homeroom representative and a member of the O-Club, Fred was one of Central's leading promoters of school spirit. When he played football, he was a handful to try and block or get around. Howard Fouts joked that "Fred had to be tough because he was the slowest guy on the team."

Despite his poor foot speed, Fred was a three-year member of the Central football team before being diagnosed with diabetes after his junior season. In the 1960s, the disease was poorly understood and treatments were primitive. The existence of two major types of diabetes was a new concept, and

Fig. 8. Diabetes kept Fred Scarpello off the football field his senior year, but the illness didn't stop him from rooting on his teammates. Reprinted with permission of the 1961 Omaha Central High School *O-Book*.

the first testing strips for self-measuring blood glucose were just being developed. Fred's medical complications forced him to give up football. He continued on with the wrestling team, his best sport, as he remembers, but it failed to completely fill the void left by football. Fred missed football greatly and he kept up with the team, watching every game from the stands.

Surrounding Sayers, Breakfield, and Gunn with tough-minded, no-nonsense football players such as Vinovskis and Fiedler made Central a formidable team. But when the Eagles needed a big play, whether it was an important tackle or grinding out a yard when there seemingly wasn't one available, they turned to Gale Sayers. In most everyone's eyes, he was a player without compare in the intercity league, perhaps in the entire state of Nebraska. It was Gale who would lead Central in 1960; it was he who would make sure that they wouldn't settle for a 4-5 record, like they did in 1959.

CHAPTER 5

MIKE MCKIM NEVER KNEW his father.

It seemed everybody knew his *grand*father, and everybody included Harry Truman.

Edward D. McKim was a Kansas City native who served as a private with future president Truman in World War I. Together they fought in Battery D of the 129th Field Artillery in battles at Saint Mihiel and Argonne Forest. After the service, McKim, whom Truman called "Eddie," spent a thirty-year career at Mutual of Omaha, the prominent insurance and financial services provider, retiring in 1957 as a vice president. He was at Truman's side in 1945 when President Roosevelt died and haberdasher Harry took office. On the night of Roosevelt's death, Truman phoned McKim at his Washington hotel to tell him that, regretfully, he had to cancel their poker game. The next morning, Truman's first day in office, McKim was the new president's first official visitor. Truman stood up from his desk to greet McKim and again apologized about canceling poker. Truman asked his old friend to stick around while he got accustomed to the new job. He appointed McKim his chief administrative assistant and later deputy federal loan administrator. McKim was one of Truman's army buddies and trusted friends, often spending time with the president around a poker table or strolling through downtown Omaha in the early morning hours during Truman's visits. In 1952 McKim became a trustee of the Truman Memorial Library in Missouri.

His son Edward McKim Jr., like many college-aged men

of his era, enlisted in the armed forces after the 1941 attack on Pearl Harbor, Hawaii, choosing to join the Marines. He was a student at the University of Notre Dame, scheduled to graduate in the spring of 1943. With the country's sudden involvement in the Second World War, McKim, once a Creighton Prep student and graduate of the Missouri Military Academy, accelerated his classes at Notre Dame so he could serve his country as soon as possible. He spent the summer between his junior and senior years at platoon leadership school in Quantico, Virginia. When he graduated ahead of schedule in December 1942, he returned to Quantico to await his orders. He was told he would be headed to San Diego, California, and was given a two-week leave, during which he dropped in on his hometown of Omaha and visited neighborhood sweetheart Frances Radford. Frances had attended Duchesne College and the University of Nebraska, where she joined a sorority.

Edward wasted little time asking Frances to marry him. She accepted, and plans were hastily set in motion for a July 12, 1943, wedding at St. Margaret Mary Catholic Church in Omaha. The couple married and lived together briefly—very briefly—before Edward shipped out for the South Pacific.

Regrettably, he never came back alive.

Second Lieutenant McKim led a rifle platoon that landed in 1944 to retake Guam. He helped overtake three Japanese-held caves in the Guam cliffs during the initial landing and sustained a wound from a mortar fragment on July 22, 1944, the second day of the campaign, but stayed with his platoon. Four days later, during the inspection of a barbed wire fence fifty yards ahead of his lines, McKim was killed at age twenty-two. His son Mike was just three months old. They never touched.

It took nearly a month for the War Department to notify his family in Omaha of his death, and four years passed before his body was returned to Omaha. A proper funeral was held on December 14, 1948, at St. Margaret Mary Church, where he had married Frances just five years earlier.

Frances became a young widow and raised her son in the mold of the man she had married. She sent Mike to the same high school (Creighton Prep), and he would attend the same university (Notre Dame) as his father. When Mike was in grade school Frances took a job working for the Byron Reed Real Estate Company. She had been an English major and was assigned to inspect all the company's new listings and write ads that appeared in the Saturday and Sunday editions of the newspaper. It was steady employment, and she was good at her job. In an era where few women worked at full-time jobs, her son said she was capable of more than basic advertising writing.

"She would have been a crackerjack saleswoman," Mike McKim said. "But women didn't do that back then. They didn't work a lot, except as secretaries."

Frances remained a single parent for eighteen years before marrying a longtime family friend from North Platte, Nebraska, who had been widowed prematurely when his wife died of a heart problem. The new couple welcomed a daughter, Mike's half-sister, into the world a few years after their marriage.

By 1960 Mike had grown into an athlete—and man— his father would have been proud of. He was the consummate jock. He was good-looking and stood tall—in fact he was the tallest player in the back row of the 1960 Creighton Prep football team photo. If his lanky frame caused observers to suspect he was better suited to basketball than to football, they were only partially right. He played basketball and was part of Prep's 1960–61 team, which reeled off an improbable string of victories en route to the state finals, but it wasn't like he couldn't hack it on the gridiron. He possessed a strong arm—"a hose," remembered one friend—that made him a natural fit at quarterback and

Fig. 9. Tall and likable, Prep quarterback Mike McKim (no. 11) was all smiles. Reprinted with permission of the 1961 *Jay Junior.*

a hard-throwing baseball pitcher. During the summer he pitched for the Murphy-Did-It American Legion team that played at Omaha's Boyd Park.

McKim's father would also have been proud of his son's work ethic, which he likely inherited from his mother. Frances's friendship with Peg Flinn helped Mike land a job with Flinn Paving, an asphalt-paving company run by Peg's husband, Matt. Mr. Flinn preferred to hire Creighton Prep students for his summer crews because they were usually hard workers who avoided trouble and showed up on time. In the summer of 1960, "on time" meant 7:30 a.m. Chuck Van Vliet, a guard and linebacker in McKim's class at Prep, left his parents' house at 100th and Center Streets each morning on his Vespa scooter and picked McKim up on Underwood Avenue to travel to the day's job site. The early start helped, but the conditions were stifling. The boiling summer sun baked down on the Flinn crew, and in combination with the hot and smelly asphalt, it made for nasty work. They scraped more asphalt into wheelbarrows than they could stand, and they sometimes strapped three-pound weights around their ankles to help beef up and get into football shape. To top it off, there was no drinking water on site. The job's main appeal was the $2.63/hour union wage, a significant upgrade from the federal minimum wage of $1.00. Each worker was presented with a laborer's union card that the bearer was supposed to be at least eighteen years old to carry, but the Flinn crew bent the rules for the boys from Creighton Prep. A year later, on a trip to Kansas City with friends, Van Vliet discovered the value of holding a legitimate photo ID when an unsuspecting barkeep let him buy beer.

McKim, Van Vliet, and other members of the Flinn crew worked at sites in and around metropolitan Omaha, including Council Bluffs. One summer they resurfaced North 30th Street in Omaha and then performed the same feat the following summer on North 24th Street—each time covering the distance from just north of Cuming Street to Ames Avenue. They also worked on North 16th Street near Boyd Park. Some days McKim would leave the 16th Street job site and return home to his Memorial Park neighborhood to change into his flannel baseball uniform and drive back out to Boyd to pitch seven innings for the Murphy-Did-Its in the late afternoon heat. He also worked a couple of summers with Prep classmate Jack Larson for the Parsons Construction Corporation. Parsons Construction helped build Mount Michael Abbey in Elkhorn and the Saint Margaret Mary Church bell tower in McKim's neighborhood. Mike assisted with both projects.

McKim's first encounter with Don Leahy came in Leahy's freshman history section. He learned immediately that Leahy was not a man to cross.

"He was very much a disciplinarian. Very tight. He was a no-frills kind of guy, and you didn't get out of line. When we all grew up and watched and listened to the Vince Lombardi teams, a lot of what Lombardi stressed, Leahy had already been stressing: execution, precision, consistency, discipline, organization."

McKim played quarterback, Leahy's position. On the practice field, Leahy drilled into McKim and his other quarterbacks the nuances of the position: how to receive the ball from under center, how to hand off, how to take a three-step drop, five-step drop. The list of maneuvers was never-ending.

"We would run a play in practice where the fullback went straight ahead, either left or right of the center," McKim said. "And he wanted the line splits to be just so. Jackson and Brosnihan worked with the linemen to get their splits—the distance between themselves and the center—just right. I would take the ball, and I wouldn't step left or right; I just turned and pivoted. As I stood sideways to the hole, my right pad, if I was turning to the left of the center, was supposed to just nick the shoulder pads of the fullback as he took the handoff and went by me through the hole. We would run that play ten, twelve, thirteen times in practice, until everybody had it just right. It was repetition, execution, again, again, and again.

"Everything was execution and precision. That was Leahy's forte. He was very committed to that. He understood it and understood the need for it."

The placement of his feet was one of the quarterbacking nuances that McKim was slow to pick up. Prep's left guard, Dan Van Ackeren, began tripping over McKim's feet, which were parallel to the line of scrimmage as he took snaps, in practice. Van Ackeren would take his first step with his right foot and push off the side of McKim's left foot like it was a launching pad. The constant beating made McKim's feet sore until Leahy intervened, instructing his quarterback to place one of his feet behind the other to give himself a head start as he pivoted away from the line of scrimmage.

It was a subtle but important modification, suggested by a man who knew success dwelt in the details.

The fix worked, and the team's execution improved.

Despite his strong arm and aptitude for the position, McKim began the 1960 season behind senior Frank Spenceri on the quarterback depth chart. Spenceri was a good all-around athlete with a knack for seizing important moments. Although Leahy never said it directly to either player, Frank suspected that McKim's passing ability made him a more desirable option at quarterback, particularly for a coach who liked to pass the ball. But that didn't guarantee him a starting job. Spenceri lacked McKim's arm strength, but he was an excellent runner and a natural leader. His basketball teammates thought of him as a guy who would make big plays when the team needed a lift. Frequently he'd drive through the lane to complete a layup when two points were an absolute must. Leahy had a decision to make, and while a strong-armed thrower seemed tempting, he voted for experience. The Junior Jays began practice in the fall of 1960 with Spenceri as the no. 1 quarterback and McKim as second string, being groomed for the following season.

Spenceri was born and raised in Omaha's Little Italy neighborhood. To be more accurate, it was one of the city's three Little Italys.

"If you were from Sicily, you grew up on Sixth Street and Pierce," he said. "If you were from the lower part of the boot, that was 20th and Pierce. Rotella's Bakery used to be there. Scarpello's Bar is still there. And if you were from the northern part, you were in Florence."

Spenceri's family was from, as he put it, the "lower part of the boot." He grew up just blocks from Prep teammates John Bozak and Bob Marasco. There were other athletically inclined kids in the neighborhood, sometimes twenty or more, and they made a habit of playing baseball, flag football, and sometimes tackle football without pads in the neighborhood as kids.

Spenceri and McKim got along well together. Whatever competition existed between them on the field did little to harm their friendship.

"I was his mentor, more or less," Spenceri said. "We became very good friends. There was never a rivalry."

In some ways, they were kindred spirits. Spenceri's family situation, like McKim's, presented a challenge. His mother died when he was just a year old and his uncle and aunt helped raise Frank and his older brother. When the family moved to a house just east of the Pacific Street gates to Omaha's Ak-Sar-Ben racetrack, Frank attended school at St. Margaret Mary, where he met McKim.

The third quarterback in Leahy's stable was Tom Heim. Heim grew up in the area of 40th and Center Streets in Omaha and graduated from Our Lady of Lourdes Grade School. His father had worked as a decoder for General Douglas MacArthur in the South Pacific during World War II while his mother raised the young family alone at home. When the war ended Tom's father became a career navy man, later serving as a civil engineer for the U.S. Corps of Engineers then eventually retiring as a distinguished civilian employee.

Tom was the third of five Heim boys, and when they were young his father took the boys to Creighton Stadium to watch Prep football games on Friday nights. The games were a welcome reprieve from Tom's other favorite pastime, riding his bike with friends past the Veterans Administration (VA) Hospital to a large dirt pile in the area of 42nd and Center that in 1955 became Center Mall, Omaha's landmark shopping center. There he would imagine himself as a motocross superstar, riding over the mound of dirt. At Creighton Stadium, he imagined himself in a different light, as a star quarterback. The smell of the popcorn and the concrete stadium's other charms made an impression on young Tom, but they paled in comparison with the impression made by Coach Don Leahy. As Heim watched Leahy's every move, including the manner in which he would instruct his players on the sidelines between series, he fantasized about the day when he would be playing football for Creighton Prep. That day came in the fall of 1957 when he joined other newcomers to the program who donned leather helmets for the freshman team. That summer, helping out on a relative's farm in Leavenworth, Kansas, Heim broke his ischium, the lower and back part of the hip bones. The accident kept him from playing football for two years. To add insult to injury, he was forced to carry around a pillow to sit on during class, which, naturally, earned him a good razzing from his classmates. It didn't stop him from helping out with the farm work, and he returned for a few weeks each summer to pick up hay bales and complete other chores that made the farm run smoothly. The intense work caused a rank sweat, and he cooled off by joining his cousins on fishing trips and bullfrog hunting excursions in nearby Stranger Creek.

Stuck behind Spenceri and McKim on the depth chart, Heim's chances of playing time at quarterback seemed slim. He took practice reps with the defense but continued on as a quarterback. Don Leahy knew the importance of having more than one, and in this case two, capable signal callers, especially over the course of an entire season, and Heim got the opportunity to learn the position under the watchful eye of his head coach.

Heim and the other quarterbacks also learned to run Leahy's best play, the trap pass. In military parlance, the Creighton Prep trap pass was Don Leahy's paramount volley. The trap pass was a sudden salvo of undetectable pigskin sleight-of-hand that broke the stride of safeties in pursuit of a game-changing play and broke the hearts of opposing coaches exhausted from a sleepless week spent drilling into their players the tells they should watch for in Prep's formations and fakes. The drilling didn't matter. The trap pass worked nearly every time.

"They were taught, 'Watch for the trap pass, watch for the trap pass,'" said Sandy Buda, another player on the 1960 team. "The trap pass was a Prep signature. Everybody got ready for it, or so they thought, and then when it came to the game, they found out they weren't ready for it."

The trap pass, also known as the 338 trap pass, was built upon two of Prep's favorite and most commonly used plays, a pitch to a fullback for an end run or a fake pitch to the fullback and a quick trap handoff to another back coming out of the backfield. The trap pass required the quarterback to fake both sequences—the fullback sweep and the subsequent trap—and step into the pocket to deliver a pass to an end, one who ran a long banana pattern down one end of the field or the other who came across at five yards for a short dump-off.

"That first fake would draw some people," said Frank Spenceri. "Then you would ride the fullback in. Linebackers would go after this guy and safeties and corner linebackers would come down. The banana was a touchdown, and if he ain't open, it ain't running really well. But just in case, the across pattern was the safety belt."

Prep quarterbacks were so good at executing the fakes, officials would frequently blow the play dead in its infancy, convinced that a ball carrier had been stopped in his tracks at the line of scrimmage. But the ball carrier in question never had the ball at all; it was in the hands of the Prep quarterback. Leahy began sending Tom Brosnihan out to discreetly alert the game officials before kickoff that they planned to run the trap pass at a certain point in the game, often once in the first half and once in the second half.

"Please—don't blow it dead," Brosnihan would plead to the officials.

"We faked out the officials all the time," said Spenceri. "So had every Prep quarterback for the previous five years."

The quarterbacks were Leahy's eyes and ears on the field, but he communicated with them—in football parlance, he "ran in plays"—through his offensive linemen, particularly the guards. Along the offensive line, his two-part process of substitution and play calling became known at Prep as the "changing of the guard." Leahy would select a play, grab one of his linemen by the helmet, and whisper the call into his earhole. The usual starting guards, Rich Vomacka and Walt Kazlauskas, who were split by center Bob Marasco, shared time with guards Dan Van Ackeren and Chuck Van Vliet. The line play was anchored by tackles Bill Heaston and Fred Hoefer, who shared time with Tom Jaworski.

Van Vliet was an air force brat who seemingly had been everywhere. His father, Charles Van Vliet Sr., transferred frequently, and the family always moved with him. The Van Vliets lived in Florida, New Jersey, Alabama, Texas, and Massachusetts, with a couple of short stints in Omaha sandwiched in between. But the Omaha move immediately before Chuck's freshman year of high school was the closest thing to permanent he had ever experienced, and when he arrived in Omaha he went down to Creighton University to take the Prep entrance exam.

"You sort of get used it, but it got old," Van Vliet said of the frequent moves. "The reason I got into sports, mainly, was so that when I went to all these new places, I could meet people. Creighton Prep was a good thing for me. That was the longest time we stayed any place, four years. It felt like home."

Van Vliet was also one of the Prepsters who got to know and befriend Father C. T. Shinners. After graduating from Creighton Prep, Van Vliet attended Marquette University. By that point, Shinners had moved to Milwaukee to take a job at Marquette High School. Van Vliet kept in touch with his old assistant principal, and Shinners responded by connecting Van Vliet with a job selling programs at Milwaukee County Stadium during the two or three annual home dates the Green Bay Packers had at the venue. He worked the job for a couple of years during college, collecting some much-needed spending money while enjoying a prime vantage point for watching professional football.

The inside tandem of seniors Rich Vomacka and Walt Kazlauskas was as feared as any in Nebraska high school football. Even underclassmen at Creighton Prep felt intimidated in their collective presence. Standing 5'10" and weighing a stocky 185 pounds, the thick-chested Kazlauskas, with bulging biceps and a no-nonsense expression on his square-jawed-face, looked and acted the part of a physically imposing player you didn't want to cross. Kazlauskas, who had come to the United States from Lithuania in 1950, was a quiet guy off the football field but the total opposite between the lines. His teammates, with apologies to Father Shinners, thought of him as Prep's John Wayne, the enforcer. When he appeared at a pep rally wearing a dress and wig to play the role of "Boom Chick," another student's fictitious date, he drew plenty of laughs from his classmates in the audience; no doubt there were many others who kept their mirth to themselves, just in case Kazlauskas caught them having a laugh at his expense. He was one of the rare young men of the era who had been working out regularly with free weights since his youth, and it showed in his rock-like physique. When he showed up in a Prep classroom as a freshman, Dudley Allen, noticing his visible strength, asked Kazlauskas if he planned on playing football.

"No, I've never played football," he said.

"Well, if you don't play football, then don't ever come back to this class," Allen bluntly told him.

Kazlauskas got the message. By his senior year, he was the guy delivering the messages. When fourteen-year-old freshman kicker Dave Bouda showed up for his first practice, Kazlauskas slugged him in the stomach and told him, "Welcome to varsity football." The punch moved Bouda to tears.

"I thought that he killed me," Bouda recalled with a wince. "He just nailed me. It was very uncomfortable. I had never been hit that hard in my life. I was just a little fourteen-year-old who was frightened to death of him."

Vomacka, standing 5'10" and weighing 172 pounds, was less imposing physically than Kazlauskas, but he compensated with a barbaric intensity that was unmatched on the Prep team. He was broad-shouldered and played with an edge that resonated with his teammates, even years later, in the same way they remembered Don Leahy's meticulous practices or Tom Brosnihan's motivational speeches. Vomacka was provocative and feisty, the sort who was always up for a good fight. He grew up in South Omaha, on Atlas Street, two blocks south of Municipal Stadium. Later, his family moved to 49th and Center Streets, and Rich attended Holy Cross Grade School from fifth through seventh grade. His parents were graduates of South High School, but when it came time to pick a high school, Vomacka followed his Holy Cross buddies to Creighton Prep. As he entered his final year of high school, a football scholarship to college seemed like a real possibility for the talented Vomacka.

At 6'0", 194 pounds, Bill Heaston was nearly as formidable a lineman as Kazlauskas and Vomacka. Named after his grandfather William Patrick Lynch, a Prep graduate and the first letterman at Creighton University, Heaston grew up at 12th and Martha Streets and went to Mass at St. Patrick's Catholic Church at 14th and Castellar before the family moved away and then returned to Omaha, settling on Hanscom Boulevard and joining the parish of Our Lady of Lourdes. Heaston was the oldest of eight children, and like his grandfather he would one day become a lawyer. Among William Patrick Lynch's achievements, he was a member of the Creighton University School of Law's first graduating class. He also shared his grandson's knack for athletics, playing baseball at Creighton and later in the minor leagues.

If you lined up across the line of scrimmage from the younger Heaston, you would have had a hard time tracking his eyes, thanks to a cage-style facemask that covered his entire face, a rarity in 1960. The extra bars were meant to protect his glasses, which had been broken the year before during a game when an opposing player took a cheap shot during a pile-up, snapping his hornrims in two. Not one to take such a stunt lightly, Heaston punched the player in retaliation and drew a 15-yard penalty flag. When he got off the field, Assistant Coach Jack Jackson chided Heaston while he waited for an explanation.

"Damnit, coach, he broke my glasses," Heaston said. "What was I supposed to do?"

Heaston patched the glasses together with athletic tape and, as he said, "looked like the perennial nerd." That changed the following year during equipment checkout when Don Leahy fit him into an extra-large helmet (he wore a size 7⅞ fitted hat) and a facemask that became the envy of every lineman in the intercity league.

Heaston spent the summer before his senior year at Prep working for a county road repair crew. The outskirts of Omaha were surrounded by numerous two-lane roads, some of them gravel, in dire need of repair, and Heaston was part of the "Prep crew" that filled holes in the road with coal patches. He worked alongside Bill Pycha, a 5'10", 240-pound sophomore-to-be who owned the biggest body on the Prep football team by 46 pounds. He may have been only a sophomore, but he didn't look like one, nor did he act like one. Heaston typically "tolerated" younger students, including his younger brother, who was also entering his sophomore year at Prep, but he got along well with Pycha despite their age difference. Pycha's immense size had something to do with it. Pycha was no slouch on the road crew, handling every bit the same workload as Heaston. Old Bill respected young Bill's work ethic.

Their supervisor was a slow-moving county employee who kept the work atmosphere light. He drove the dump truck and made every effort to buddy up with his teen-aged crew. The county road repair job was a fun way to spend the summer. It was quiet, for one thing, and the assigned territory was mostly bordered by farmhouses and cornfields in the outskirts of the city. The supervisor made sure the crew maintained a gentlemanly pace to their work, never accomplishing enough to earn promotion to a fuller workload.

Bill Pycha was well liked by everyone who knew him, older and younger alike. The *Jay Junior* ballyhooed his "vibrant and vigorous personality," calling him "the kind of boy who gave all he had to whatever he undertook." He wore a closely cropped haircut, and his large frame was hardly chiseled. One teammate called him a "big, roly-poly" kid. But he was strong underneath, and with that strength came great potential. Don Leahy saw it and hoped to fashion Pycha into a dominant lineman, powerful and agile on offense and immovable on defense. But it would take work, and sweating out under the hot summer sun with the county road crew was a good way to prepare for the start of football practice.

Before practice officially began, players from Creighton Prep and other Omaha high schools took part in pre-season conditioning at the University of Omaha, located at 60th and Dodge Streets. In the 1960s, some sarcastically referred to Omaha U. as "West Dodge High." In the days before seven-on-seven scrimmaging became the off-season standard for football practice, these summer workouts were the only way players stayed connected to the sport over the summer. These were known as captains'

FIG. 10. Size matters. *Clockwise from top*: Assistant Coach Tom Brosnihan, Walt Kazlauskas, Bill Pycha, Rich Cacioppo, Sandy Buda, Mike Fitzgerald (manager). Reprinted with permission of the 1961 *Jay Junior*.

practices because Don Leahy and other coaches had no part in how they were run, at least in principle. Players ran wind sprints to build endurance, and in the process teams built camaraderie. The captains' practices were informal and not a requirement, but any player, sophomore through senior, who planned to play a significant role on his school's varsity squad made sure he showed up for the captains' practices. Chuck Van Vliet best put their importance in context when he said, "They were unofficial, but Omaha was just a small town then. If you weren't there, you were in trouble."

CHAPTER 6

Twelve thousand seats were made available Friday, September 9, at Omaha Municipal Stadium for Creighton Prep's 1960 season opener against Omaha South. Kickoff was scheduled for 7:30 p.m. Tickets could be purchased at Rush Drugs in South Omaha, Russell Sporting Goods downtown, or at either school for one dollar apiece.

Since 1950, Municipal Stadium (later Rosenblatt Stadium) had been home to the NCAA-run College World Series. During that time, and in the decades that followed, generations of Omahans and visitors to the city had made lifelong memories at the ballpark. The neighborhood surrounding the stadium embraced the event and the visitors that flocked to it every year. They opened up their driveways and lawns to baseball fans with barbecue grills and coolers full of cold refreshments. The whole event fostered a family atmosphere that helped cement Omaha's reputation for fine Midwest hospitality.

Stadium Manager Charles Mancuso and his staff made the changeover so the baseball stadium was ready to accommodate football usage. That included supplementing the stadium's regular grandstand seating with additional bleachers in the bullpen area along the third base line. For football, Mancuso set the field running north and south from left field to home plate. The east side of the playing field, normally center and right field, was spared of bleachers. In an effort to save the outfield grass from the heavy traffic of football cleats, Mancuso placed the sideline benches on platforms a few inches off the ground.

Charlie Mancuso had known Don Leahy for years. Leahy recalled it as "a pretty decent friendship." Mancuso, remembered by many for always having a cigar in his mouth, worked for the city of Omaha. In addition to his duties operating Municipal Stadium, he was in charge of the Omaha Civic Auditorium. He was well connected, had a good head for sports, and knew how to manage crowds. He also had a knack for making things happen. During one of Tom Brosnihan's years as basketball coach, Mancuso and Leahy partnered up to host a Prep basketball game at the Civic Auditorium. Mancuso's knack for promotions helped bring eight thousand fans to the Civic that night. Later in 1960 he earned a noteworthy public appointment when the National Baseball Congress selected him as one of fifty state commissioners responsible for overseeing state and district baseball tournaments for the 1961 season. Years later, he helped Bernie Berigan, coach of the semiprofessional Omaha Mustangs, by erecting lights around his practice field so the team could practice at night—a feat he accomplished just forty-eight hours after Berigan's request.

Managing Municipal Stadium was no small chore. The stadium opened its doors on a chilly October day in 1948. It played host to a baseball exhibition between a professional All-Star team, which included Central High's Assistant Coach Jim Karabatsos and Omaha's own Johnny Monaghan Storz team. Opening day at Municipal Stadium was the culmination of three years of work and planning by the city of Omaha, an effort that began during World War II. The thirteen-member Municipal Sports Stadium Committee that planned the function of the stadium included Johnny Rosenblatt, for whom the stadium would eventually be renamed. A 1945 architectural rendering of the proposed stadium from the Leo A. Daly Company dubbed it Omaha Memorial Stadium, but the name didn't last. The new stadium replaced Western League Park, a ten-thousand-seat facility south of downtown Omaha that had succumbed to a 1936 fire.

During the stadium's construction, another architectural rendering emerged showing how the stadium would be configured to host football games. The field ran north-south from left field to home plate (just as Mancuso set it up in 1960), and large portable bleachers sat along the far sideline in center and right fields. The west stands provided suitable viewing sight lines for football, but those who saw games from the south side of the stadium often wished they had stayed home to watch on television.

Although it was built primarily to host baseball, over its first few years Municipal Stadium saw its fair share of football. In 1949, the Los Angeles Rams played an exhibition game against the New York Giants, drawing 13,110 fans on a mid-September afternoon. Other professional exhibitions followed, including a 1950 visit by the Chicago Bears that drew about 10,000 fans and a 1951 visit from the Chicago Cardinals. The stadium hosted its first high school game in 1949, a duel between Boys Town and out-state power Scottsbluff. Boys Town won by 2 touchdowns in front of a large crowd estimated at 10,000.

Mancuso's expectations for the Prep-South game—and those of *Omaha World-Herald* sportswriter Don Lee, who forecast a crowd of at least 10,000—were a little on the high side, but it wasn't as if nobody showed up. In fact, an estimated 8,500 fans turned up to see the traditional season opener, an impressive crowd to see high school football anywhere.

Omaha South was a first-game opponent that had Creighton Prep's attention. The Packers were in their second season under the tutelage of Head Coach Merle Applebee. 1959 began poorly for Applebee. His team dropped 6 of its first 7 games and managed just a tie in the seventh. Things started to click after that. A dominant 51–0 win over Abraham Lincoln High School in week eight followed by a 7–6 victory

FIG. 11. Don Leahy demanded respect and execution, especially from veteran players like Rich Cacioppo, *right*. Reprinted with permission of the *Omaha World-Herald*.

over Omaha North in the season finale was good enough for seventh place in the intercity league, but more important, it provided Applebee and South fans reason to hope that 1960 would be a better year for Packers football.

South was led by returning lettermen Duane Novak (end), Leo Kennedy (tackle), and John DeGeorge (guard). And there were the Crums—that is, the offensive-minded Crum brothers: Larry (fullback), Don (quarterback), and Dennis (halfback). If the Junior Jays had any notions of steamrolling through their first opponent in the week of practice leading up to the game, they needed only open their 1960 yearbooks to be reminded that the mighty two-time defending intercity league and Nebraska state champions had managed only a 6–0 win over South the year before. Not that it mattered, because both teams were from Omaha and the game was being played on a supposedly neutral field, but South was given the distinction of being the game's "home" team. The Friday edition of the *Omaha World-Herald* helped draw attention to the game by running a photo of Prep co-captains John Bozak and Walt Kazlauskas opposite a photo of South end Duane Novak lining up in a three-point stance with a determined look in his eyes. Sportswriter Gregg McBride, a member of the newspaper's Lincoln Bureau, predicted another close contest and even expected that Prep's graduation losses would seal a South victory.

Creighton Prep's players and coaches had other plans.

"Creighton Prep taught one emphatic football lesson to South Friday night. To wit: You can't make mistakes against the lively Junior Bluejays. They are a go-go bunch, ready to strike any time you make an error." Those were the words Don Lee used to open his recap of the game, which the Junior Jays had mostly put away by halftime. In what Lee dubbed a "give-and-take contest," South did the giving and Prep the taking. Prep let South make all the mistakes and capitalized in surgical fashion. Prep's execution was the sort that some armchair quarterbacks would call "opportunistic," but Don Leahy just thought of it as clean football. Prep played sharp, error-free, and fundamentally soundly.

The first South mistake was a Larry Crum fumble on his 31-yard line, which was recovered by Prep's Bob Gaeta, who seemed to have a knack for recovering fumbles. Gaeta was always in the right place at the right time. He was also the ultimate competitor. He wore a game face as well as anyone on the Prep team; he stood 5'7", but he always seemed to stand a little taller and position himself in just the right place to make an important play. Nobody could intimidate him. Off the field, he was well liked and respected by his fellow students. The first time teammate John Bjelland met Gaeta, while warming up for baseball practice, Bjelland asked Gaeta where he was from.

"Gaeta, Italy," he said. "My dad says it's a beautiful fishing village."

"I meant what neighborhood," Bjelland said.

The two shared a laugh, but Bjelland could tell Bob proudly wore his Italian heritage on his sleeve. He played football with that same sense of pride in where he went to school.

Eyeing the end zone on their first possession with Frank Spenceri under center, the Jays opened with a pair of running plays for Rich Cacioppo and John Bozak, then a 10-yard Spenceri pass to speedster Mike Wiley, which took Prep to South's 4-yard line. Spenceri then handed off to Cacioppo, who shed a shoestring tackle attempt by South's Leo Kennedy and fell into the end zone for the game's first score.

Prep's momentum continued later in the first quarter when Chuck Van Vliet recovered a botched handoff between South quarterback Don Crum and Bill Rose on South's 16-yard line. With the goal line within close reach, Prep methodically drove in for another score, this time care of John Bozak from 1 yard out.

Down by two scores, South began piecing together a decent drive of its own, even crossing into Prep territory, but a Larry Crum fumble on the 43-yard line was recovered by Bob Gaeta, putting a quick end to a promising South drive. The night was quickly becoming a forgettable one for the Crum brothers, and Larry began audibly airing his frustrations. Referee Bob Adwers noticed the temper tantrum and called all eleven South players together to calm them down.

"Trying to help 'em, not penalize 'em," Adwers told Don Lee. "And it works, too."

Cooler heads may have helped the Packers avoid unnecessary penalty yardage, but they couldn't keep Creighton Prep out of the end zone. Prep made South pay for its third first-half fumble by driving 57 yards to a third touchdown, this time care of a Rich Cacioppo run from the 3-yard line.

The only thing South could feel good about as it headed to the locker room was the defensive stop it made after another turnover—this time a Mike Wiley interception—on its own 10-yard line. Merle Applebee had seen enough football to know that spotting a Don Leahy team 20 points at halftime was a poor recipe for victory. There were a few bright spots for South in the second half—a 39-yard run by Reggie Jackson in the third quarter down to the Prep 6-yard line and a 43-yard run by Phil Taylor to the Prep 14-yard line—but each scoring attempt came up empty. Prep's defense responded to Jackson's fine run by digging in its feet and holding South out of the end zone on four straight plays. After a procedure penalty moved South back 5 yards to the 11-yard line, Rich Vomacka and Fred Hoefer blasted into the South backfield to drop Bill Rose for a 2-yard loss. Two incomplete passes spoiled second and third downs, and on fourth down, Chuck Van Vliet and Bob Marasco stopped Don Crum short of the goal line. Taylor's long run was undone on the very next play by another South fumble, this time care of Bill Rose, which was recovered by Chuck Van Vliet, who seemed to be in the right place all night long.

One last gasp, a 34-yard run by Reggie Jackson to the Prep 22, came to a familiar end on the next play when Jackson fumbled on the Prep 17-yard line and Marasco was waiting to scoop up the mistake.

FIG. 12. Prep runner Rich Cacioppo and the Junior Jays took advantage of sloppy play by their first opponent, Omaha South. Reprinted with permission of the 1961 *Jay Junior.*

When the final buzzer sounded, the 20–0 Prep verdict must have made South players sick to their stomachs. Five fumbles and 1 interception were mostly to blame for the loss. When the final statistics were tallied, overall yardage was much closer than one might have guessed in such a lopsided score (196–170 in Prep's favor). Prep managed 14 first downs to South's 6, and the Junior Jays accumulated most of their yardage on the ground, completing just 3 of 9 passes for 22 yards.

Quietly, another bright spot for Prep was the play of freshman kicker Dave Bouda, who kicked 2 successful extra points in his first taste of varsity football. Bouda's rise to varsity kicker as a freshman was somewhat inexplicable. He was a graduate of Edward Rosewater School, located across the street from Municipal Stadium, but had been cut from the football and basketball teams as a seventh-grader. After making the football team the following year, he joined the nearest YMCA branch that spring with hopes of improving his athleticism. He knew that he was a clumsy kid, and he wanted to do something about it. He also wanted to attend medical school, and his father, William, a supervisor at the Omaha Post Office who sometimes worked alongside Central coach Frank Smagacz, would have had a hard time affording the tuition. Even Creighton Prep tuition was a lot to ask on Mr. Bouda's $5,000 annual salary, so young Dave took a summer job unloading boxcars for Ceeco Steel to earn the $250 annual tuition needed to attend Prep.

Bouda thought an athletic scholarship would be his ticket to college and medical school. He spent the summer before his freshman year at Prep kicking and throwing a football through an old tire at an abandoned lot near his house at 17th Street and Deer Park, affectionately called "the dump." He walked a city block down to "the dump" nearly every day, carrying his football and kicking tee, ruining several footballs in the process thanks to the property's cyclone fence. The extra practice paid off. So did a growth spurt. Just as he finished eighth grade at Edward Rosewater, he won his age division in the citywide 100-yard dash. He also won the broad jump, high jump, and shot put. Don Leahy was an interested spectator at the city meet, and Bouda's performance must have made an impression, because when he showed up for football practice as a freshman he was fast-tracked straight to the varsity. He would never play a down of freshman or junior varsity football. At a time when most Prep frosh floundered through the hallways carrying more textbooks than they were able, Bouda occupied a different universe, worrying only about scouting reports and nailing his next kick.

The win over South High felt especially gratifying to sophomore Sandy Buda, one of three sophomores who were part of the varsity squad (John Bjelland and Bill Pycha were the others). Sandy's father Carl Buda was a South High graduate. Carl had played college football at Creighton University until the program was dropped, then at Tulsa University, earning first-team All-American honors. As a member of the college All-Star team that played the Green Bay Packers at Soldier Field, Carl played the entire game, sixty minutes. After college he played professionally for the Pittsburgh Steelers, but he quit pro football for financial reasons after Sandy was born. When he returned to Omaha, Carl opened a bar near Omaha's Old Market district called Buda's Bar. He opened for business at three o'clock every morning to catch bar traffic from shift changes in the nearby warehouse district. Later he moved the bar to 49th and Underwood Streets and called it Golden Buda Cocktail Lounge. To make extra money, Carl opened up his house to three students from Creighton University. One of them was Johnny Carson's brother, and from time to time the future late-night talk show host would stop by to visit.

Carl Buda cared deeply for Sandy, his other son, Joe, and their two sisters, but he probably would have preferred that his sons follow his path to South High. For one thing, the Budas lived in South Omaha, near South High and just two blocks from Municipal Stadium. Sandy's uncle Dr. Sam Buda was the first family member to attend Creighton Prep. He was a successful athlete and became a dentist, and his influence drew Sandy to Prep.

"My dad said, 'You want to go to Prep? Fine, but you pay for it,'" Buda said.

Sandy was able to save money for his Prep tuition by working at Municipal Stadium in the summer selling popcorn, operating the manual scoreboard, and helping out the grounds crew. The summer he left for college, Sandy was replaced on the grounds crew by Jesse Cuevas, who would one day become the stadium's head groundskeeper. Instead of paying bus fare, Sandy rode to school each morning with Prepsters George Sullivan, Carl Salanitro, and Burnie Bisbee, all of whom became priests. During the school year he washed dishes in Prep's cafeteria each day over the noon hour to help pay his tuition.

"My dad owned a bar. We weren't rich at all. We were lucky. That made my experience at Prep even more rewarding because it wasn't given to me. I had to earn it. I had to pass the entrance exam. I got accepted, but when I got the notice, it said that I was going to be in D class. My dad loaded me into the car and took me up to Prep to see Father Sullivan. He wanted to know why I was in D class. Father Sullivan, who was a man of short words, looked at my test results and said, 'Well, Mr. Buda, your son Sandy is in D class because we don't have an E class.'"

Carl Buda supported his son's academic and athletic career, making it to all his football games. But he wasn't above the occasional cutting remark if warranted. In 1962, as a senior, Sandy served as the team's co-captain. Prep lost its opener to South and quarterback Marlin Briscoe at Municipal Stadium, and when Sandy walked in the door of the Buda residence that night expecting sympathy, Carl was sitting in his favorite worn-out reclining chair, staring into the newspaper. Then he broke into song: "South High will shine tonight, South High will shine tonight."

"He jabbed me," Sandy said. "Good guy, Dad. He liked to have fun. He was from the old school."

One man who probably would have appreciated Carl Buda's old-school ways was Don Leahy. Although much of his coaching philosophy felt cutting-edge, his approach to player discipline was decidedly throwback. During the season, that meant Saturday practices at Creighton Prep. But before practice, the players reported to Room 112 at Prep, the Chapel.

"That's where we would go to Mass after football games on Saturday mornings," remembered Bill Heaston. "We had to. Everybody. I don't care who you were. Saturday mornings around 8:30. We would have Mass and then we'd go out, and not have practice as such, but work out a little bit to get the stiffness out. Then we'd talk a little bit about who we were going to play."

Leahy was adamant about the Saturday routine. The coaches would check on any injuries that were sustained during Friday night's game and then take the players out for some light running. The routine also included receiving a report from Steve Costello about the next opponent on Prep's schedule. Steve Costello was Leahy's advance scout. Costello was a sort of football whisperer to Leahy, a man in whom he placed a great deal of trust. That trust was rooted in familiarity. Costello had been the starting center on Prep's undefeated 1953 football team. He had been a good player on a championship team, the sort that was used to winning. Leahy was an assistant coach on the '53 team and got to know Costello well. Steve played with a measure of pluck that impressed Leahy, especially given his size. Bernie Berigan remembers Costello weighing "160 pounds dripping wet, but he was tougher than hell and a good blocker." One game in particular impressed Leahy and Berigan—Boys Town. Costello lined up across from a much bigger player—Leahy remembered him as "an absolute mountain" and Berigan recalled he weighed at least 240 pounds—and held his own for the entire game.

"He got knocked around and everything, but he held up tough in there," Berigan said.

Leahy thought Costello's football acumen would make him a good scout, and he was right. He also became a volunteer coach. "He was very good," Leahy said. "When he came back with a scouting report, he didn't color it. He told you like it was. He'd say, 'We're going to have a tough time with this team.' Then I would say, 'All right, Steve, tell us why.' He was just outstanding. He took a pad and pencil. The first thing he'd do was get numbers and names and positions. Then, of course, he'd try to figure out the defensive schemes and the major offensive plays. He would come back and you'd be surprised how detailed and how accurate it was. He was very well known among the football people in Omaha."

"He was a really good scout," said Dudley Allen, who by 1960 had left Prep to coach at North Platte. "We always looked at basic formations. We looked at anything that was special about the team other than personnel. What did they do well? What did we have to stop? We always zeroed in on one, two, or three plays that we had to deal with."

What a team did well was something scouts at any level of football were keen to identify. Most football coaches, maybe all football coaches, believed every football team established a pattern of execution. Each team had strengths and weaknesses, and coaches went to great lengths to stop what an opponent did best. They subscribed to the philosophy that you should make your opponent try to beat you by executing something they normally didn't do . . . or something they didn't do well.

Everybody who was associated with Prep football knew how integral a role Costello played in the Junior Jays' success. And his work with his alma mater was a great sacrifice, too. He worked a full-time job at Omaha's Western Electric plant, one of the manufacturers for the Bell telephone system. Costello rearranged his work schedule so his shifts could accommodate games and practices during the season. When he watched games, he preferred to stand behind one of the two end zones so he could monitor the line play, his forte. At halftime, he would find Leahy in the locker room and explain what he was seeing on the line and suggest adjustments. The pair mined into the tiniest details, such as the placement of a lineman's knuckles on the turf before the snap or the plays a team was most likely to run out of a given formation. Costello knew what he was doing, and Leahy trusted him. He also fought through a noticeable stutter. Players and coaches became accustomed to phrases such as, "F-f-f-flex the t-t-tight end" in the locker room during halftime pep talks. The players, particularly the linemen, loved him. The level of detail in his scouting reports was exhaustive, and everyone took notice.

"He was probably the best scout in the state of Nebraska," said quarterback Frank Spenceri. "And nobody ever brings his name up. He came back with his scouting reports and we knew when the other team sneezed, when they farted, and which side of the line they were going to do it on. And Don Leahy was always prepared. He was a part/whole teacher. He segmented into parts the whole of what he was going to teach. Good coaches do that."

Costello's scouting work in later years included assisting future University of Nebraska football coach Frank Solich when he coached Omaha's Holy Name High School and scouting for the semiprofessional Omaha Mustangs. The Mustangs sent Costello to Chicago and other cities to scout, and each time he came back with a thorough report that the coaches could begin implementing immediately into the week's game plan. One of his other sporting interests was horse racing. The *Omaha World-Herald* ran a photo of a smiling Costello a few weeks before football practice began in the summer of 1960 at the Ak-Sar-Ben racetrack wearing binoculars around his neck and holding a race form and a handful of cash. The latter, supposedly, was borrowed for sake of the photo.

Costello was candid in explaining the scouting report

for Prep's next opponent, the Benson High School Bunnies. "That Benson team was tougher than nails," remembered Rich Vomacka. They had size, talent, and a capable quarterback. And more importantly, the Bunnies, after a surprising 13–12 victory Friday over intercity league preseason favorite Tech High, had momentum. The Bunnies were going for their first victory over Creighton Prep since 1941, and after their upstart victory over Tech, it suddenly seemed possible.

Football, at least high school football, took a temporary backseat to politics on Saturday, September 10, when Nebraskans opened their morning newspapers to learn of the sudden death of Governor Ralph Gilmour Brooks, sixty-two. The *Omaha World-Herald* spared any suspense with its oversized headline: "BROOKS' HEART FAILS." Brooks's untimely death from congestive heart failure that Friday afternoon came just a few hours after he announced that he was planning to continue his campaign for U.S. senator, despite a three-week stay at Lincoln General Hospital. Brooks was Nebraska's twenty-ninth governor, the first Democrat in the office for nearly two decades, and the first to die on the job. Sixty-eight-year-old Lieutenant Governor Dwight W. Burney, a Republican, took over the state's gubernatorial duties upon Brooks's death.

Football went on as planned for Omaha Central Saturday night, and that meant a visit from Lincoln High School and state sprint champion Bobby Williams. Like Creighton Prep, Central would open the season under the lights at Municipal Stadium.

Stopping a talent the caliber of Bobby Williams had to keep Frank Smagacz awake at night. Born in 1942 in Alabama, Williams grew up in Lincoln, where he developed a flair for many sports. He finished third in the state wrestling tournament as a sophomore before deciding to spend his winters on the basketball court, where he was second on the team in scoring as a senior. Smagacz was familiar with Williams's tremendous speed from seeing his performances in track and field. Williams won the 100-yard and 220-yard gold medals at the state meet in 1960 and won the 100 again in '61. That spring at the Hastings, Nebraska, Invitational, Williams was the noteworthy champion of a 100-yard dash he ran in 9.5 seconds that saw the next four finishers run in 10 flat or better.

Then there was Williams's jumping ability. It's safe to say the only athlete in the state who could match Williams's leap was Gale Sayers, and the story of the 1961 Nebraska state high school track meet confirms it. Williams and Sayers spent the better part of the season besting each other at track meets, continually topping each other in the broad jump, one meet after another. At the 1961 state meet, held indoors underneath the University of Nebraska Memorial Stadium, Williams jumped 22 feet, 11 inches on his first jump, breaking the state record by a quarter of an inch. Sayers topped him on his third jump with a mark of 23 feet, 3 inches, only to see the lead disappear after a Williams jump of 23 feet, 3¼ inches. With one jump left, Sayers called in Frank Smagacz for assistance. Smagacz laid a handkerchief off to the side of the jumping pit to give Sayers a visual guide of how far he needed to jump. As Sayers turned his back and walked down the runway to begin his jump, Smagacz kicked the handkerchief forward slightly. He then instructed Sayers to take a slightly different angle of approach as he began his jump. Smagacz took a seat parallel to Sayers's jumping-off point, surrounded by a crowd of interested spectators, to watch the jump.

Sayers sprung forward, kicking his legs, and landed dead even with the handkerchief. 24 feet, 10½ inches. Officials called for a remeasurement to make sure they had it right. They did. Gale's new record would stand for forty-four years. Sportswriter Larry Porter called it "the greatest track per-

formance ever achieved by a Nebraska high school athlete."
Perhaps he should have called it one of the greatest motivational performances ever by a Nebraska coach. Smagacz's
homespun methods of motivating athletes to do great things
was perhaps his greatest trait as a coach, and it rubbed off
on even his greatest athlete. Another veteran Omaha sportswriter once wrote that Smagacz "probably talked more athletes into good performances than any other prep coach."

Williams wasn't about to let his broad-jump loss to Sayers ruin his promising athletic career. After high school,
he attended Central Oklahoma University (then known as
Central State), a National Association of Intercollegiate Athletics (NAIA) football power that won a slew of conference
championships and two small college national championships in 1962 and 1982. At Central State, Williams became
a four-year starter in the backfield and a valuable member of the '62 national championship team. He also won a
letter in track in 1964 as a member of a conference champion relay team. With astounding statistics, including a 5.7
yards-per-carry average and 3,094 all-purpose yards, Williams propelled his collegiate success into a six-year career
in the National Football League, where he starred as a kick
return specialist.

If they could somehow master the Bobby Williams pre-
dicament Saturday night, the Lincoln High game offered
Central a chance to notch some style points against a highly
regarded opponent. But Frank Smagacz kept things low-
key, even telling a student reporter before the game that he
expected just an average season. He knew how big a first
test stood in front of his team. Lincoln High, Central's traditional opening-game opponent, was absent from Creighton Prep's schedule, and a victory for the Eagles would be
an impressive early-season coup.

As they trailed 6–2 while heading into halftime after
two uninspired quarters, a coup was probably the furthest

FIG. 13. Gale Sayers was as devastating in track and field as he was in football. Reprinted with permission of the 1961 Omaha Central High School *O-Book*.

thing from the minds of the Central players. The score was closer to that of a baseball game about to get out of hand than a football contest. The Lincoln High players deserved much of the credit. They ran a single-wing offense similar to what L. G. Friedrichs used to run at Creighton Prep, but by 1960 it seemed everybody in the state had abandoned it, except for the Links. Central's coaches knew how to defend the offense, but on this night, at least early on, it was giving them fits. Central's only score was a gifted safety care of the Links in the second quarter during an attempted punt. The first time Lincoln High possessed the football, Williams caught a long pass in stride and took it the distance for a 50-yard score. Lincoln's next score came in the third quarter after a Central fumble was recovered by Roger Campbell on the Central 35-yard line. A 23-yard pass followed by a 4-yard scoring run on a sweep play for Leroy Hunter put the Links up 12–2 with five minutes and twenty-three seconds left in the third quarter. The next four minutes and twenty seconds of game action changed the course of the game and Central's entire 1960 season.

Following the Leroy Hunter touchdown, the Links kicked off to Gale Sayers, who took the ball and handed it off to Ardell Gunn on a reverse. Gunn "wriggled" and "zigzagged" his way through would-be Lincoln tacklers, according to Don Lee's newspaper account of the game, all the way to the end zone for an 84-yard kickoff return. The Lincoln High fans, scattered throughout the crowd of two thousand in attendance that night, were stunned by the first scoring strike from Central. Surely they were completely dumbfounded by what they saw next, a Mark Firestone pass intercepted by Central's Gayle Carey (who was on the field at safety in place of injured Vernon Breakfield) that the junior returned 48 yards along the field's east sideline for a touchdown.

"Breakfield, I got your *touch*down," Carey joked to his teammate as he ran back to the sideline.

Central now led, 15–12, and had offered its first taste of a bloodthirsty ball-hawking secondary. The second taste came on Lincoln High's very next pass attempt, this time by Marc Danekas, which was intercepted by Gale Sayers and returned 53 yards along the west sideline for another Central score. The extra point made it 22–12, with Central having taken the lead without executing a scoring play from scrimmage.

Don Lee characterized the dramatic change of events as a "brief but smashing display of the burning speed which the Eagles have in the defensive secondary." Things could have been even worse for Lincoln High had Central's Johnny Bruce not dropped a potential touchdown pass that was headed for his hands. Teammate Eugene Barker, a sophomore, was even positioned to help escort the "over-eager" Bruce toward the end zone, but it was not to be. Unfortunately for Bruce, a *World-Herald* photographer was in position to snap a shot of his drop, preserving the gaffe for the Sunday newspaper.

Lincoln High was shell-shocked, and not even Bobby Williams could bail them out. Backed up on their own 10-yard line in the fourth quarter, Williams fumbled, and Central's Don Fiedler recovered the ball, setting up a 5-yard scoring run up the middle of the defense by Gale Sayers that put the game out of reach.

"Lincoln High was a signature game for us," said Gayle Carey. "And we were on a roll."

Despite being outgained in total yardage 197–128, Central scored the game's final 27 points to steal a 29–12 win from Lincoln High. All of Central's yardage came on the ground, as the sore-shouldered quarterback duo of Howard Fouts and Jim Capellupo failed to complete any of their 4 pass attempts, but offensive balance was not among the ingredients for the Eagles' winning recipe on this night. The win was Frank Smagacz's sixth consecutive victory over the Links. For Coaches Smagacz and Karabatsos, the vic-

Fig. 14. Huddled up—the 1960 Omaha Central Eagles. Reprinted with permission of the 1961 Omaha Central High School *O-Book*.

tory was as informative as it was necessary. They now knew how their kids would fare against stiff competition. It didn't get much stiffer than Lincoln High.

"We knew we had a good backfield and a couple decent tackles," Karabatsos said. "So we had the build-up of a potentially good team. Now, what they were capable of really doing, we didn't know. And we found out in the first game against Lincoln. We beat them fairly soundly, so we knew we had the makings."

Lincoln High's play the rest of the season proved just how good of a win it was for the Central Eagles. The Links would reel off eight consecutive victories to finish the season 8-1.

While Don Leahy spent his weekends after football games studying his next opponent, Frank Smagacz focused on another task: public relations. That isn't to say he didn't game-plan—he certainly did—but his favorite weekend pastime, according to his son Mike, was calling Don Lee and his fellow sportswriters at the *Omaha World-Herald* to discuss Friday night's game (or in some cases, Saturday's game) and rap about the next week's opponent. Smagacz called Lee once a week without fail during football season and frequently during the spring track season.

"He always wanted to have oneupmanship on everything," Mike Smagacz said of his father. "The only way to do that is to have friends who are in the know. Don Lee was happy to have somebody to talk to him like that. And Don Lee was a guy, as are all reporters, that loved to talk. He appreciated that, I think.

"Dad was the same way in track. They'd have meetings before track meets, and he always wanted to get the best lanes. So the track coaches would get together and figure out what lanes they were going to get in. He'd always speak up for himself. Boy, I tell ya, you didn't pull any wool over his eyes. He knew exactly what was going on, I'll tell you that. He was very outgoing. He wasn't inward or quiet or anything."

Lee, for his part, was the perfect pal for Smagacz. He was also the perfect sportswriter for high school football, according to his fellow writers. With a round face and thinning red hair, Lee was a sweet man with a perky, peppy, kid-like personality. He was always laughing and smiling. Everybody seemed to love his company and respect his work. High school sports fit him like a glove. That isn't to say he was a pushover. When he put ink on paper, Lee could cut right to the heart of a team's (or coach's) strengths and weaknesses, another reason why Smagacz was smart to keep Lee as a friend.

F<small>IG</small>. 15. Don Lee, *far left*, was the perfect beat writer for high school sports. Also pictured, *from left*, are *Omaha World-Herald* staffers Bob Tucker, Jerry Kane, Jim Ivey, and Marvin Thomson. Photo by Sebi Breci (1972), courtesy of James Fogarty.

"His style was old-school," said fellow Omaha newsman Henry Cordes, a Central High graduate. "Unlike a lot of writers, particularly sportswriters of that era, Don didn't make quotes up. When you read something from Don Lee, you knew it was legit."

Whether Smagacz called Lee to curry favor for his Central High football teams or simply liked having someone he could talk football with, his weekend conversations helped keep Central relevant in the minds of sportswriters. There were other benefits, too. After earning a family award sponsored by Wonder Bread, Smagacz decided the achievement merited a photo in the newspaper. He got a hold of Don Lee and a *World-Herald* photographer, who showed up at the Smagacz residence to take a photo of Fran and the children. It ran as a full-fledged advertisement in the paper, with a photo of the healthy Smagacz family and a statement from Fran extolling the virtues of Wonder Bread: "Wonder Bread helps build strong bodies eight ways! No mother would skimp on her children's health! We all enjoy Wonder Bread so much."

Years later when Smagacz left football coaching, the lives of the Omaha journalists became a little bit duller during the fall season. He was a hard guy not to like. Columnist Wally Provost wrote as much, noting at the time of his retirement that he would be missed. Smagacz was a straight-talker and generally a pleasant man for the sportswriters to deal with. "If he had a beef, he stated it bluntly—you didn't hear it from 'a friend of a friend,'" Provost wrote.

Smagacz's other weekend hobby was listening to professional football on the radio and watching games on television. If he heard or saw a play or scheme or gadget he liked, he would come to practice Monday and try to implement it into the Central repertoire. It didn't matter if the play was run by the best team in professional football. If Smagacz saw it, he thought *his* teams could run it too.

"Frank was the type of guy who wasn't afraid to try different things," said Jim Karabatsos. "He loved to watch pro football, and he'd see things that he'd try to bring to the high school level."

Smagacz left the scouting to Karabatsos. Jim loved it. The challenge of unraveling an opponent's motives through their play selection was like trying to solve a riddle. One year, while scouting a South High game from high atop Creighton Stadium, Karabatsos turned to the assistant coach with him and declared that he could predict which way South was going to run on every play. By closely studying the South quarterback, he observed the signal-caller taking a staggered stance under center. Sometimes his left foot would sit 6 or 8 inches behind the right, and with other plays, vice versa. Karabatsos noticed that the staggered foot was the quarterback's base foot. To his discerning eye, it was a tip-off. On plays running left, he would pivot around his staggered right foot; on plays going right, he pivoted around the left. It was a small detail, but the sort that could make the difference between winning and losing. In their game against South that season, a particularly weak Central squad nearly upset the Packers. Using Karabatsos's scouting report, they shut down the South running attack, except for one play, when a South runner got loose for a long run and the Packers won the game by a touchdown. In later years, the Central coaches used a camera, on loan from a local camera shop, to scout opponents. Filming games was a growing trend, but in 1960 most high schools didn't have a proper camera or the means to get one.

The players thought of Karabatsos as their own personal Vince Lombardi, a taskmaster. He was never too quick to throw out a compliment, yet the players all loved him because he was always finding ways for them to improve. When Gayle Carey and Tim Dempsey cracked the varsity roster as sophomores, Karabatsos made sure they didn't get too full of themselves. He told them, "This is an unusually soft year, guys. Others years, you wouldn't have made it." In fact, he was quite impressed by their ability. One day at practice, he told Carey to split out wide at flanker for the next play. Carey split out wide of the line of scrimmage about five yards, and Karabatsos yelled, "No, no! Out farther." Carey took two more steps over, and Karabatsos ran across the field, grabbed Carey by the collar, and dragged him out of bounds. "Get down," he told Carey.

"He sat on my head and yelled back to the others, 'Okay, you all run the play now.' But from then on, I knew what a flanker was supposed to do. Split out. The coaches were rough sometimes, but they made us better. We didn't have any panties on out there."

Another day at practice, Karabatsos was instructing the running backs when he lined up as quarterback behind the line of scrimmage. He tapped Fred Scarpello on the backside for the snap, but the ball never came. "Then he kicked me in the ass," Scarpello said. "And I said, 'Coach, I'm the guard, not the center.'" Karabatsos apologized and slid over a yard, behind the center.

Smagacz was no Lombardi-type. Karabatsos called him "a lovable man. Kind of loud, but not a screamer." His greatest strength was convincing his players they were better than they thought they were, and he would do it in his own imitable way. When he wasn't looking, his players loved to impersonate their coach. "Geez, guys. Golly, gee whiz," they would say. The peculiar cadence of his speech, rolling from one word into another, seemed to permanently imbed itself into his players' memories. "Smagese" became a private language shared between the players, and it seemed every class through the years had a chief Smagacz impressionist. Once when he was coaching defense at practice, Smagacz explained to his team the importance of a defensive huddle. "Now we're going to huddle up, guys," he told them. "Nothing really goes on in the huddle, but when it's cold out you just kind of do it to keep warm, see."

Smagacz's always-hustling ways were more than just a show he put on for his football players. With ten kids to raise, he needed every dime he could get his hands on. To do it, he worked three jobs. He taught at Central during the day, coached during the afternoons once school let out, and worked a nighttime shift at the Omaha post office as a mail sorter. The post office shift usually ended at midnight. Other times he took an early morning shift. And then there were the refereeing and umpiring jobs he picked up on the side. Anything to make a buck.

"He was a hard worker," said Mike Smagacz. "He'd teach, then coach, then go to bed until one or two in the morning and then go to work until about seven. Then he'd go teach and do it all over again. Those are the kind of things he did."

His busy work schedule made Frank Smagacz something

of a ghost to his kids, especially the older ones, who hardly ever saw him during the week. But he brought home valuable paychecks that put food on the table and clothes on their back, and in doing so he provided his kids with an example of what hard work looked like. "That's why we're all workers," Mike Smagacz said. "He was a good example in that respect."

The post office job was a year-round commitment. Smagacz tried to make it a forty-hour-per-week job, and a friendly timekeeper helped him fashion a schedule that left room for his teaching and coaching commitments while still allowing him to put in enough hours to bring home a steady check.

"Many times when he was supposed to be at the post office, he'd be up at Central," remembers Roger Sayers. "I'd say, 'Coach, what are you doing here?'

"He'd say, 'Oh, I'm checked out now.'

"I don't know how he did it, but he got away with it. He would coach football every day and then work until whatever time he got off, then when I'd show up at school the next day, he was there."

If Creighton Prep was to beat Benson High, it would have to stop Bunny quarterback Chris Beutler. The Bunnies' fine defensive effort in week one, holding preseason favorite Tech High to just 12 points, was impressive, but Beutler's arm stole the show. In his efficient come-from-behind dismantling of Tech, he completed 6 of 10 passes for 142 yards. His first scoring throw was a 64-yard strike to Dave Johnson, which Johnson caught at midfield and raced to the end zone. Even more impressive was Benson's second scoring drive, which came with time running out in the first half. The Bunnies took over with just one minute left before intermission after recovering a fumble on Tech's 41-yard line. Trailing 12–7, Beutler then completed passes of 9, 12, and 20 yards to Johnson, William Donahoo, and Gary Hart. The Hart catch came as time expired in the half and put Benson up 13–12, a score that held up as the final.

Beutler was the real McCoy. He weighed just 150 pounds, but he was the heart and soul of the Benson team—"their big hero," remembered Prep lineman Bill Heaston. Beutler's post–high school career took him to great places, too. He attended Yale University and the University of Nebraska College of Law, eventually serving two terms in the Nebraska legislature. In 2007, he became the mayor of Lincoln, winning a tight general election by 845 votes. Had Beutler known of his future in politics, he might have awoken early the Friday morning of the Prep game and ventured down to the Omaha Civic Auditorium to hear a speech from Vice President Richard M. Nixon, who was in town for "Coffee with Dick and Pat," sponsored by the Douglas County Republican Central Committee. For one dollar, anyone could grab coffee and a roll and listen to the views of the presidential candidate.

In his pregame column, Don Lee forecast a game that likely would be decided by the passing game. It made sense that Benson coach Rex Johnson would put the game in the hands of his star player, Beutler, but the Bunnies had yet to experience the 1960 Creighton Prep defense. Perhaps Lee put it best when he wrote, "It's out of the pan and into the fire for the Bunnies."

When the game got underway, it became clear that Benson's game plan was to try and win the game not through the air but behind the strength of its bigger bodies. And for a while, at least, the strategy worked.

The first time Benson possessed the football, the Bunnies scored quickly on the ground thanks to Beutler, 145-pound halfback Kenneth Kortright, and Dave Johnson, who scored from a yard out to polish off the 59-yard opening drive. Prep returned the favor on the ensuing series, moving the ball with big chunk plays, particularly a 17-yard pass reception by Vic Meyers and a 19-yard John Corrigan run. John Bozak finished off the drive with a 1-yard scoring run early in the second quarter.

Moving the football offensively was hard work for Prep for the rest of the second quarter and most of the third. Benson's defense was stingy, thanks mostly to 183-pound linebacker Terry Ronne, who was a familiar face in the Prep backfield. During one series late in the third quarter, Ronne helped Benson stop Prep for negative plays on three consecutive snaps. Deadlocked 7–7, Prep's Bobby Gaeta set up to punt on Prep's 28-yard line. He was dropped for a 14-yard loss, Prep's fourth consecutive negative play, and Benson took over deep in Junior Jay territory with eyes on the goal line and a go-ahead score. Benson's Dave Johnson gained 4 yards on first down, and Beutler threw an incomplete pass on second down to set up an important third-and-six at Prep's 10-yard line. Benson called for a delayed quarterback keeper, and Beutler had barely made it past the line of scrimmage when he ran into a wall of Prep defenders led by Bill Heaston, who hit Beutler hard enough to knock the football loose. Bobby Gaeta, a former classmate of Beutler's at St. Bernard Grade School and a teammate on the Brandeis midget team, alertly plucked the ball out of the air before it hit the ground and took off toward the end zone, 90 yards away. Flanked by a convoy of blockers including Walt Kazlauskas, who single-handedly blocked the pursuit of two Benson players, Gaeta's speed and hunger for redemption soon pulled him ahead of the pack and he was never caught.

Touchdown Creighton Prep. Talk about sudden change.

The score put Prep up 14–7 with three minutes and fifty-seven seconds left in the third quarter and totally changed the complexion of the game. The fumble recovery earned Gaeta the *Omaha World-Herald*'s Star-of-the-Week award, a noteworthy honor in a week when Bobby Williams ran for 4 long touchdowns against Omaha North and Charles Schweiger of Grand Island had a 76-yard punt return to help beat Scottsbluff.

For Bill Heaston, the Gaeta play was one highlight in an all-around well-played game. His rooting section, the entire Heaston family, was sprinkled in among the crowd of eight thousand at Municipal Stadium that night, and according to a family account, they were "a wild bunch for a while" after his big hit. After suffering an early-season rib injury in practice, Bill wore a brace to prevent further injury. The combination of sore ribs and the cumbersome brace made it difficult for him to breathe from play to play, and another tackle he made in the fourth quarter completely winded him and knocked him out for the rest of the game. But by then he had already made his mark on the contest.

The Prep touchdown took the wind out of Benson's sails. The next time Prep possessed the football, the Junior Jays strung together an 86-yard drive, culminating in a 5-yard John Bozak touchdown run with five minutes and forty-four seconds left in the game that sealed Benson's fate.

Bozak was one of Prep's co-captains, and he took the honor seriously. He was responsible for relaying the defensive calls that came in from the sideline and keeping his teammates in a positive state of mind. For Bozak, playing for Prep was like living a dream. He had grown up listening to Prep games on the radio at night, and soon he fell in love with the entire program. His father, John Bozak Sr., was a police sergeant who stopped by to watch Prep practice from time to time. Growing up with a father who was a cop had its advantages and disadvantages.

"I had to be careful," Bozak said. "I could never get in trouble."

The 20–7 Prep victory was impressive in many ways. For

starters, the team had shown the ability to pull out a tough game late. Prior to Gaeta's fumble recovery, the score was tied and Benson had all the momentum as it pushed toward the end zone for what would have been a go-ahead score. Prep's defense limited the Bunnies to just 111 yards of total offense, and their much-feared passing attack was virtually nonexistent (Beutler completed none of his 3 attempts). Prep, meanwhile, got its aerial game on track, completing 4 of 9 pass attempts en route to the victory.

The Benson rooters, hungry to end the losing streak to Creighton Prep, would have to wait another year.

Visitors to Benson Field Friday night would have a hard time deciding what part of the action between Omaha Central and Omaha South was most impressive: the sudden scoring ability of Gale Sayers, the equally sudden big-play capability from South, or the sheer volume of penalty flags that covered the field. One thing was certain: the game was entertaining.

Don Lee's pregame write-up, which billed the Central-South matchup as the night's second-most-attractive prep contest (behind Creighton Prep vs. Benson), forecast an "explosive game" between the Eagles and Packers, and that's just what they delivered.

The two teams combined to produce 658 total offensive yards, 23 first downs, 23 attempted passes, and 85 yards of penalties. However, when the game finished, the Central Eagles were dominant en route to a 32–18 victory.

The first quarter ended without a score and with both teams lamenting missed opportunities. A Central drive that went deep into South territory was undone by an untimely fumble. The hard-luck Packers squandered two scoring chances of their own thanks to penalties on long pass completions. Just as they had the week before against Creighton Prep, South had difficulty staying out of its own way, committing penalties and letting scoring chances slip by. It was a shame, because once Gale Sayers shook loose, the Packers had little chance of victory. Central led 13–0 at halftime and tacked on another 13 points in the third quarter to all but put the game out of reach. Sayers exploded for touchdown runs of 74, 43, and 42 yards to cement his already developing reputation as a scoring threat from anywhere on the field. All three plays were end runs, and nobody from South could catch the speedy back once he turned the corner. Gayle Carey also aided the scoring, taking in a 5-yard sweep for a score and tacking on the extra point. The South game was a bright spot for Carey as a runner; he amassed 104 yards and 2 scores.

South's quarterback, Don Crum, one-third of the Crum trio, did his best to help the Packers keep pace, including bolting for a 61-yard touchdown run where he faked a pass and followed blocker Don Garrison's path into the end zone. He also returned a kickoff 86 yards behind the block of Garry Marley for another touchdown and connected with Marley on a 46-yard pass that went the distance, but his valiant play brought South High no closer to victory.

When the final buzzer sounded, the Eagles had notched another double-digit victory and made a clear statement that they were playing on a different level from Omaha South. For South coach Merle Applebee, there was little reason to berate his players. Sure, there were unforced errors and sloppy penalties, but his team had played hard for two consecutive weeks against two teams shaping up to be the state's best. Any beef he had should have been with his athletic director for scheduling Prep and Central in back-to-back weeks to open the season.

When sportswriter Gregg McBride released his first edition of statewide prep football rankings in the Monday edition of the *Omaha World-Herald*, Creighton Prep was ranked first and Omaha Central was second. The full top ten went as follows:

FIG. 16. The Central High cheerleaders—full of school spirit. Reprinted with permission of the 1961 Omaha Central High School *O-Book*.

1. Creighton Prep
2. Omaha Central
3. Lincoln High
4. Omaha Benson
5. Omaha Tech
6. Hastings
7. North Platte
8. Kearney
9. Grand Island
10. Falls City

Clearly, Central's decisive victory over Lincoln High in the first week earned the Eagles significant clout in McBride's eyes, especially after the Links blanked Omaha North 32–0 in week two. The Links were paced that night by Bobby Williams, who scored 4 touchdowns, all runs, of 37, 16, 71, and 43 yards.

Despite the notoriety of their high ranking and the two

hard-earned victories, the Central players avoided cockiness and maintained their focus on next Friday's opponent, Omaha North, Frank Smagacz told a newspaper reporter on Wednesday after the South game. Injuries were also a concern, but Smagacz downplayed their effect, too.

"We have the usual number of bruises," he said, "but the bruises don't hurt as much when you're winning."

One such concern was starting center Tim Dempsey, whose malady was not a bump or bruise but an internal medical ailment. Dempsey, a junior, had been one of the team's surprises early in the season. After a summer of intense conditioning, he arrived at practice in excellent shape and impressed coaches enough to earn starting jobs at center and defensive guard. After playing his sophomore season at 195 pounds, he dropped to 185 that summer, mostly solid muscle full of athletic potential, and the coaches loved the production he offered on both lines of scrimmage. Dempsey played against Lincoln High and Omaha South but came down with a mysterious illness the following week. He first suspected the stomach flu, but after spending a few days at home convalescing, he noticed he wasn't feeling better. And he had unusually low energy to boot. A few days off turned into a full week, and he returned to the doctor suspecting a more serious diagnosis. Tests revealed infectious mononucleosis, and he was admitted to Omaha's St. Joseph's Hospital.

Dempsey's bout with mono would end his 1960 season. His pancreas had been damaged, and doctors recommended an extended hospital stay. Dempsey's father, Joe, a Creighton Prep graduate, worked at Central as the school's head engineer, and he was a close friend of Frank Smagacz, the other coaches, and many of Tim's teachers. As head engineer, Joe Dempsey was responsible for supervising the school's entire staff of janitors and the engineers who fired the boilers. He and his staff handled all of Central's maintenance.

Dempsey's absence was a major blow to Frank Smagacz's roster, no doubt, and as the Eagles set their sights on North High, they looked within their ranks for someone capable of filling his spot in the starting rotation.

CHAPTER 7

FITTINGLY FOR A SPORTS-CRAZED town like Omaha, the mayor in 1960 was John Rosenblatt, a former athlete and the man for whom Municipal Stadium would later be named. Rosenblatt became mayor in 1954, and his tenure, which lasted through 1961, came at an important time for Omahans and their governance. A landmark change took place in city government in 1957 with a major revision to the city charter, switching Omaha from a commission form of government to what was essentially a strong-mayor system, where the mayor and city council representatives were directly elected. Rosenblatt's tenure was a bridge between the two systems. He was the last mayor appointed under the commission system and the first elected under the new charter.

Rosenblatt, by most accounts, was a sweet, streetwise man, slightly built, and well known and admired by most all Omahans. Even the press seemed to like him, probably because he was known to offer car rides to reporters from time to time. The likable mayor was a graduate of Omaha Tech, where he had played baseball. In 1927 he had participated in an exhibition game alongside Babe Ruth and Lou Gehrig. He played sports as a collegian, and he was active in Omaha baseball for many years. In the 1940s he led bond drives for new stadium funds, and when a committee was formed to help get Municipal Stadium built, Rosenblatt was a natural choice to chair it.

The population of Omaha in 1960 was a shade more than three hundred thousand, a 20 percent increase from a decade before. Surrounding communities not within city limits (Council Bluffs, Iowa, for example) made Omaha feel even more robust. The population boom would continue for at least another decade, but by 1980 the growth would temporarily halt, likely as a consequence of the demise of the city's meatpacking industry.

But in 1960, the livestock industry in Omaha was booming. By 1955, the city had surpassed Chicago as site of the world's largest stockyards, and a large sign over a prominent South Omaha bridge let visitors know it. So did license plates throughout the state, which carried the words "Beef State," letting the outside world know what industry buttered the state's bread. Every day, livestock came to the city by the thousands: cattle and hogs, mostly. In the stockyards they would be penned until one of the many prosperous meat packinghouses would buy the livestock for slaughter. Bushels and bushels of government grain were stored at the stockyards to feed the animals, and millions of dollars were exchanged every day. It was a booming industry that supplied jobs to a significant portion of the city's workforce. Many parents who sent their children to high school at Omaha Central or Creighton Prep held jobs in the packinghouse industry, and they were grateful for the opportunity.

The decision to build the new Creighton Prep campus on 72nd Street, west of downtown Omaha, made sense for numerous reasons. Perhaps most importantly, there were space issues on the campus of Creighton University that could be remedied by moving the high school. But the city was rapidly growing from east to west, away from the packinghouse district. Land was available to the west, and the march of suburbia in that direction began when soldiers came home from World War II and started moving into small starter homes in growing neighborhoods between 50th and 72nd Streets.

In a sense, Omaha felt like two or even three distinct cities. There was old Omaha to the east and new Omaha to the west. South Omaha—home to the livestock industry, ethnically distinct neighborhoods, and years of political influence—functioned as its own political reality. In fact, it once had been. South Omaha had been a separate city, distinct from Omaha, until it was annexed in 1915. During that time, one of the city's mayors, C. P. Miller, was found one evening at 8th and Dodge Streets injured from a 45-caliber bullet wound that tore out his left eyeball. He died a day later; some suspected the event was suicide, while others looked for answers in the city's gambling houses. That part of the city, largely partisan Democrat in its political ideology, dominated county government offices for what seemed like forever. Yet, the area's strongest bastion of political influence was a noteworthy conservative, Roman Hruska, who for twenty-two years served as a U.S. senator. In South Omaha, Hruska was a sort of Bohemian god, revered by almost everyone. Perhaps there was no greater tribute to his influence than the location of the U.S. Navy Personnel Center at Fort Omaha, whose nearest body of water was the Missouri River. The navy trained its reserves and occupied the fort until 1974, two years before Hruska's retirement.

In 1957, the mayor's Planning and Development Committee proposed what became known as the Omaha Plan, a series of projects designed to modernize Omaha as a city with a new airport terminal, a new police headquarters, a main library, and various phases of street and highway construction. The origins of the plan, it seems, date back to 1945, when *Omaha World-Herald* publisher Henry Doorly used his widely read newspaper to tout Omaha's plusses and minuses, and the latter got people motivated to reshape their city in a postwar motif. Mayor Rosenblatt supported the Omaha Plan, but most Omahans did not and shot it down in a June 1958 vote. It wasn't until 1971, thirteen years after that vote, that Omaha finally got a new police headquarters.

Of the many parts of the Omaha Plan, the airport issue lingered. A decision was made to create an airport authority, separate from other aspects of municipal government, and place the airport development under its jurisdiction, without the aid of tax dollars. Following the creation of the Omaha Airport Authority, the Federal Aviation Agency (FAA) granted $885,000 to build a new passenger terminal in Omaha. The figure was boosted by an additional $1 million from the Eugene C. Eppley Foundation. The new terminal, named the Eppley Air Passenger Terminal, was nearly three times the size of the old facility and would open in 1961. In October 1960, construction of the terminal was 30 percent complete. That August, Omaha began commercial jet service, signaling a new era of air travel into and out of the city.

In the fall of 1960, a golf-crazed war hero from Kansas, General Dwight David Eisenhower, was president of the United States. His time in office, 1953–61, roughly mirrored John Rosenblatt's time as Omaha mayor. In mid-October, Eisenhower, seventy, became the oldest man to ever occupy the White House, eclipsing President Andrew Jackson's record. In 1956, Congress authorized construction of the Dwight D. Eisenhower National System of Interstate and Defense Highways, named after Ike, a longtime champion of the project. A 1957 map in the *Omaha World-Herald* showed Omahans the maze of routes they could expect to see crisscrossing through their city once construction was finished. In 1974, Nebraska would claim to be the first state to complete all of its Interstate construction.

In 1960, most Omahans got their news from radio station 1110 KFAB. Kids listened to KOIL, which played popular rock 'n' roll music and weekly top-forty selections. Those who were lucky enough to own television sets—and that number was growing fast—could catch newscasts and sitcoms on KETV, KMTV, or WOW-TV.

In June, thrill-seeking moviegoers experienced Alfred

Hitchcock's "new and altogether different screen excitement" with the release of *Psycho*, starring Janet Leigh and Anthony Perkins. Billing it as a "special attraction," newspaper advertisements for the film warned that "No one . . . BUT NO ONE . . . will be admitted to the theatre after the start of each performance of *Psycho*." The ad, written in true Hitchcockian prose, explained, "This is to help you enjoy *Psycho* more. By the way, after you see the picture, please don't give away the ending. It's the only one we have." In August, movie theaters around Omaha and the country welcomed a two-hour adventure movie called *Ocean's 11* to the big screen, starring Frank Sinatra, Dean Martin, and Sammy Davis Jr. Its plot, in which a group of ex-military buddies attempt to burgle three Las Vegas casino hotels, was both attractive and timeless. It was remade, with great commercial success, in 2001.

Moviegoers in Omaha had many options for movie houses in 1960, including the Admiral, the Chief, and the Omaha. There were many drive-ins available, too, including the Airport Drive-In, the 84th and Center Drive-In, and Sky View on North 72nd. Teenagers who went to the drive-ins employed a special cost-saving strategy of piling into the trunks of cars to avoid paying admittance; of course once they were safely on the grounds of the drive-in, they would unload from the trunk and scatter like mice.

If you wanted to go out for a steak dinner before or after your trip to the cinema, Omaha was your city. Every part of town was home to at least one great steakhouse. Some even had live music on occasion, to the delight of the regulars. These establishments were part of the city's identity. Ross's Steakhouse at 909 North 72nd Street, owned by the Lorello family, was brand new in 1959. Nearby was Angelo's Studio Inn, where the menu bragged about serving "the finest steaks in the world!" In 1960, those steaks cost between three and eight dollars, depending on the cut. There were others, too: Caniglia's Italian Steakhouse, open since 1946; Mister C's, open since 1953; Cascio's, open since 1946; Gorat's, open since 1944; Piccolo Pete's, open since 1934; and Johnny's Cafe, which the Kawa family opened in 1924 on South 27th Street. Teenagers preferred fast food hangouts such as Tiner's, Otoe's, or Shada's. Others spent their free time in bowling alleys such as Kelley's Hilltop Lanes, the Ranch Bowl, and West Lanes, located near Creighton Prep.

As each summer came to a close, students and their parents headed to the stores to shop for new school clothes. Without rival, the J. L. Brandeis & Sons department store dominated the shopping scene in Omaha. In October, the store opened a branch operation at the new Crossroads Shopping Center at 72nd and Dodge Streets. The *Central High Register* warned girls that skirts were getting shorter, hitting just above the knees, long enough to be called "knee-ticklers." For more conservative girls, a *Register* advertisement recommended slacks. The boys, meanwhile, were encouraged to wear leather or suede, both of which were masculine enough to appeal to the opposite sex.

Without argument, Omaha's primary entertainment draw was the Ak-Sar-Ben racetrack, where pari-mutuel betting had been legal since 1935. Subtleties aside, pari-mutuel gambling can be described simply as betting among bettors. Effectively, a bettor's wager is made against other bettors, not against the house, or, in this case, the track. The track, for its role in handling the action, took a cut. If you strolled through the parking lots surrounding Ak-Sar-Ben in 1960, you would see license plates from all over the country—Kansas, Kentucky, Florida, Tennessee. If you strolled through the stands, on occasion you would see Mayor Rosenblatt, who entertained anyone who stopped by to say "Hi, Johnny." High schoolers would sometimes lie about their age to get admitted to the track, and there was an ongoing battle between the police and Omaha's many bookmakers who would take cover outside the track's gates, hoping not to be seen while they anxiously awaited race results. Police officers would chase them away until they retreated to a large hill northeast of the track where they could look in on the action using binoculars.

In 1959, the racehorse called Omaha, winner of the 1935 Triple Crown, was buried on the Ak-Sar-Ben grounds. (Years later when the property was slated for commercial development, the horse's whereabouts had been lost and were a subject of controversy. One longtime track employee speculated that the remains had been unearthed by accident during work on a clubhouse expansion in 1974.) The indoor Ak-Sar-Ben coliseum was home to the Omaha Knights Minor League hockey team and hosted popular concerts, large-scale municipal events, and of course the annual Ak-Sar-Ben coronation ball for the upper crust of Omaha society, an event that Nebraska novelist Mari Sandoz once called "Omaha's big make-believe." On crowded nights at the coliseum, ribbons of cigarette smoke could be seen wafting through the upper levels of the arena and pooling in conjunction with the facility's air currents until a large cloud of smoke hovered over the arena floor. It was truly an unhealthy sight to behold, but few recognized the dangers therein.

Sports betting was one of the city's favorite pastimes, the one nobody talked about. The bookmakers who hovered outside the Ak-Sar-Ben gates came in all shapes and sizes. Most Omahans knew or had heard of the big-timers; these men were mostly well-liked, family- and civic-oriented, churchgoing members of the community. Some used other occupations, such as salesman or store owner, to front their illegal bookmaking activity. If you wanted to place a bet on a football or basketball game, horse race, or even a boxing match, these were the men you went to see. Or you visited one of the hundreds of small-time bookies who worked under them. It wasn't hard to find a bookie in Omaha.

Omaha's biggest bookmakers grossed hundreds of thousands of dollars every month, the police said. To stay in business, they had to win at least half the time to have enough money on hand to handle the rough months that accompanied big losses. Most of them, it seems, did very well. From time to time, the police would jump in and squash their illegal activities, at least temporarily. One such raid in the early 1970s was carried out by the Omaha Police with assistance from fifty-four other officers from the state patrol and neighboring counties. Twenty-five gamblers were arrested, and the police found evidence of gambling and large amounts of cash. Most of these sorts of arrests, which usually took place without incident, would only temporarily slow gambling activities. The small fines the bookies paid in court kept them out of jail and amounted to a slap on the wrist for these men who dealt in large amounts of cash every month. The police knew the fines would do little to deter the bookies. So did lots of average Omahans, who, frankly, preferred to see them left alone. These people found nothing wrong with betting on sports. This attitude was shared by the judges of the local courts, who found nothing morally wrong with gambling and knew what an insurmountable challenge it would be to prevent people from betting on sports. Their duty was simply to apply the law. District Judge Theodore Richling suggested that the state revisit its laws on gambling; the fix he suggested was to force bookmakers to get licensed by the state and then to penalize individuals who continued taking bets without a license.

In 1977, Omahan Jerry Subject, who had changed the spelling of his name from "Sobczyk," tried to start a betting service for horse racing called Pegasus of Omaha. The service, modeled after others in Illinois and California, allowed bettors to come to a downtown storefront window to make a bet, which Pegasus would then place directly with the track. Subject, who previously (and later) worked for former Omahan Jackie Gaughan at the El Cortez Hotel in Las Vegas, immediately became a target of the Douglas County Attorney and the City Prosecutor.

But as targets went in Omaha, he was one of many.

Omaha was a city that changed with the times. In 1955, the once-crucial city streetcar system made its last run. There was a new kid in town called the automobile, and cars were becoming better-looking, more affordable, and easier to operate. It seemed every family was getting one, and the streetcar became a thing of the past in Omaha—a little bit like city commissioners, the old airport, and three-dollar steaks.

The buildup to the Creighton Prep–Omaha Westside game felt like an ambush. The Westside Warriors entered the game, like the Junior Bluejays, with a perfect 2-0 record, having shut out Council Bluffs Abraham Lincoln (19–0) and Lincoln Southeast (7–0). Better yet, Westside was breaking in a brand-new football stadium, which would be dedicated that night during a halftime ceremony. So new was the stadium, in fact, that workers were rushing through the facility's final touches on Thursday and Principal Ken Hansen openly discussed potential glitches that might pop up during the game. The concrete stadium, built into the hillside just south of 87th and Pacific Streets, included a new lighting system and capacity for 4,040 spectators; school officials added an additional 1,500 bleacher seats on the opposite side of the field to accommodate visiting fans. Despite the potential for opening-night bugs at the new field, Hansen and the rest of the Westside fan base sounded excited to welcome Don Leahy and the two-time defending state champions.

It seemed Westside had set the perfect trap.

Adding to the dilemma, Prep would be without backup center and tackle Bill Pycha. The *Omaha-World Herald* Thursday reported that the 240-pound sophomore was ill and confined to a local hospital. Sadly, Pycha's illness was more serious than the newspaper let on.

Pycha's problems first started to surface around his close friends, namely Thomas Kearney, a neighborhood pal who liked to hang around Pycha, mostly because Pycha was a big kid who looked after his smaller friends, like Kearney. The pair often walked home together after school, sometimes hitchhiking, and Kearney sensed something was wrong when Pycha asked him to carry his books because he felt tired. He seemed like a shadow of the kid who had worked all summer long in blazing temperatures for the county road crew. Toward the end of the summer, Mike Spinharney, another friend, ran into Pycha one afternoon at the Miller Park neighborhood swimming pool. He thought something about Pycha looked different but couldn't put his finger on what it might be.

"Just tired," Pycha told him. He wasn't the sort to make a fuss over himself.

Pycha was losing close to ten pounds during each practice in the late summer heat. But he tried his best not to complain. Things escalated at football practice during a particularly hot afternoon when he collapsed while trying to run off the field, barely making it to the sideline. This came after some teammates remembered him complaining that day of debilitating headaches, shortness of breath, and vomiting.

"Jeez, I feel lousy," Bill Heaston heard him say. "I feel so weak."

Coaches and teammates initially figured it was just heat exhaustion. Football coaches in those days frowned at giving players water breaks during practices, viewing the need for hydration as a form of weakness.

"That's the way it was when I started coaching," said Don Leahy. "'You've got to be a Spartan.' We'd really drive them hard, out there in hundred-degree heat with full pads on. No water—how stupid can you get?"

Leahy's philosophy on water breaks evolved over the years, eventually to the point where team managers came around to players with water bottles whenever they were thirsty. However, Bill Pycha's collapse was caused by more than just poor hydration. It was the end to a rougher-than-normal day for the sophomore. Assistant Coach Jack Jackson chewed out Pycha in front of the entire team after he was beaten on consecutive plays by smaller, weaker players during a scrimmage. It looked to Jackson like the young lineman was giving less than 100 percent effort, something the Creighton Prep coaches refused to tolerate.

After Pycha's collapse, a student manager ran into the school to phone a rescue squad from the front desk. The squad showed up at Prep and took Pycha downtown to St. Joseph's Hospital for an examination. He stayed there for observation. A few days later, Don Leahy visited Pycha in the hospital, where he received bad news.

"Coach, I think I've got something—something *like* leukemia," Pycha told Leahy from his hospital bed.

Something *like* leukemia, in fact, turned out to be leukemia. It was a grim diagnosis, yet Leahy sensed optimism in Pycha's voice. Pycha was a big, strong, strapping young man, and Leahy left the hospital feeling upbeat, albeit concerned.

Leukemia is a type of blood cancer that affects blood-forming tissues such as bone marrow and the lymphatic system. It's a disease with many forms, some commonly found in children and young adults. In 1960, doctors knew little about the disease and were unsure how to treat it. The survival prognosis for young children during that time was incredibly grim. Some doctors wouldn't even take on children with the disease as patients. Not until the discovery of chemotherapy and certain anti-leukemia drugs was it even thought possible to treat young people with the disease. It was a heavy load to put on the shoulders of a high school sophomore, especially one as fun-loving and admired as

Pycha. It seemed he had no enemies at Creighton Prep, only friends. Over the next few days, rumors about Pycha's condition began circulating around school. Most students had heard he couldn't stop vomiting at practice, so he was sent to the hospital to get better. Despite the setback, the Prep football team turned its attention to Friday night's opponent, Westside.

Westside had its own set of ailments, all of them much less severe than leukemia. The team's top fullback, Chuck Mumma, was nursing a sprained ankle. Mumma would play, but in limited duty. His backup, Ron Aurbach, also had injured his ankle during the team's Wednesday practice, and halfback Tom Wolff was ill with the flu. Wolff, too, would recover in time to play.

An "overflow" crowd numbering 6,500 turned out that night for the Westside-Prep game, most of them Warriors supporters on hand to dedicate the new stadium and help derail Prep's march to another state title. The weather failed to cooperate, as a driving rainstorm had turned the field to mush. Players were covered head to toe in mud, and so were the coaches and some fans. It was an important night for ball boys and student managers, and Creighton Prep had one of the intercity league's best in senior Mike Fitzgerald. As a child, Fitzgerald had been diagnosed with a heart murmur that doctors suspected was related to problems with his mitral valve. They cautioned against his playing sports, and Fitzgerald complied. (In adulthood, he would receive a different diagnosis and have his aortic valve replaced.) As a freshman at the "old" Creighton Prep, the flattop-wearing Fitzgerald approached Dudley Allen and asked for a job as the football team manager. Fitzgerald was installed as the junior varsity manager, and as older managers graduated, he was promoted. By his senior year, he was the man to whom all the younger managers reported with questions about equipment or game day management. It was a busy job, especially working for someone as precise as Don Leahy, and Fitzgerald loved it. It kept him involved in athletics and provided a valuable apprenticeship.

Westside failed to convert a first down on the game's opening possession but found a ray of light after Prep fumbled the ensuing punt on the 34-yard line. The Warriors converted a first down, but a penalty and two incomplete passes ended the drive without points.

Starting on the Prep 24-yard line, Don Leahy called six straight running plays, eventually causing the Westside secondary to inch closer to the line of scrimmage for run support. It was an adjustment Leahy expected and wanted. He next called for a pass, which looked like a stroke of genius after Frank Spenceri hit speedy Mike Wiley for a 41-yard bomb that moved the ball all the way to the Westside 10-yard line. Two plays later, Rich Cacioppo went in for a touchdown from a yard out, and Prep was on the scoreboard first.

In the second quarter, Prep went on a nine-play, 70-yard drive that included two Spenceri passes for 35 yards and a 9-yard quarterback keeper for the touchdown: 13–0 Creighton Prep.

The first two quarters were a clinic in sequencing plays, a skill that Don Leahy felt was more art than science. "I called plays based on how the game flowed. You hear coaches today talk about scripting plays. Some of them script the first fourteen plays of a game. Well, how do you know if you're going to have a pass intercepted on the second play? There goes the script. I didn't believe in that at all. From the first play on, I just felt the game unfold. Our philosophy was that we're going to throw the football and we're going to run the football. We're doing both—but we're not scripting. And it seemed to work."

Although he steered clear of scripting plays, Leahy used a few techniques to aid his in-game management of the offense. One innovation was a clipboard, and on it was a

FIG. 17. Don Leahy, *center*, kept in constant communication with his
assistants during games using military-style walkie-talkies, like the one held
by Mike McKim, *right*. Reprinted with permission of the 1961 *Jay Junior*.

sheet of offensive plays he expected to call during the game.
That way, if he ever forgot what his next call was going to
be, he needed only scan down his call sheet. Another aid
was an army-issue walkie-talkie that one of his backup quarterbacks held on the sideline. A Prep assistant coach, usually Jack Jackson, would find a spot high above the stadium,
either in the press box or on top of the stadium grandstand,
where he could get an eagle-eye view of the entire field, making it easier to decipher formations. The backup quarterback
would keep the walkie-talkie close by, and he would hand
it to Leahy if he wanted a word with Jackson or vice versa.
Leahy later called it a "prehistoric communication device,"
but in 1960, the walkie-talkie was rather cutting-edge.

Frank Spenceri was an active participant in Leahy's play
calling wizardry and gained a great deal of admiration for
his coach's ability to sense the right play for a given situation.

"He knew the down, the distance, how far we were from
midfield. He even knew how 'on' we were on that particular night," Spenceri said. "Many coaches, once they get

into games, become spectators. Leahy wasn't. He was an orchestrator. When you coach, it's like being the leader of an orchestra. You have tubas, clarinets, violins. The backs and receivers are like violins, and the tubas are the offensive and defensive lines. They all have to work in harmony. Leahy did that."

Leading 13–0 at halftime, maestro Leahy and his orchestra had silenced the home crowd and put a damper on the dedication festivities. "About the only thing Westside fans had to cheer about Friday night was a new stadium," reported Don Lee. A Creighton Prep yearbook writer dubbed it a "sad day in Mudville."

Creighton Prep continued its rout in the third quarter. Spenceri capped off a twelve-play, 60-yard drive with another touchdown run. The methodical manner the Junior Jays used to control the game was made possible by its defense, which held Westside to just 3 first downs through the game's first three quarters. For the game, Prep limited the Warriors to 145 yards of total offense. The late score the Warriors picked up in the fourth quarter, care of three Terry Rusthoven passes and a 3-yard touchdown run by Tom Wolff, mattered little to the game's outcome. Creighton Prep, having played an entire game of penalty-free football, was victorious, 20–6. Ironically, by staying within 14 points of Prep, Westside entered into Gregg McBride's top ten the following week at no. 6. Prep, now 3-0, next would face Omaha Tech.

Gregg McBride's prep football rankings in the *Omaha World-Herald* on Monday, September 26, went as follows:

1. Creighton Prep
2. Omaha Central
3. Lincoln High
4. Omaha Benson
5. Omaha Tech

6. Omaha Westside
7. Hastings
8. Lincoln Southeast
9. Lincoln Northeast
10. Falls City

Central High held onto its second-place spot despite not playing Friday night. Their game with Omaha North, perhaps due to venue issues, was postponed and moved to Monday night at Benson Field. McBride decided the postponement hardly warranted dropping the Eagles in the standings, especially since Lincoln High, who trailed immediately behind, had lost to Central on opening weekend.

Careful readers of the Monday sports section also noticed a small news item crammed in next to McBride's rankings. Tom Osborne, a graduate of Hastings High School and little Hastings College, had made his professional debut that Sunday with the Washington Redskins. This came after the future University of Nebraska coach had spent two seasons with the San Francisco 49ers but had never seen the field. It would not be the last time Osborne merited mentioning in the local sports pages.

As for the Eagles' contest with Omaha North, fans eager to watch some Monday night football should have arrived early. "Little Charley Gunn," as the *Omaha World-Herald* called him, let the North High Vikings know the kind of night they were in for on the very first play from scrimmage when he intercepted a pass that gave the ball to Central. A few plays later, Gale Sayers "loped" into the end zone from 10 yards out to put the Eagles ahead 6–0. And thus began Sayers's dismantling of North.

That night, Sayers scored 3 touchdowns—currency for six Pookie Snack'n Burger patties at Otoe's Drive-In—and quelled any hope North had of staging an upset. Sayers's other touchdown runs were even more electric than his first: a 36-yard "change of pace" scamper and a 74-yard strike where he reversed his field during the play and still couldn't be caught by any North defender. North's offense could do little to keep Central off the field, mustering just 1 first down in the entire first half.

Vernon Breakfield added to the scoring barrage, first with a 3-yard touchdown run and later with a 32-yard cutback run. At the end of three periods, Central led North 34–6, and the game was all but over. If Central missed the play of starting center Tim Dempsey, it never showed. "Strong and tough," backup center Lee Brentlinger was proving himself a "fine replacement" for Dempsey, noted a writer for the *Central High Register*. North's lone touchdown through three periods was a noteworthy bright spot, however. It started when Calvin McGruder intercepted a Central pass to give the ball back to the Vikings. The scoring play, which was 1 of 7 passes the Vikings completed in the game, was an 11-yard aerial connection between North quarterback Ted Sanko and John Burger. A newspaper photographer captured the play, a Willie Mays–like over-the-shoulder catch that Burger plucked from the outstretched hands of Central cornerback Gayle Carey, and the photo made the Tuesday night *Omaha World-Herald*. The score was too little, too late for North, who added another touchdown and point after in the fourth quarter to put 13 points on the scoreboard. Central quarterback Jim Capellupo joined the Central scoring binge with his own 21-yard touchdown run in the second half.

Central finished off North by a score of 40–13, piling up 17 first downs and 369 yards of total offense, most of which came on the ground, and holding the Vikings to just 115 yards of total offense. It was another impressive win for the Eagles, who were making a habit out of not just winning but pummeling their opponents.

Creighton Prep running back John Bozak and a few

Fig. 18. Thanks to blocking from linemen like James Brown, *left*, speedy Vernon Breakfield and the Central backs usually found running room. Reprinted with permission of the 1961 Omaha Central High School *O-Book*.

friends and teammates were in attendance that night at Benson Field, watching the game from the sidelines. They wanted a firsthand look at the much-hyped Central back-field. The onslaught they saw was jaw-dropping.

"They were rolling up and down the field. I was like, 'Holy cow. This is unbelievable,'" Bozak said.

With just four days between games, Frank Smagacz was worried about the Eagles' upcoming game Friday night against Abraham Lincoln. In addition to the quick turn-around, the injury bug had again bitten Central, at least mildly. End Mike Pederson was suffering from a shoulder injury, tackle (and senior class vice president) Maris Vinovs-kis was slowed by a bad ankle, and Gale Sayers, seemingly invincible to this point in the season, had an infection on his arm. No doubt Smagacz was also worried that his young team would look beyond A.L. and instead focus on the Octo-ber 7 matchup with Creighton Prep. Adding to these issues, the World Series, contested between the New York Yankees and the Pittsburgh Pirates, would begin the following Wednesday. There were ample opportunities for distraction.

The injuries and potential diversions, real or imaginable, did little to slow the Eagles. They were on a roll. On their first possession against Abraham Lincoln, the Eagles, beginning on their own 41-yard line, effectively moved the ball down to the A.L. 14-yard line, where Gale Sayers took a handoff off tackle and into the end zone to give Central an early lead. The rest of the first half was a three-man show: Sayers, Gunn, and Breakfield, each with blazing speed, put touchdowns on the board, pacing Central to a 26–0 half-time lead. The highlight was a 94-yard strike from Gunn right up the gut, aided by a block from Sayers at midfield.

After Sayers got to the corner and scored from 54 yards out in the third quarter, Abraham Lincoln was all but finished. So were the Central starters, who happily made way for backups to finish the game. One beneficiary was junior Harold Smith, a speedy runner who scored 2 touchdowns of his own when the game was out of reach. So was quarterback Don Buresh, who came in and completed a 30-yard pass to Mike Pedersen during the final Central scoring drive. When it was over, Central was victorious 54–0, but the final score only told part of the story. The Eagles gained 561 yards of total offense, including 522 on the ground. Forced to pass most of the game, A.L. completed just 1 of 16 pass attempts against the dominant Central defensive secondary. The *Central High Register* called the game a demolition, and rightly so.

Now the Central players could turn their attention to the much-awaited October 7 matchup with Creighton Prep. So could the *Register*'s sportswriters, who should have received a scholastic press award for their headline in anticipation of the Prep game. Even in an era of snappy sportswriting, this one stood out: "POWER PACKING PURPLES PLOT CHASTISEMENT FOR CREIGHTON ELEVEN."

Beautiful afternoon sunshine and temperatures in the seventies greeted players and fans from Creighton Prep and Omaha Tech on Saturday, October 1, at Municipal Stadium. With Omaha Central's victory over Abraham Lincoln on Friday night, Prep players knew that the Junior Jays had to win to keep pace with the undefeated Eagles; otherwise, next Friday night's game would suddenly seem a lot less important. Tech had talented players, good enough to beat Prep on a given day. Sportswriter Don Lee even thought Coach Dick Christie's ball club had more talent than any team in the intercity league. However, that talent had fallen on hard times during the week of the Prep game. Sprint champion and starting halfback Fred Farthing was nursing cracked ribs and two-way player Don Dober had an injured hip. Farthing planned to play with specially taped ribs and extra padding to protect his chest, and backup C. B. Miles was getting extra coaching from Christie during the week of practice, just in case. As for Dober, his backup, David Hall, weighed just 120 pounds, providing seemingly little resistance against the stout Prep line.

Prep versus Tech was a seesaw game that was ultimately decided on a few key plays. A first-quarter Tech fumble was recovered by Prep junior Tom Letter on the Trojan 38-yard line, which set up Mike McKim and the Prep offense. McKim, recently installed as Prep's starting quarterback, played one of his better games against Tech, and it started with a 12-yard completion that moved the ball deep into Tech territory. Don Leahy then called four consecutive run plays, the first to Rich Cacioppo and the next three to John Bozak, which moved Prep down to the Tech 5-yard line. Cacioppo then took a handoff into the end zone for a touchdown, which gave Prep the lead with seven minutes and eleven seconds left in the first quarter.

McKim's solid play made Don Leahy look brilliant. However, the lineup change was the result of more than just a hunch. When fullback John Corrigan went down with an injury before the Tech game, Leahy decided that moving Frank Spenceri to fullback and inserting McKim at quarterback gave him the only thing better than one capable quarterback on the field—two capable quarterbacks. It also added an element of surprise to the Prep offense. McKim may have been the *better* thrower, but Spenceri still had an adequate arm and lots of game experience. Now Leahy could call plays with two throwers on the field at once. For a coach that liked to pass, it opened up endless possibilities.

Tech took the ensuing possession and went on a long drive that lasted into the second quarter. The march began with a James Harbin completion of 29 yards to Huey Jackson, which advanced the ball to the Prep 37. It was the only Tech pass completion all day, but an important one, and the Trojans were on the move. The rest of the drive chewed time off the clock and yardage on the ground, mostly care of Fred Farthing, who was thriving despite his cracked ribs. His ground gains included a 17-yarder and an 11-yarder. A 4-yard touchdown plunge and the point after—kicked by Farthing—evened the score at 7–7.

With the score tied at halftime, the mood in the Prep locker room, according to the *Jay Junior*, was "tense." Don Leahy took off his sport coat and sat against a wall underneath a propped window in the corner of the locker room to give his players instructions. His bevy of assistants, including Tom Brosnihan and Jack Jackson, looked on anxiously during Leahy's talk.

If panic had enveloped the Prep locker room, it didn't show in the way the team played the second half. Patiently, Prep saw the third quarter expire without any scoring. Its defense was impenetrable as always. The fourth quarter started with promise when elusive senior John Bozak, having one of his best games for the Junior Jays, returned a punt 27 yards to start Prep's drive near midfield. A few plays

Fig. 19. With the outcome still in doubt, Don Leahy, *far left*, rallies his team during halftime of the Tech game. Reprinted with permission of the 1961 *Jay Junior*.

later, McKim dropped back to pass and unleashed a bomb to slightly built Tom Murphy, who hauled it in at the Tech 1-yard line. For Murphy, a junior who stood just 5 feet, 5 inches tall, the catch was his first ever in a varsity game, and it couldn't have come at a more urgent time. With McKim in at quarterback, this was the sort of big-play potential he provided the Junior Jays. Don Leahy sent in Frank Spenceri to go under center and handle a quarterback sneak, which he executed cleanly, sending Prep into the end zone to grab a 13–7 lead with six minutes and forty-nine seconds left in the game. Dave Bouda's extra point made it 14–7, a margin that held up in the final minutes as Prep's defense stopped the Tech scoring threat to seal the victory.

Prep came out victorious thanks to its steady defense and mistake-free offense. The Junior Jays gained 218 total yards in the game (113 passing, 105 rushing), nearly approaching Don Leahy's mythical perfect balance of running and passing. Creighton Prep also completed 7 of 14 passes. Mike McKim's ascension into the starting lineup had proven to be a wise choice for Leahy. Still, when the game was on the line late, he reinserted Spenceri at quarterback to handle the keeper.

Now—finally—Prep, 4-0, could concentrate on Omaha Central and stopping Gale Sayers. Thanks to the Saturday game, they would be preparing for the high-scoring Eagles with one less day of practice than normal. Attention to detail was a priority.

Prep students returned to class on Monday as usual, but it was not a typical week. It would not start that way, and it certainly wouldn't end that way. The Central game generated considerable buzz on campus. So did other, less pleasant news. At St. Joseph's Hospital, sophomore Bill Pycha, ailing with leukemia, was fighting for his life. It was a fight he was losing. For a young man with such prodigious physical attributes, his sudden decline was hard to imagine.

On Monday evening, Pycha's buddy Thomas Kearney and some other friends from Prep visited Bill in the hospital. They could sense the situation was dire. Bill's extreme weight loss was apparent. Someone in the group asked Pycha's mother about his prognosis, and she told them he was terminal. "None of us really knew what leukemia even was," Kearney remembered. "We had never heard the word 'terminal' before and didn't even know what it meant."

"Well," Pycha's mother told them, "we think he's going to die."

Bill Heaston and John Corrigan were among Pycha's visitors that night. They left the hospital unsure whether they would ever talk to their friend again. "We didn't hear anything more about it until we came to school the next morning," Heaston said. "Corrigan and I carpooled, and we pulled into the back parking lot at Prep. That was where everybody was standing outside with the news that he had died." It was a bittersweet moment for Heaston, who was coming off the high of playing one of his best games against Tech. Now he was mourning a teammate's death.

Officially, William E. Pycha Jr. died in his sleep at 1 a.m. on Tuesday, October 4, 1960. He was just sixteen years old. Bill was survived by his parents and three sisters. On Wednesday night, a special Creighton Prep rosary was held in Pycha's honor, led by three hundred students. Funeral services were scheduled for Thursday morning, beginning first at John A. Gentleman Mortuary and continuing with a requiem mass at Blessed Sacrament Church. Again, three hundred Prep boys were there. Services concluded with a burial at Calvary Cemetery.

News of Pycha's death hit the Prep community hard. Perhaps nobody, family members excluded, was hit harder than Assistant Coach Jack Jackson, who had so loudly voiced his displeasure with Pycha's performance on the day he collapsed at football practice. The death tortured Jackson.

"I almost quit coaching," he said. "It really bothered me. Bill Pycha was a great kid. He was from north Omaha. He was a big, jolly kid. He had just made some mistakes, and as a sophomore—jeesh. I should have remembered that the kid was only a sophomore. He wasn't a junior or senior; he hadn't been playing for three years ahead of that scrimmage. He was just learning. He just had gotten taken by a few guys he shouldn't have been taken by. It took me a long time to get over that. Bill was not really well known yet because he was just a young kid, but he was liked by everybody, and it stung those kids. Had that kid lived through his four years of high school, he would have been unbelievable. He had so many things going for him; he just didn't know how to use them all yet. And that's one of the great things about athletics. You learn from those experiences, and you learn how to handle them."

"We were just kind of thunderstruck," said Mike McKim. "That was really a shock, how somebody our age was so sick that he died. It's just not something you comprehend. You read about people getting in accidents and dying, but

FIG. 20. With tremendous size and physical gifts, sophomore Bill Pycha had all-state potential. Reprinted with permission of the 1961 *Jay Junior*.

you don't think of anyone at age fifteen or sixteen getting sick and dying."

"He was one of the funniest human beings I ever met," said friend Mike Spinharney. "There was a lot of self-deprecation in his humor. If he was ever kidded about his size, he'd say, 'Oh, I'm just fat.' He could leave you in stitches.

Football saved him at Creighton Prep. He wasn't into big crowds, so it gave him a group to associate with. Had he kept playing, there's no doubt he would have been a two-time all-state selection."

"It took him in a matter of days," said Don Leahy. "It came very fast. What a great prospect he was. He was one of the bigger linemen, and he held his own with this team, which was very good. He was a good student, too. Oh my gosh, he would have been something special. He was such a good kid. He could have named his college."

Scoreless

CHAPTER 8

DON LEAHY'S APPROACH TO game planning and practice made the results of games almost a foregone conclusion. It was as if the team was simply staging a performance, one that had been rehearsed throughout the week of practice with such attention to detail that the end result was as predictable as the third act of a Broadway play performed by the same troupe of actors night after night, week after week, year after year.

This concentrated level of preparedness gave the team an added confidence each time it played. For years, Prep teams had taken the field and executed another Leahy opus with such regularity that it only made their coach's methods seem all the more reliable because they worked. Game after game. Week after week. Season after season.

Prep sophomore Sandy Buda said that such sophisticated preparation gave the team a psychological edge. "We knew going into a game that the game plan we had put in place at practice was sound and gave us an opportunity to win. That was just something we always knew. We were always well conditioned; that's another thing. At the end of practice, we had to run sprints up a hill at Prep that went up toward 72nd Street. We sprinted up the hill and then rolled down. You'd get up feeling dizzy, sick. When I tell people this, they say 'What?' Nobody else did that, but we did it."

Prep student manager Mike Fitzgerald, who went on to become a student manager at the University of Notre Dame when he was a college student, saw in Leahy's methods the same things he saw in coaching icon Ara Parseghian, with whom he worked during the legendary coach's first year at Notre Dame. "The similarities between Leahy and Parseghian are unbelievable," Fitzgerald said. "Both were very competitive. Both wanted to win. And they surrounded themselves with outstanding assistants. Leahy was a genius, and Parseghian was a genius when it came to football. The two of them just did everything about the same, and they got the most out of their ballplayers."

Leahy viewed his intensive preparations in a less romantic light. It was a means to an end: the best way to solve the riddle of consistency in teenage boys—young men whose minds were already occupied by other distractions such as chemistry tests, sports cars, pimples, puberty, and girls.

However, the death of a close friend and teammate was something those young minds had never encountered before, at least not during game preparation. Leahy was a rookie at handling the tragedy, too, and he wondered how his players would respond. Deep inside, he didn't know. He was just as susceptible to emotion. One rumor purported that Leahy caught one of his junior varsity players smoking a cigarette outside Blessed Sacrament Church on the day of Bill Pycha's funeral and Leahy threw him off the team on the spot.

Did he give any thought to using Pycha's death to rally his team? "No way!" he recalled. "I would never have used 'Win one for Bill Pycha' with that team. Never. That would have been a dishonor to Bill. To use his misfortune would have been the wrong thing to do. We didn't have to use any extra motivation anyway. We were playing Gale Sayers and Omaha Central."

Pycha's death undoubtedly affected the Prep players, remembered Student Manager Jim Phillips, but there was no question about the team's true motivation. "You played for Don Leahy or else," Phillips said. "There was no lack of motivation when he was around."

On Wednesday, Leahy "charmed" (according to a *World-Herald* reporter) a crowd of three hundred when he spoke to the Creighton Prep Mothers' Club on the subject of participation in athletics, becoming the first member of Prep's athletics staff to ever speak to the Prep Mothers. The Prep Mothers were a do-good organization that helped raise and donate money to the school and offered extracurricular activities for students such as dance lessons. If Pycha's death was weighing on his mind, Leahy didn't show it. Nor did he indicate that his brain was pinballing different strategies to contain Gale Sayers and the Central Eagles' offense. According to Don Lee, the silver-tongued Leahy told the mothers not to push their sons into athletics. However, he told them sports provided young men with an opportunity to get involved in a school activity and mirrored many of the same lessons teachers hoped to impart to students in the classroom. Sports provide a "rallying point for school spirit," Leahy told the crowd. "We play to win, yes, but we never compromise with rules or ideals. As competition gets tougher, the boy must get tougher with it."

The competition was about to get a lot tougher Friday night at Municipal Stadium. Don Leahy knew Omaha Central would be as up for the game as any team Prep had faced all season, and he told his team as much. The secret to containing Central's offense, Leahy figured, was keying on Sayers. If he could be stopped, or at least corralled, Prep would have a chance to win. Leahy dug into his memory bank and decided to employ a 4-3 defensive alignment that he had learned at Marquette. The 4-3 was new to high school football in 1960. Prep, like most teams, normally ran a five-man front.

"We had to take a risk," Leahy recalled. "We told all three linebackers to key on Sayers, and we told the four down linemen that it would be their responsibility to take care of the other running backs. They had some good ones, too."

All week long, practices were devoted mostly to defense and implementing the new scheme.

If loading up against the run had a flaw, it was that it left Prep's secondary shorthanded in pass coverage. It was a vulnerability the Prep coaches were willing to concede. It was reinforced in their scouting and a simple review of Central's passing statistics. The coaches stressed to their defensive players the importance of taking good angles in pursuit of the Central runners, who were fast enough to shift sideways and run right past tacklers. Leahy told his defense stopping Sayers would be like penning in a chicken. Keeping him inside the edge of the defense would be critical. If he got outside the Junior Jay defenders, it would be a long night. "Don't chase him. He'll come back to you," he shouted all week at practice. "Just do your job! Play where you're supposed to be, and he'll come back."

Offensively, Leahy and his assistants made one notable game-specific tweak. Certain that Central would be watching and waiting for Prep's famous trap pass, Leahy decided to turn the play into a deep three-man route. He instructed both his ends to run straight downfield—instead of sending one across the field on a short 5-yard crossing pattern—and he sent running back John Bozak down the middle of the field on a third "go" route. Leahy figured that the two ends streaking down the field would split Central's safeties toward the sidelines, leaving a large hole in the middle of the field for his running back. However, the key would be baiting Central's linebackers, especially Sayers, with convincing play action. If Sayers didn't take the fake, any pass thrown over the middle would almost certainly be intercepted. Leahy told McKim throughout the week to throw the pass long, giving Bozak—and only Bozak—a chance to make the catch.

The adjustments now made Prep's famous trap pass a boom and bust proposition. Leahy saw it as that sort of game, and he wanted to be the aggressor. Bullet points from the game plan were written in yellow chalk on Leahy's green chalkboard in the Creighton Prep locker room. All week long, players could walk by and read the following list, which Leahy told them would lead to victory:

- Key on Sayers, keep the ball away from Central
- Minimize mental mistakes and penalty yards
- Maximize practice effort, eliminate mis-execution
- Maintain superior field position
- Dominate special teams
- Establish running game, then play-action pass
- Never, ever forget the power of prayer

If Frank Smagacz had picked up the phone to call Don Lee at the *Omaha World-Herald* during the week before the Prep-Central game, the conversation probably would have turned to Prep's famous trap pass and Smagacz's plan to stop it. Lee expected Creighton Prep to pull out a victory, even forecasting a score of 21–13 in his Friday morning column. Few high school teams threw the football as well as Prep, so coaching against a pass-capable offense was something of a rarity in 1960. It gave Don Leahy a tremendous advantage.

"High schools were always behind," said Jim Karabatsos. "Everybody ran the ball in those days. Hardly anyone threw it, so you didn't put much time in on the passing game— but Prep did. Prep had refined it. While they tried for perfect balance, they probably ended up running more than passing. But they were dangerous. They picked their spots to throw perfectly."

For other coaches in the intercity league, this is how the week of practice usually went before the Creighton Prep game. A fired-up coach, frustrated and weathered through years of failed attempts at stopping the staple of Don Leahy's offense, vows that "this is the year" we shut down the Junior Jays. The coach tells his players not to fall for Prep's play action fakes; he pleads with his secondary not to let any of the slippery Prep receivers get behind them on a pass route; he yells and contorts and bellows to get the point across that the trap pass is nothing more than a simple two-receiver route shrouded in football eye candy designed to get them to look the wrong way. The coach, certain he has gotten his point across, looks to his assistant coaches for affirmation that they finally got it right. Then the game begins. The coach watches from the sidelines, and waits, knowing that at any second his week of preparation will be put to the test. Prep runs a series of sweeps and traps, grinding out yardage and slowly causing the opposing team's secondary to inch closer and closer to the line of scrimmage for tackling support. Then, just as the coach and his team feel secure in their defensive game plan, the trap pass is unveiled. *Fake, fake, drop back, zip, touchdown.* The coach, dejected, stands on his sideline, unsure whether to yell or pout. *Not again,* he thinks to himself. Then he mutters, "That god-damn-trap-pass!"

Frank Smagacz didn't want to be that coach, not again. Yet he knew no other way to stop Prep's famous pass than to drill into his team, over and over, what to guard against. The rest, he figured, would be up to the players.

Stopping Prep was about more than just the trap pass. The Junior Jays' defense was allowing just 5 points per game, and even Central's high-scoring offense would have its hands full scoring points. Smagacz pined for a gadget play to surprise Leahy and Prep, and he thought a pass would be just the ticket. He had been eyeing Gale Sayers as a passer throughout the season but had yet to try the concept. This was the week, he thought. He and Karabatsos no longer wanted to coach a game handicapped by their team's inability to throw the football. But throwing was just one problem; catching was another, and just as important. Play after play, Central's receivers kept dropping the ball in practice. Smagacz was "madder than hell," remembered Jim Karabatsos, until finally Howard Fouts approached the coaches and asked to try his hand at receiver. Fouts split out wide, Sayers threw the pass, and he caught it. Once, twice, three times. Pass, catch. Pass, catch. Pass, catch. Sayers to Fouts couldn't miss.

Smagacz had seen enough. "That's it," he shouted to the team. "We'll use it if we need to."

"I wanted to try and get Leahy into a passing game," Smagacz recalled years later. "We had a pretty good pass defense, and I wanted to try to score first and then force him to pass."

Smagacz and Karabatsos tried to keep the rest of their team's preparations as normal as possible. "For us, it was just a standard football week," Karabatsos said. "Get ready, do the routine we were used to every day and prepare for that night. We didn't get caught up in the hype. Everybody outside the game got caught up in the hype."

The hype was proving difficult to ignore. By starting 4-0, Central suddenly found itself in the enviable position of being a marked team. Other schools took note of their scores each week, and the added attention held the potential to stifle the team and its high expectations. This was something new for Frank Smagacz's players. Omaha Central was the nouveau riche of high school football. Prep, with its back-to-back state championships and years of rich tradition, was old money.

The Don Lee effect, if you believed in the power of the press, was also hard to ignore. Lee's bullish take on the game served to only further the hype.

It seemed anyone who had at least a lukewarm interest in high school football had an interest in the Prep-Central game. As Smagacz and Karabatsos went about their normal business, friends and colleagues kept asking them how the

Fig. 21. Howard Fouts, one-half of the Central quarterback platoon.
Reprinted with permission of the 1961 Omaha Central High School *O-Book*.

game was going to play out. Many thought offense would rule the day. Central's coaches weren't so sure, and they warned their friends not to be surprised by a low-scoring game. The hype even spilled into local eateries, including the Golden Spur, a grill on the bottom floor of the Blackstone Hotel, where a crowd of Central players had gathered one night. Upstairs, the fancier Orleans Room entertained a more adult crowd, but high school and college-aged students preferred the Spur. Students from Creighton Prep sometimes came there to meet up with girls from other high schools, including Central. On this night, the Central players were discussing Creighton Prep. They shared a few tidbits from their scouting report, but mostly they raved about the play of Prep's nose guard, Rich Vomacka, whom they identified simply by his jersey number, 75. Every play, it seemed, 75 was in the opposing team's backfield at the snap of the ball. Prep student manager Jim Phillips was at the Spur that night and overheard the conversation. Had anything provocative been spoken about the Prep team, he may have passed it along to his buddies. But hardly anything about the conversation was controversial. The boys from Central respected their counterparts at Creighton Prep.

The Prep-Central rivalry was heated, despite its limited history. The two teams started playing football in 1922, and the early games were one-sided contests. Central was dominant, winning the first two games by an average of 37 points. Then, in 1924, Prep blanked the Eagles 13–0. The two squads never met again until 1950, and they resumed their annual game from that point forward, yet nobody is certain of the reason for the long gap in the series. The 1955 game was packed with intrigue and controversy. That year Central was trying to prevent Prep from capturing a third straight intercity title. The Eagles hung tough but ultimately came up short, 47–20. The game was less than memorable for Frank Smagacz, who came onto the field to protest a Prep onside kick after a touchdown. So heated was the dispute that officials ordered Smagacz off the field and tacked on a 15-yard penalty.

When Central and Prep got together, it was always an important football game. In 1960, the game's importance reached an all-time high. At one South Omaha grocery store, the proprietor, who took bets on sporting events out of his back room, got word that the city's Italian bookies, who controlled most of the action in Omaha, were, for apparently the first time, placing odds and accepting bets on a high school game—Prep versus Central.

Typically, high school games in Omaha were off limits for bookmakers, but college and professional games were a different story. At this grocery store and at others like it across the city, male patrons crowded in every Saturday morning during the fall to pick up their wives' meat orders and other groceries ordered by phone the day before. Sometimes the line at the meat counter stretched fifteen people long. While their place was held, some went into the back room to make their bets on college and professional football games.

The practice was illegal, yet it was prolific in backrooms such as these all around the city. It seemed everybody in South Omaha knew where to go to place a bet, yet nobody talked about it publicly. Even Omaha police officers were occasional customers. It's not as though law enforcement turned a blind eye to illegal gambling; the *Omaha World-Herald* later reported that the city's top bookmakers had been arrested hundreds of times in their careers, yet not one had spent a day in jail. They always paid a small fine in the corrupt municipal court to avoid serious punishment.

The line makers who set the points handicapped Prep-Central at -1, -1. That meant they expected a very close game, and any gambler who wanted to bet the game needed his team to win by at least 2 points to collect on the bet. If neither team prevailed by such a margin, the bettors were losers and the money stayed in the hands of the bookmakers. This market's proprietor always transferred the bets he collected to one of the city's larger bookmakers, thus reducing his liability. Essentially, he functioned as a middle man for bettors in his neighborhood, transferring the bets he collected to the big-time bookies. Bets began rushing in for Friday night's game, and he passed them along to his Italian bookmaker friend. The Italian told him this was the first time, best he could recall, that points were set and money was exchanging hands for a high school football game in Omaha.

The Prep-Central game, the state's most-anticipated high school contest, now had all the key ingredients of a memorable sporting event: two evenly matched teams, first-rate coaching, talented, headline-grabbing athletes, and ubiquitous fan interest. And a lot of action.

Game day arrived. At Creighton Prep, players began arriving in the locker room shortly after four o'clock. Like everything else that was part of his football program, Don Leahy took all the guesswork out of his players' pregame routine. Players attended classes on game day just like any other day. There were no special privileges.

"The Jesuits didn't cut us any slack in that regard," remembered one player. "They expected us to be on task and pay attention."

Earlier that afternoon, after class had let out, the players joined the student body at a pep rally in the gymnasium. Frank Spenceri was the team's speaker that day, and he stood up to deliver the following message to his fellow students: "Omaha Central—they got Sayers. They got Breakfield. And they have Gunn. That's some pretty good speed. But we have something they don't have—Prep speed!"

The students erupted with applause. Prep speed was more than just a clever cheer to the student body. It was an ethos. Doing things Prep speed meant doing them a little bit faster, a little bit harder, a little bit better than everybody else.

After the pep rally came the homecoming parade, described in the Prep yearbook as "the largest ever put on by

Prep." Forty-five cars caravanned from the school to Municipal Stadium that day, many of them decorated with streamers and crepe paper. The caravan left Prep, headed south on 72nd Street until it reached Center Street, then headed east to 32nd Street. From there it was south to Ed Creighton Avenue and east toward 13th Street until it finally arrived outside the stadium.

The first thing players did when they arrived in the locker room was paint their shoes. After a week of practice, their once-black football cleats had turned an un-Leahy-like shade of dusty brown, and their coach wouldn't stand for such a ragged appearance, even on his players' shoes. His solution was a secret mixture of high-gloss black shoe polish and paint that his players called "Black Magic." It came in gallon-sized, oil can–looking vats. Student managers placed paintbrushes and bowls of "Black Magic" outside the locker room door, and as players arrived one by one they grabbed a brush and applied an even coat of the secret paint to their shoes. When they finished, their shoes carried a blinding glint that looked like spit-shined patent leather. To a casual fan, it appeared that the team took the field each week with brand new spikes. To Leahy, a neat uniform was as much about substance as it was about style. Inside the locker room, clean jerseys and pants awaited the players. Those who needed ankles or wrists or other body parts taped had their taping done before they dressed.

"I always felt our uniforms were the best in town," remembered quarterback Mike McKim. "They snapped underneath in your crotch, so you never had any shirttails flapping. Your shoes had to be shined. You didn't have any extra chunk on. We rarely played in the daytime, but when we did we wore eye black under our eyes. It was a routine we followed every week."

Once in uniform, players lined up for a dress inspection before boarding the bus. Leahy's coaching counterpart

Frank Smagacz may have been the man with actual military experience, but it was Leahy who ran his football program like the armed services. From the moment they entered the locker room to suit up for the game, Leahy expected the team to adopt his serious attitude. He advised his players to begin thinking about the game, about their individual responsibilities and the role they'd be required to play in different situations.

For some players, Leahy's serious management style left them extra nervous. McKim was one of them. "If that style has a shortcoming, it forced us to focus so hard that it hurt us until we had our first hit or played our first series of downs. After that we loosened up and typically came out of it. He expected an awful lot out of us. It was a burden to carry that around. We knew there were great expectations and didn't want to let anybody down. But it worked."

The tightness in the locker room had a similar effect on Bob Gaeta—and, worse yet, on his stomach. Gaeta was among the first players to arrive and the first to coat his shoes with "Black Magic." As he reached for a paintbrush, Student Manager Jim Phillips, sensing his unease, asked Gaeta how he was doing.

"I just threw up," Gaeta said. "That's how nervous I am."

Gaeta's pregame heaves were nothing unusual. Players had by this point in the season grown accustomed to hearing him release his nerves in thunderous retches that echoed throughout the locker room.

Where McKim and Gaeta struggled getting comfortable around Leahy, the seniors on the team—particularly John Bozak, Rich Cacioppo, Walt Kazlauskas, and Frank Spenceri—kept the others loose. They seemed more at ease around their coach.

"What was good about the senior class was they had some real jokers," said McKim. "Johnny Bozak and Frank. They knew that there's a limit to how much of a game face you can put on. They knew that you had to play well, and to play well you had to be more or less relaxed. I found it difficult to relax. Maybe that was because Leahy had been a quarterback, and he expected so much out of his quarterbacks."

McKim could recall a game where, after he had thrown an interception that led to a touchdown for the opposition, Leahy approached him and put his hand over one of the earholes in McKim's Riddell football helmet. With great authority, he screamed into the other earhole, "That was a 14-point mistake! Fourteen points, you understand?"

The sound of Leahy's voice lingered inside McKim's helmet for what seemed like an eternity. "Don't make me feel any worse," McKim thought to himself. "Seven is bad enough."

"He did that to a lot of players," McKim recalled. "He made sure to cover one earhole so the sound wouldn't exit. It just spun around inside your helmet."

On this night, it seemed even the jokers on the Creighton Prep team were a little tight. Student Manager Jim Phillips lived just two blocks from Creighton Prep, and from time to time he would invite a few members of the team over to his house after school on game days for his mom's spaghetti dinners. On the day of the Central game, he could sense that nobody was joking around. "I remember thinking, 'Boy, is everyone more quiet and serious than usual,'" he said. "When we got back to the gym and the locker room I noticed the whole team seemed to be in the same serious and thoughtful mood, especially on the bus ride to Municipal Stadium."

As the players were dressing, Leahy pulled a few aside, including Bill Heaston, for a small motivational tactic. Starting tackle Fred Hoefer had partially pulled a hamstring, and the training staff was applying athletic tape to restrict his ability to pull his leg forward. Leahy was impressed by Hoefer's desire to play, and he wasn't going to miss out on a chance to use it as motivation.

"Look—this is what this guy's willing to do to get into this game," he told his players.

After the dress inspection, the Prep team boarded the bus for the ride to Municipal Stadium. The bus rides were always the same. The bus came down 60th Street until reaching Grover Street, then headed east on Grover all the way down through Deer Park and eventually to the stadium, always parking behind the bleachers on the first base side of the ballpark.

Barely a word was spoken on the bus ride. That was the same every game. Even cracking a laugh or a smile would have been frowned upon. Players were instructed to think about the game. Some did, and others just let their minds wander. But nobody said a word.

The mood at Omaha Central was lighter. All week long, student council representatives had sold Central beanies in the hallways for a quarter apiece. "Get your purple 'n' white beanie!" they shouted. School spirit was alive and well.

The players were serious, sure, but not tight. Frank Smagacz wouldn't let his team take the field bound up with emotion, especially in such an important game, but he also wanted them focused. Smagacz, who was known by his players to be "a little bit of a bullshitter," got together with Joe Dempsey to cook up a plot to help motivate his team. By game day, Tim Dempsey's mononucleosis was getting better, and his condition was no longer threatening. However, he was still in the hospital, so, without his son knowing, Mr. Dempsey sent Smagacz a bogus telegram to read in front of the team in the locker room before the game. As Tim remembers, it contained words to the effect of "Tim's not doing too good. We don't know if he's going to make it."

Smagacz stood up in front of the team and held up a piece of paper. "I've got a telegram here from Joe Dempsey," he said. "And I'm going to read it."

Fig. 22. Central quarterback Jim Capellupo gets a pregame tape job.
Reprinted with permission of the 1961 Omaha Central High School *O-Book*.

"That was purely motivational," Tim Dempsey said. "That's the kind of guy Smagacz was, a character."

If you chose to spend your Friday night parked in front of your radio—or, if you were lucky enough, your television set—and not at Municipal Stadium watching Omaha Central and Creighton Prep, there's a good chance you would have listened to the TV or radio broadcast of the debate between presidential candidates Richard M. Nixon and John F. Kennedy. This was the second of four scheduled televised debates between the two candidates, and after his showing in the first debate, Vice President Nixon had ground to make up.

Viewers of the first debate found Nixon pale and unhealthy-looking, while his counterpart Kennedy came off as vibrant and appealing. Republican national headquarters blamed Nixon's appearance on poor lighting and makeup, and his backers vowed to make him look healthier during the second debate by calling in New York makeup man Stan Lawrence. A Republican spokesman claimed Kennedy's good looks in the first debate were aided by an appearance expert in Chicago, but the Kennedy camp denied the charge and cited their man's suntanned skin as the reason for his good looks. Debate number two was scheduled for TV viewing at 6:30 p.m. Friday, an hour after it was scheduled to air on the radio and an hour before the Prep-Central kickoff. Viewers would be seeing a split screen, as Nixon would answer questions from Los Angeles and Kennedy from New York. Although most, it seemed, were in favor of seeing a televised debate for the first time, Minnesota senator Eugene McCarthy disagreed, calling the concept "risky and dangerous."

If you were a Nebraskan on the fence about your political choice in 1960, there's a chance you might have sided with Kennedy, thanks not only to his appearance but also to a strong local tie. Nebraskan Theodore C. Sorensen—"Ted"—was Kennedy's top aide. Just thirty-two, he was known as Kennedy's jack-of-all-trades man—speechwriter, organizer, trusted adviser—yet he carried no formal title. Born in Lincoln, Nebraska, Sorensen attended the University of Nebraska, was the top graduate of his law school class and editor of *Nebraska Law Review*, the student-edited legal journal. He hooked up with Kennedy in late 1952 after Kennedy defeated Henry Cabot Lodge in a Senate race. Sorensen instantly became an important member of the Kennedy political team, earning greater responsibility as the candidate headed toward the 1960 election year.

Nixon handled himself better in the second debate, trading barbs with Kennedy on topics ranging from civil rights to foreign policy. The agreeable manner he had used with little success in the first debate had been replaced by an aggressive, sometimes sarcastic, tenor. Years later, the sarcastic tenor would make an about-face, sometimes at the hands of sharp-tongued bumper sticker writers who warned voters to "Dick Nixon before he dicks you" and to "Honk if you think he's guilty." On this night, however, Nixon seemed to be gaining ground on his opponent.

For Nixon, however, the change in debating tactics might have come too late. A week later, Kennedy drew headlines when he kissed his first baby on the campaign trail, planting a smooch on the cheek of seven-month-old Annette Luci in New Brighton, Pennsylvania. Young Annette wasn't the only person noticing Kennedy's sudden momentum. Oddsmakers in Las Vegas, who had tabbed Vice President Nixon as a nine-to-five favorite after the national conventions, changed their thinking during the first weekend in October, pegging Kennedy somewhere between a six-to-five and seven-to-five frontrunner to capture the presidency. Debate coaches attending an annual meeting in Pittsburgh, Pennsylvania, agreed with the bookmakers in the desert, citing candidate Kennedy's superior debating techniques as the reason for his sudden boost in popularity. Jackie Robinson, the former major leaguer who had broken professional baseball's color barrier, told an NAACP crowd in Greensboro, North Carolina, that he favored Nixon, "a champion of civil rights." *Omaha World-Herald* readers were slow to join Kennedy's sweeping momentum; the first of several informal polls made Nixon a large favorite, and he increased his lead in the second poll. Whether the newspaper men were as handy at predicting elections as they were prep football outcomes remained to be seen.

At Omaha Central, students took part in a straw poll a few weeks before the national election. They favored Nixon (54 percent) over Kennedy (46 percent). The ballots included sixteen write-in votes. Among them was Mr. Frank Smagacz, who received one vote for president of the United States. It's doubtful Smagacz had any true political aspirations. If so, he would have been a darling with the media. On this Friday, he had a different campaign in mind—one for a football state championship.

CHAPTER 9

SHORTLY BEFORE KICKOFF, THE phone rang at Omaha's Central Police Station at 10th and Dodge Streets. The man on the line, perhaps an out-of-town scout or a wisecracking attorney from the upstairs Municipal Court or maybe just a practical-joking student, asked, "Just where is this Municipal Stadium where they're playing football tonight?"

It's unknown whether the caller ever made it to Municipal Stadium that night. If not, he sure missed a hell of a show.

Overflow crowds swarmed outside the stadium gates in the hours before kickoff. Don Lee forecast the season's largest crowd yet, but even his prediction of twelve thousand spectators fell short of the actual turnout. So overwhelming were the hordes that the stadium's six regular ticket windows couldn't keep up with the demand, and five additional stadium staffers were dispatched into the crowd to sell tickets by hand. Nobody, it seemed, was willing to miss this Prep-Central game.

Mother Nature had bought into the pregame hype and responded with beautiful fall weather, officially forecast by the United States Weather Bureau as a sunny day with highs in the mid-seventies and a low temperature near fifty degrees. Firsthand recollections of the weather varied, but not by much.

"Kind of a cloudy day," remembered Prep assistant coach Jack Jackson. "The weather that night wasn't very cold out. The temperature was maybe in the low sixties. It wasn't a bad night for football."

"Nice day—warmish," remembered Jim Fogarty, then a Prep sophomore who arrived at the game early with Tom Cavel and other classmates. The ticket taker punched their student passes and they climbed up the main grandstand on the preferred third-base side until they found a row of seats even with the 40-yard line.

Elsewhere in the stadium, Fred Scarpello and his date, Barbara Gossin from Mercy High School, found their way to seats in a section of Central rooters. One young man recognized Scarpello as a football player and yelled out, "What are you doing up here? You should be down on the field." The young man didn't know about Scarpello's diabetes or how miserable the comment made him feel. Fred's date and future wife, Barbara, did.

"Fred was not the happiest person that night," Barbara said. "He suffered through every play that happened out there on the field because he wasn't down there. It was terribly hard for him to not be able to play his senior year because he loved football. His coaches said he was one of the toughest guys they'd ever coached. That was a hard, hard thing to not be able to play that last year. All those guys, even on the other team, grew up together and played midget football together."

High up in the stadium, almost directly behind the home plate backstop, Fran Smagacz and her oldest son, Mike, found two seats together "pretty far away, but we could see everything," Mike recalled. Two younger Smagacz boys, Pat and Pete, were down on the sidelines with their dad for the game, where they could help out as water boys.

If you arrived late like Bill Heaston's family, finding an empty seat, never mind a row of seats together, was nearly impossible. No seats were reserved, so an early arrival was enviable. Forced to separate, the Heaston contingent spread throughout the stadium looking for good vantage points. Finding a good seat was no problem for Rose Vomacka and

Emma Charvat, Rich Vomacka's grandmother and aunt, who were always among the first spectators to enter the stadium. They found a couple of seats on the south side of the stadium, many rows up where they could get a good view of the entire field.

Frank Spenceri's older brother Pat and a friend—a future judge in the Nebraska Supreme Court—sneaked into the third base dugout with a pack of Lucky Strike cigarettes and a concealed bottle of bourbon. The contraband held out, and they stayed there the whole game.

Cheers of "Let's go, Prep speed . . . Let's go, Prep speed" wafted through the stadium as spectators continued filing in. Down on the sideline, Prep paraded in its good luck charm, a llama that had been present at the Westside and Tech games. The llama appeared more interested in eating candy than watching football, but Prep was not about to forego the psychological edge that the well-socialized pack animal provided to its fan base. Central cheerleaders Judy Eichhorn and Mary Lucht joined the fun, posing with the llama for a newspaper photographer and holding a Central baseball cap over the animal's head.

When all the heads were counted, some 14,500 people and one llama were crammed into Municipal Stadium. Some people remember seeing fans turned away at the gates. Others recall traffic on Deer Park Boulevard backed up to 24th Street. All this for a high school football game. In Nebraska, no less. The *World-Herald* reported that it was the largest football crowd in stadium history. By night's end, the crowd would number at least one less, care of an apparent heart attack that claimed the life of sixty-six-year-old Wilbur Pringle of Omaha. A rescue squad rushed Pringle out of the stadium, but sadly he was dead on arrival at a hospital ninety minutes after kickoff. He wouldn't be the rescue squad's only call that night. Central pep squad member Judy VanDeventer was injured while cheering after she leapt up and fell back on a stadium seat. Her injuries also required a trip to the hospital.

The teams filed off their respective buses and headed out for warmups. Typically, the specialists—kickers and punters—went out first before the linemen and skill players joined them to finish the warmup. As the teams ran through a few plays, the rest of the players formed a long wall, sideline to sideline, to gain a psychological edge over their opponent and prevent opposing coaches and players from watching their plays. Prep assistant coach Jack Jackson headed up to his familiar perch atop the stadium, where he could see the entire field from a bird's eye view. There he communicated with coaches and players on the sidelines with a walkie-talkie.

Throughout the warmup, the crowd continued to grow as anticipation mounted. Fans continued filing into their seats well into the first quarter.

"The atmosphere that night was very special," said Don Leahy.

"Of course when you walked in, the raucousness—the noise, the yelling, the cheering—was obvious," said Central assistant coach Jim Karabatsos. "But once the game started, you kind of don't pay attention to that. You block it out. A lot of people talk about that in baseball and football. That's what happens to you. You're so focused on what happens on the field that background noise doesn't bother you at all. It's a sport where you can communicate mouth to ear, sending instructions in with a guy or bringing a couple guys out. You just tell your kid, 'Run this play and have so-and-so split out on the left side,' or whatever you want to do. Same way with defense. Your mind is on the game."

Central kicked off to Creighton Prep to begin the game. Don Leahy liked to play with a lead, and he wasted little time going for the first score. On the second play from scrimmage

Leahy called for the trap pass that the team had been practicing all week, sending right halfback John Bozak circling out of the backfield, into the slot for a slight pause before streaking down the middle of the Central secondary. The ball was snapped, and Mike McKim stepped back to throw. All week long, Leahy's instructions to McKim had been simple: "Don't throw that pass short." Leahy knew a short throw would likely fall into the hands of Gale Sayers and he would be off to the races for an interception-turned-touchdown.

Leahy's instructions were ringing in McKim's ear as he surveyed the defense. *Don't throw it short. Don't throw it short.* Central was aligned in its Oklahoma, or 5-2, defensive formation. Frank Smagacz all week had instructed his defenders to knock the Prep ends off their pass patterns early. The trap pass was a slow-developing play, and he figured knocking the receivers off their routes would keep them from getting behind the secondary.

Prep's two ends ran down-and-out patterns that pulled the two safeties toward opposite sidelines, and Bozak was wide open down the middle of the field, past the linebackers with nobody else in sight. McKim let the pass sail, but he overthrew his receiver by 3 feet, and the play was a bust. A reception would have been a score, everyone on the Prep sideline was sure of it, but the pair had failed to connect.

"I could have scored easily," Bozak recalled. "There was nobody around me."

"It was too bad," McKim said. "I'm told that was one of the last plays that we had anybody open."

Prep failed to convert its third down attempt, and John Bjelland came onto the field to punt the ball to Central, a scene that would become familiar throughout the evening. Leahy had warned his punt unit of a crisscross pattern that Sayers and Gunn ran during returns, fearful that one missed assignment could lead to a game-breaking play. John Bozak lined up on the far right side of the field and raced down to make a tackle. He charged Sayers as hard as he could and landed a body block that seemed to stun Bozak as much as its recipient. The hit knocked Sayers down and prevented a big return.

The Eagles failed to muster up anything on a conservative opening series, and when Prep got the ball back after a Central punt, Leahy again tried to find pay dirt on second down. McKim faded back to pass, looking to connect with end Pat Hogan, who was dragging across the middle of the field. This time Smagacz's defenders had taken the ends off their routes, and McKim's intended receiver was covered, so he left the pocket and began scrambling to the right sideline. As he neared the boundary, Hogan attempted a block on Gale Sayers, who was in hot pursuit across the field. The block slowed him down, at least for a few moments. Vernon Breakfield was next in pursuit for Central, and he was able to get a hand on one of McKim's legs to bring him down. McKim looked down and noticed that the sideline chalk was just a few feet away. That was the last thing he remembered before catching a full-speed helmet to the jaw care of Central's 165-pound Steve Cenk, knocking him to the ground and out of the game. Thankfully for Prep, McKim held onto the ball.

Prep's longtime trainer Matty McGrath rushed onto the field, along with Student Managers Mike Fitzgerald and Jim Phillips. McKim was out cold, and they used smelling salts to wake him, eventually standing him up and walking him off the field and straight to the locker room. It was obvious to the training staff that McKim was suffering from cognitive impairment, likely a concussion, and he would not be returning to the game. McKim remembers none of the questions the trainers asked him. His next conscious memory was emerging from his fog in the Prep locker room. He was laid out on a training table, covered in a stack of long rain parkas. McKim tried to sit up when he noticed

McGrath slicing through an orange with a knife right above his nose. It was a few minutes into the second quarter, and it was McGrath's job to cut orange slices for the players at halftime. Fitzgerald kept a close eye on the quarterback while McGrath prepared the snack.

By the time McKim sat up under his own power, an ambulance had arrived outside the Prep locker room to transport him to St. Joseph's Hospital for a full evaluation. There he would spend the night, but he wasn't alone. His friend Dan McGinn, quarterback for Omaha Cathedral, broke his jaw that night and was sent to the same hospital. McGinn's injury was serious enough that the doctors had to wire his jaw shut. The two quarterbacks spent the night on different floors in the same hospital. After high school, they would spend their next four years together at the University of Notre Dame, both as students and McGinn as a scholarship athlete.

McKim's jaw hurt all the way up to his ear the next morning when he awoke. He remembered the first few series of the game but remembered nothing from the time of the hit until he came to in the locker room. He only vaguely remembered the ambulance ride to the hospital.

For his Creighton Prep teammates, the game would continue. Don Leahy was now without his starting quarterback and had a choice to make. The McKim injury changed the capabilities of his offense and the way he called plays the rest of the game. It also placed even greater responsibility on the shoulders of the Prep defense.

Leahy turned to Tom Heim at quarterback, deciding to leave Spenceri in the backfield, where he had spent the week practicing. Heim was a senior but had very little actual game experience, and the gravity of the moment made him nervous. So did his eyesight, which he remembers as not being so good, especially under the lights of Municipal Stadium and in front of fourteen thousand people.

As the first quarter came to a close, neither team had scored. As the two teams traded sides of the field, Gale Sayers met eye-to-eye with Bill Heaston. Rich Vomacka stood nearby with his palms resting on the back of his hips and his elbows kinked out to the side.

"He's chicken shit," Vomacka said. "Chicken shit."

"Okay, Rich," Heaston said, trying to calm the temperamental Vomacka.

Sayers's eyes opened wide when he appeared to hear the remark. By this point in his high school career, he was familiar with nearly all of Creighton Prep's strategies to slow him down. During his junior year, he became upset with Prep players taking extra time to get off him once the whistle had blown a play dead. It was a subtle but annoying trick to wear Sayers out.

"Get off me, man, play's over. Get off me," he kept telling the Prep tacklers.

Another Prep tactic was to deploy a blocker on Sayers every play, no matter where on the field the ball was headed.

"If I was the off tackle and the play was going someplace else, I was to find him," Bill Heaston said. "If it was within 5 yards of the line of scrimmage and between the tackles and I could get him from behind, I was to get him from behind. He was all over the place at middle linebacker, and he could run faster backwards than I could run forwards. Several times I chased him, almost out of bounds. Neither one of us was really involved in the play. He would look at me like, 'What the hell are you doing?' Every play that did not directly involve a tackle, we had to contact him and punish him."

Howard Fouts, who had watched Sayers take the brunt of every team's best defenders for three seasons, noted that against certain teams Gale would purposely act lethargic, sometimes even hurt, to ensure he saved his energy for the fourth quarter when the game was on the line. "He kind of reminded me of Jim Brown," Fouts said. "He would get tackled and get up like he was hurt. Sometimes he would lie there and it would seem like he would never get up. Then he'd get the ball again and go off. Gale played quiet like that."

Having thwarted multiple Prep drives, Central settled into its comfort zone on offense, grinding out yards—and sometimes inches—with its sturdy running game. "They mixed it up," said Prep assistant coach Jack Jackson. "But whenever they wanted sure yardage, they gave it to Gale." The yards piled up, mostly on Central's side of the field, and so did the first downs, but the Eagles were unable to create any explosive plays. They were finding out just how tough it was to penetrate a defensive front anchored by Rich Vomacka and Walt Kazlauskas. Don Leahy's 4-3 alignment and his strategy of assigning all three linebackers to Gale Sayers both proved effective.

"It was a little new at the time," Leahy said of the defensive concept. "We knew we had to take a little bit of a risk. We told the four down linemen that it would be their responsibility to take care of the other running backs. But if you don't stop Sayers, you don't win. It's that simple."

The risky maneuver was working, thanks in part to sure tackling by the Prep front seven. It seemed that every time a Central running back tried to turn the corner, a Prep tackler was waiting for him and a convoy was close behind. It made prophetic Don Leahy's words, *Don't chase him . . . he'll come back to you.* In one such play, captured perfectly by *Omaha World-Herald* photographer Maurice Shadle, Sayers took a handoff and broke to the left side of the line of scrimmage and tried to turn upfield. Prep safety Frank Spenceri was there waiting for him, in perfect tackling position, using the sideline as another defender until his teammate Fred Hoefer, trailing the play from behind, could catch up to help make the stop. Sayers lowered his right shoulder, securing the football between his left forearm and armpit, and the play gained 12 yards. Prep was willing to allow a few 12-yard runs as long as it could limit long scoring plays. However, the rough-and-tumble tackling came at a price. Rich Cacioppo, attempting a tackle on Gale Sayers, got his hand stuck in the wrong place on Sayers's helmet and broke a finger. Tom Heim got onto the field at right linebacker and assisted a tackle that left him with a scar on his wrist. It was a blood-and-guts type of game, remembered Rich Vomacka.

"You could hear that cracking and popping and the hard hitting," said Gayle Carey. "Right up center and off right tackle. It was furious. We were really scared of their passing game, at least until McKim got knocked out. Then they ran, ran, ran. The game was played from tackle to tackle. I was kind of disappointed because they never ran or threw it at my end. They had a little flat pass they usually threw. I was ready for that. I thought, 'This is gonna be a pick six.'"

The sore-shouldered quarterback duo of Capellupo and Fouts did not scare Prep. Don Leahy knew neither quarterback was likely to beat his defense throwing the football. Frank Smagacz knew, too, and so, after running a series of sweeps, he broke offensive tendencies by calling a halfback pass for left-handed Gale Sayers.

"Thirty-nine pass. Gale throwing," he told Howard Fouts on the sideline.

Central did little to disguise the gadget, lining Fouts up as an end and sticking Jim Capellupo under center. Sayers received the pitch from Capellupo, and Fouts ran a post route, streaking down the field. Prep, so preoccupied with stopping Sayers, fell for the fake completely.

"Nobody was even close to me," Fouts recalled. "I was in my own zip code."

Sayers rifled a pass, his first attempt ever in a varsity contest, according to Don Lee, that hit Fouts squarely in the hands, but he dropped the ball. He could have walked into the end zone untouched.

FIG. 23. Omaha Central coach Frank Smagacz platooned
quarterbacks Howard Fouts, *left*, and Jim Capellupo, *far right.*
Reprinted with permission of the *Omaha World-Herald.*

"Our team was hit with very few surprises over the years,"
said Don Leahy. "One of them was that pitch-out pass to
Gale Sayers. I don't know why we didn't look at it. My God,
it worked. We were so intent on getting to him to make
the tackle."

Most Central offensive drives, like those of Creighton
Prep, ended with a punt. In Central's case, those duties
belonged to Fouts, who quickly learned that even punting
came at a price.

"I can remember punting the ball, and the next thing I
knew, I was on my ass," he said. "They had a guy who was
charged with knocking me down so I wouldn't go down and
make a tackle. They were so well coached and disciplined;
you could just tell. They didn't do anything screwy, didn't
play dirty. They just played hard."

By halftime, neither team had scored, and the game action had been limited to clean tackling, lots of punting, and missed opportunities in the passing game. Punters John Bjelland and Howard Fouts had emerged as the unexpected stars of the game, successfully swapping field position with booming kicks. Bjelland had also saved a touchdown on one of his punts, reaching out and catching speedy Ardell Gunn by his shoelaces before Gunn could break through the last line of Prep tacklers blocking his path to the end zone. Recalling the play, Bjelland said the thought went through his head that Gunn could either cut left or right, and so he figured he had a 50/50 chance of making the tackle. He guessed right. Bjelland's sophomore classmates cheered loudly when they realized who had saved the touchdown.

Don Leahy came into the Prep locker room at halftime and emphatically told his team, "We are going to win this game!" He smacked the back of his clipboard for emphasis. So profound was Leahy's statement, it made John Bozak wonder whether Leahy might have doubted that his team could win all along. After the first half, he now had proof that they could at least play to a stalemate.

"It was dead even," Leahy recalled. "We had the one opportunity for a touchdown pass, but we were totally holding them defensively. But I imagine their coaches were saying the same thing in their locker room."

In the Central locker room, Coaches Smagacz and Karabatsos were, as Leahy guessed, essentially telling their players the same thing. They made sure to alert the defensive backs and linebackers to the adjustment Leahy had made to the trap pass. In such a tight game, one missed assignment could spell defeat. The coaches stayed true to their personalities, Karabatsos the intense one and Smagacz relaxed. Had they broken character, it might have signaled trouble to the team.

"He was never a nervous coach," Mike Smagacz said of

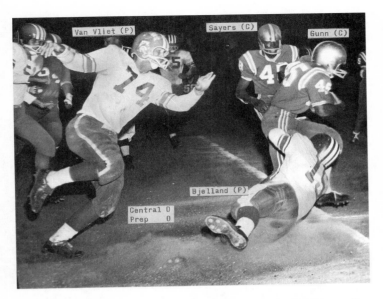

FIG. 24. Ball carrier Ardell Gunn had a touchdown in sight until punter John Bjelland's shoestring tackle tripped him up. Reprinted with permission of the *Omaha World-Herald*.

his father's in-game manner. "He could be domineering and loud, but he never got nervous. Any calls the referees made, he didn't hold back. He always knew the officials, but he didn't mince words with them."

The third quarter played out much like the first half, but more conservatively. Each team kept the play calling straight-forward, knowing one mistake could spell doom in such a seesaw game. The entire quarter, neither team crossed the goal line. Everyone in the stadium hung on the results of each play, even the student managers, whose job normally kept them from watching the on-field action.

"I cheated during that game," said Prep student manager Jim Phillips. "I saw almost the entire game. I did my duties in between plays, but I stopped and watched almost every play."

"As the game progressed, it was a dogfight," said Prep's Sandy Buda. "There was heavy hitting. People see the results of that game and say, 'What's the big deal?' But you had to be there to see the athleticism on the field."

"It was just a defensive battle," said Prep assistant coach Jack Jackson. "We'd get the ball and they'd stop us. Then they'd get the ball, and we'd stop them. They were sucking up dirt on darn near every play."

"The guys left everything on the field," said Central quarterback Howard Fouts. "You could just see it in their eyes when I walked into the huddle and called plays, and the same when we came off the field at halftime. It was two sets of guys just punching each other's brains out. Nobody gave up in that game. You could see it on their faces."

The jawing between Rich Vomacka and Gale Sayers continued, but as the game wore on the verbal discourse turned respectful. Neither player left the field. On one particular play, Sayers received a handoff and cut back between a tackle and a guard, but Vomacka was able to shed Don Fiedler's block to make the tackle. Sayers gave Vomacka an appreciative pat on the butt after the play, and the memory has stayed with Vomacka ever since.

"I'll never forget that," Vomacka said. "That's the way he was. Gale kind of complimented you. He appreciated the fact that he couldn't get through because they were not going to be able to block me. There was nobody like him on the football field. There was nobody."

Sayers continued disrupting Prep's offensive rhythm. Prep center Bob Marasco had difficulty snapping the ball and getting nose tackle Dennis Tiedemann blocked before Sayers read the direction of the play. Gale was gone at the snap of the ball, and Tiedemann was a hearty force to resist. Marasco said Tiedemann was the best defensive lineman he faced all year. "He was the only guy I played against that made me see stars. I guess today you would call that a concussion," Marasco recalled.

In the fourth quarter, "things began to pop seriously," wrote Don Lee in the *World-Herald*. The first to pop was Creighton Prep, who took possession of the ball in its own territory on the north end of the field. Prep had managed little offensive firepower, having completed just 1 pass thus far in the game, and Central's defensive front, led by Don Fiedler, Maris Vinovskis, Dennis Tiedemann, and Malcolm Young, had put a stop to Prep's running game.

From Prep's 31-yard line, reserve quarterback Tom Heim took the snap from center and faked the trap sequence before dropping back to pass. He found John Bozak open downfield and threw a pass that Bozak hauled in amid Central traffic at the Eagles' 43-yard line for a 26-yard gain. The price for Bozak's catch was a vicious hit, but he hung onto the football. As co-captain of the two-time defending state champions, he didn't want to leave the field. He just needed a moment. He later learned he cracked his ribs on the play.

First down Creighton Prep.

As Bozak tried to pull himself up from the turf, he could make out the sound of a girl's voice calling out from the stands. It was his homecoming date, Peggy Gassman, a Mercy High School girl who wanted to make sure he was fit for his duties escorting her to the dance later that night.

"Don't get hurt, Bozak, you have to take me to homecoming," she yelled out.

Leahy stayed aggressive, next calling for a pass designed as a sweep. Heim pitched to Spenceri, who looked for an open receiver. Vic Meyers sprinted downfield, running a flag route toward the home plate end zone in the south end of the stadium. Spenceri could have broken off to run but instead chose to loft a risky pass toward Meyers, who was closely covered by three Central players. The ball fell just over the three Eagles and into Meyers's outstretched hands, right near home plate and in perfect view for much of the large crowd. The catch was "tremendous," reported Don Lee.

Suddenly Prep's offense was no longer dormant, the end zone just 12 yards away. But in the shadow of its own goal line, the Central defense stiffened. On first down, feisty Don Fiedler, as he had done so many times that season, broke through the line of scrimmage and stopped a Frank Spenceri run before it even got started. No gain. Second down.

Don Leahy sensed this was no time to get fancy, so he called another Spenceri run, but again the senior was stopped for no gain by Vernon Breakfield and Ardell Gunn. Third down.

Creighton Prep, which had played such disciplined football all night long, was called for a procedure penalty on third down, backing them up 5 yards to the 17-yard line. After the play, the line judge approached Bill Heaston to tell him that he was the one who had lined up offsides. As a result, Pat Hogan, at the end of the line of scrimmage, was also offsides, and for a moment Hogan caught the ire of the Prep coaches. With confidence in his freshman kicker Dave Bouda, Leahy did not want to risk a turnover so close to the goal line, so he called for another handoff, this time to Rich Cacioppo, who was taken to the ground for a 2-yard loss by Malcolm Young and Jim Capellupo. Fourth down.

Leahy called for a field goal, and Dave Bouda trotted out for a 36-yard attempt. Bouda would now be kicking off of infield dirt near second base. Despite the penalty, there was still a kick to be tried, possibly to win the game. There were nervous faces on both sidelines, but Central's Jim Karabatsos was not one of them. He turned to Smagacz and said, "Shit, that kid'll never hit it."

Had Karabatsos known Bouda's talent, or the future in football that awaited him, he might have rethought the remark.

Frank Spenceri received the snap from Bob Marasco and put the ball down for a nice, clean hold. Bouda kicked, and the crowd watched the ball in the air, awaiting a verdict. So did players and coaches on both sidelines. So did Spenceri and others on the line of scrimmage. Only Bouda kept his head down, as Leahy has coached him to do, until the kick had completely left his foot.

No good, signaled the officials. The 0–0 score remained intact with six minutes and fifty-five seconds left on the game clock.

Spenceri suspected someone on the line of scrimmage got a finger on the ball, possibly Sayers. Bouda thought the kick hit the crossbar. Don Lee reported that the kick missed short but by a few yards. Karabatsos, from his vantage point on the Central sideline, agreed with Lee.

As they came off the field, Leahy and Tom Brosnihan approached Pat Hogan about the penalty. "Offsides?" they asked, visibly upset.

Bill Heaston was not about to let his teammate take the rap for his mistake.

"Coach—it was me," he confessed. "The line judge told me. I was the one offsides."

Leahy looked at Heaston and said, "Thanks. Thanks a lot."

Full of energy and sensing an opportunity to clinch the game, the Central offense took the field, hoping to crack the riddle of the previously unsolvable Creighton Prep defense. On their first play from scrimmage from their own 20-yard line, it appeared they had the riddle cracked cold. Sayers took a handoff around the right end and headed toward the centerfield sideline, right in front of the Creighton Prep bench. As he approached the sideline, he appeared to hand the ball off to Ardell Gunn, who shot forward with a burst of speed and went the length of the field, dashing toward the north end zone and the distant downtown skyline for an apparent touchdown.

Atop the stadium's main grandstand, a livid Jack Jackson threw his clipboard down in anger. As he struggled to regain his composure, he saw the clipboard sliding toward the edge of the grandstand roof, and in a matter of seconds he instinctively bent down and reached out for it before it fell into the mass of spectators below. Jackson lost his balance and slipped and found himself staring down at the overflow crowd, his life and an image of a Central touchdown run flashing before his eyes. Thankfully for Jackson and the spectators below, he regained his balance and pulled himself up and avoided tumbling over the edge of the stadium. Just that morning, readers of the *Omaha World-Herald* had seen on the front page a photo of a baseball fan sliding down the top tier of Pittsburgh's Forbes Field to grab a foul ball that had lodged in a rain gutter above home plate during game two of the World Series. A headline beneath the photo read, "This is real hustle."

Jackson later called his tumble the closest he ever came to killing himself.

"It was just a reaction thing," he said. "I'm glad that I caught it before I went over or I probably would have been lying in the stands below. It was scary enough that from then on, when we scouted up there, I stood in the middle of the grandstands because I didn't want to be that close to the edge again."

In the grandstands, the Creighton Prep students thought the Gunn touchdown had ended their chances of winning. Throughout the stadium, other Prep rooters felt their hearts stop, if only for a moment. Central fans, meanwhile, felt the high of impending victory in the season's most important contest and began celebrating the game's first score.

Then a flag came out. It was a penalty that Sayers, and others, would never forget.

The official call will go down in history as an illegal forward pass, or forward lateral, on the Sayers to Gunn exchange. Had the call been made more promptly, it might have spared fans of both teams a lot of yelling and screaming—and Jack Jackson a harrowing near-death experience. The incident in question happened directly in front of the Creighton Prep sideline and the discerning eyes of Don Leahy, who was just 6 feet away.

"Bob Marasco was in on the play," Leahy said. "It was right in front of me, and I saw the forward lateral, so when the guy continued running down the field, I wasn't worried. The flag was thrown. It was a forward lateral, and we didn't worry about it."

Prep lineman and future head coach Tom Jaworski was standing on the sideline next to Leahy and saw the same thing. "It was clearly a forward lateral from my viewpoint and right when I saw the lateral, the referee's flag came out and whistled it back," he said.

Sandy Buda, also standing near Leahy, heard his coach yell out, "Hey—forward lateral!" as soon as the ball changed hands. From the Prep sideline, it seemed there was little controversy.

Gale Sayers and his Central teammates viewed the play differently, contending that Sayers had fumbled the ball and Gunn scooped it up and scored. In the moments and years that followed the game, opinions of the penalty varied, mostly along party lines. Sayers, without question, maintained that he fumbled. Perhaps never has a running back so willingly admitted to a fumble.

"I know my rules," Sayers recalled later. "I was hit and the ball flew up in the air. Ardell got it and went for a touchdown."

On Bill Heaston's first day of law school at Creighton University, more than four years after the game was played, he walked into a classroom and sat down next to Don Fiedler, who looked at Heaston and greeted him by saying, "It was *not* a forward lateral!"

"That's all he said," Heaston remembered. "No, 'Hey, how are you doing?'"

Jeff Wohlner, a student writer for the *Central High Register*, also took issue with the call, noting that the head linesman who was running parallel to the play and in position to make such a call did not signal a penalty. The official who did signal the penalty, Wohlner claimed, was in front of the runner, and Wohlner wrote that "no referee can call a decisive play as that when he is in front of the runner." If his account was correct, Wohlner made a strong point.

Despite the differences of opinion and any unrest that hung over the stadium, the penalty stood and the game continued. To their credit, the Central players kept their focus and continued to march down the field on one of the game's best offensive drives, piling up rushing yardage behind their talented backfield of Breakfield, Gunn, and Sayers, who contributed as the Eagles moved the ball to the Prep 14-yard line, taking important time off the clock in the process.

On first down from the Prep 14, Smagacz opted for another Breakfield run, which gained 5 more yards. On second down, Central put the ball in Sayers's hands but modified its blocking scheme. Smagacz advised Fiedler and Tiedemann to cross block rather than run a straight zone block that was part of the usual Central repertoire. The talented linemen hadn't properly rehearsed the play and were unsure who was supposed to pull first. Jim Karabatsos warned Smagacz that the cross block made little sense on such a quick-hitting play, but Smagacz stuck with the call. Sayers ran right into a trio of Prep tacklers—Marasco, Van Vliet, and Gaeta—who dropped the Central star for a 2-yard loss. Third down.

Vernon Breakfield carried for a few yards on third down, but Prep was feeling the momentum swing in its favor and the play was never destined for a score. That left the Central Eagles with a fourth-down attempt and 5 yards to gain. The clock was ticking toward the end of the game. If they could convert, Central would establish a new series of goal-to-go downs at the 4-yard line. A field goal attempt was never considered; Central didn't even have a set of uprights on its practice field, never mind a regular placekicker. A handoff to Gale Sayers might have seemed logical, but Smagacz was betting that Creighton Prep would have such a play snuffed out, so he instead opted for trickery, giving Sayers one more shot to prove himself as a passer.

The game now rested in the hands of the state's best player and his coach's imagination.

Sayers received the pitch and sprinted out looking to throw. He tossed a pass, described by Don Lee as a "bullet," that went incomplete, ending the Central scoring threat.

Forty-two seconds remained in the game. The scoreboard still read 0–0.

On the Creighton Prep sideline, Don Leahy pulled quarterback Tom Heim aside with instructions to finish the game.

"All you do is take the ball and go to a knee," he told Heim. "We don't want to fumble."

A cunning Heim considered abandoning the instructions in lieu of dropping back for a last-second heave, for a moment anyway. Then he pictured returning to the sideline and having to explain the audible to his coach. As for Leahy, the decision to take a knee was the easiest call he made all night.

"It's just common sense," he said. "We're on the 5-yard line. We've got 95 yards to go with a minute to play and we haven't scored yet. In this case, the tie with Central was a win."

Heim took the snap and fell on the ball. The game was over. In front of a record crowd at Omaha Municipal Stadium, the two best teams in Nebraska high school football had just played a classic game. And neither one had scored a single point.

After the final seconds ticked away, Don Leahy went onto the field to congratulate Gale Sayers on the game he had just played. The Creighton Prep defense had been nearly impenetrable in shutting him down offensively, limiting him to about 80 yards rushing, but Sayers had been a menace at linebacker, disrupting plays and making tackles all game long. It was the only time in Leahy's coaching tenure that he chose to speak with another player before his own team, and in typical Leahy fashion, it was a classy, albeit understated, exchange.

"Great game," Leahy told him. "You're a very fine football player. Good luck."

Sayers accepted the congratulations. Despite being held off the scoreboard, he later called the Creighton Prep game the one he had most enjoyed playing in.

Gale spotted Prep running back John Bozak across the field and called out his name. They met and shook hands. "Great game," Sayers told him.

Everyone in the stadium, it seemed, had watched the game from the edges of their seats, and they weren't disappointed by what they had seen. When it ended, an eerie silence settled over the stadium. The infield dust, which had been swirling all night, seemed to hover over the field. Some spectators wondered among others in their section what they had just witnessed. Others had nearly lost their voices from screaming and didn't try to talk. "Then we realized, 'Damn—this is the way it's supposed to be,'" said Jim Fogarty, who had watched the game among other Prep sophomores on the edge of his seat. "This is as good as it gets."

Final Statistics

	Omaha Central	Creighton Prep
First downs	13	7
Rushing yardage	204	93
Passing yardage	0	60
Total yardage	204	153
Penalty yardage	45	20
Pass attempts	8	6
Pass completions	0	3
Interceptions	1	1

Source: Statistics courtesy of the *Omaha World-Herald*, October 8, 1960.

Bill Heaston sat in the locker room at Creighton Prep, looking for a hole to crawl into. He wasn't alone, but he felt that way. The game action was still fresh in his mind. He kept thinking back to his offsides penalty that had preceded Dave Bouda's late field goal try, feeling that he had cost his team the game. Even worse, he couldn't shake his memory of Don Leahy's reaction when he found out who committed the penalty. *"Thanks. Thanks a lot."*

Leahy noticed something was troubling his lineman and sat down by Heaston.

"What's wrong?" he asked.

"I'm just really, *really* sorry about being offsides," Heaston said, struggling to speak.

Leahy put his arm around Heaston.

"Look—things happen in the heat of battle. Don't let that bother you."

It was a short, simple conversation, and in typical Leahy fashion, he had wasted few words. He stood up and left Heaston to change out of his uniform. Then he turned around.

"What class you in, Heaston?"

"A class," Heaston said, referring to his position in the top rank of Prep students.

"Really? You're in A class?"

Leahy smirked, shook his head, and walked away. The exchange helped Heaston relax, "at least enough that for the rest of the evening I could tolerate things," he said.

He could have used another pep talk an hour later when he and his homecoming date walked into Gorat's Steakhouse at 50th and Center Streets and were greeted by Don Fiedler and what seemed like half the Central team. He had hoped for more anonymity as he ate his dinner. Surprisingly to Heaston, Fiedler seemed happy, almost amused, with the game's result.

"A tie!" Fiedler said. "It's too bad we can't have a playoff game to decide this."

"A tie, God bless it," Heaston thought to himself.

He and his teammates were used to winning. Over the course of their four years at Prep they could count their losses on one hand. They hadn't lost this game, but not winning felt a lot like losing. The week had been filled with emotion. Now there was no victory to thrill over, no loss to stew about. Only a tie.

The bus ride back to Creighton Prep felt like the team was on its way to a funeral, its second one of the week. Players were feeling down and unsure how to react to a game with no winner. Leahy would not stand for such a reaction after such a tremendous effort, so he stood up in the bus and waited until he had everyone's attention. Then he told his team they had played a fantastic game against a great opponent. It was a game, he told them, that they would remember and be proud of for the rest of their lives. The 0–0 result was, in fact, a great achievement. Later, Leahy would call it "the best defensive game ever played by a Prep team."

Spirits were lifted, at least slightly, by the time the football players joined several hundred of their classmates and dates at the homecoming dance in the Creighton Prep gymnasium. They were greeted by a long row of blue-and-white crepe paper streamers dangling from the ceiling and bouquets of multicolored balloons hanging from each basketball hoop, giving the evening an "air of gaiety," according to the '61 *Jay Junior.* The decorating had been completed entirely by a group of volunteers after the school day. Students danced to live music care of the Rockbrooks while they awaited the end-of-night coronation ceremony to crown homecoming co-queens Judy Enis of Mercy High School and Pat Oglesby of Marian High. Football co-captains Walt Kazlauskas and John Bozak helped crown the co-queens, who were each presented with a decorated commemorative football.

For Rich Vomacka and others of like mind, the homecoming dance was drudgery. "It just made me sick because it was all so much, so fast," he said. "We didn't really have any time to enjoy anything. I had a hot date that night, a gal from Cathedral, but my mind wasn't on homecoming, I'll guarantee you that."

"It was homecoming, so some of the players didn't care about the outcome by then," said Frank Spenceri. "It was time to go back to Prep and find your girl. For myself, it was just right there in our grasp, and if only I could have done this or that . . . what if. Central was the same way, I'm sure."

Central quarterback Howard Fouts shared Spenceri's feelings. "It felt like we didn't do anything," he said. "We didn't win. We didn't lose. It was kind of an empty feeling really. We were kind of numb to it."

Across town at St. Joseph's Hospital, a crowd of Central players—estimated at twenty—gathered around Tim Dempsey's hospital bed to wish their teammate well and relive the game. They told him about the disputed Sayers-to-Gunn forward lateral, Prep's missed field goal, and Sayers's late-game halfback pass attempt that would have won it outright. Their mostly congenial mood was confusing to Dempsey, who had expected a gutted reaction to the tie. He was unaware of the phantom telegram his father had sent to Frank Smagacz or that Smagacz had read it aloud in front of the team.

Fortunately for Dempsey, his infectious mononucleosis would soon wear off and he would be back to his normal self. He would leave the hospital in a matter of days, but as the *Omaha World-Herald* reported, he would have four to five weeks of bed rest ahead of him. After running its course the illness would leave a noticeable mark: he dropped to 160 pounds (he was listed at 185 on the 1960 Central roster), and his damaged pancreas, which couldn't afford to sustain physical punishment, would keep him off the field for the rest of the season. However, his football playing days were far from over. He put some weight back on (he wrestled at 175 pounds the following year) and returned to the field in 1961 for his senior season, where he earned all-intercity honors for his play at center. Then in the fall of 1962, Frank Smagacz petitioned on Dempsey's behalf for a semester of hardship eligibility, and he was allowed to play in all but two games of the '62 Central season, giving him, in effect, two senior seasons.

In his bonus season of high school competition, Dempsey led his team with 56 tackles, despite missing the first two games. It was a standout performance in what was otherwise a disappointing season for Central football.

Following his recovery, Dempsey returned to school and a mountain of makeup schoolwork that became a chore, but he was excited to be around his friends again. However, money was tight at home, and his father was stuck with a sizable medical bill from Tim's hospital stay. Frank Smagacz was chatting with Joe Dempsey in the hallways of Central one day and asked him about the hospital bill, which was several hundred dollars.

"I'll be a little short, but I'll find a way to get it paid off," Dempsey told him.

Smagacz told Gale Sayers the story and planted the seed to organize a fundraising drive. Using his celebrity, Gale and his teammates organized an effort to raise money to help pay Dempsey's bill. He patrolled the student body, collecting anything he could, a quarter here or a dollar there, whatever his friends could spare. Gale Sayers was a hard man to say no to, especially if you were a fellow student. A box with the words "Tim Dempsey Fund" began appearing in the lunchroom to help collect the money. In all, he raised a couple hundred dollars for the Dempseys.

"My dad was a blue-collar guy," Dempsey said. "It was a little embarrassing for me at the time, but when I look back on it, it was pretty much Sayers's idea. When I later saw the movie about Sayers and Brian Piccolo, I had a pretty good sense that Sayers was truly a caring person, and that was not an anomaly. He was and probably still is a very caring individual. You don't find those stories every day. That's just an example of the kind of guy he was."

The following morning, at his parents' house in Council Bluffs, Creighton Prep punter John Bjelland got out of bed and walked into the kitchen. His parents were waiting there with the morning edition of the *Omaha World-Herald*. They told him a surprise awaited him. Bjelland sat down and read Don Lee's headline: "14,500 SEE CENTRAL, PREP BOTCH LONE TOUCHDOWN CHANCES, BATTLE TO 0–0 TIE." Then he read the recap of the game in its entirety. It was hard not to fall under a spell from Lee's writing: "Creighton Prep's shot at a field goal died short of the uprights. Central's last-minute pass was spoiled in the shadow of the end zone. And neither of the football giants had a whiff of the goal any other time. So it was a gasping 0–0 tie between Nebraska's two best teams at Municipal Stadium Friday night."

When he finished, Bjelland looked up at his parents.

"That's great. But what's the surprise?"

Then Bjelland took a second look at the article. Directly above the headline on the front page of the sports section was a large Maurice Shadle photograph. It captured Bjelland's shoestring tackle of Ardell Gunn on the infield dirt at Municipal Stadium. In no small way, the tackle, as had so many other plays during the game, preserved the 0–0 tie. A photograph with such billing had the potential to make Bjelland, just a sophomore, a celebrity among his peers, at least for a week. He was pleased.

At St. Joseph's Hospital that morning, Central linebacker Mac Young dropped by to see his buddy Mike McKim, who was still lying in a hospital bed with a sore jaw. Young gave McKim details of the game, but the whole thing was still a little fuzzy for the Prep quarterback. He remembered nothing from the game after the shot to his jaw.

The harmony of an otherwise perfect 1960 season was disrupted by an imperfect note—each team still had more games to play, three for Creighton Prep and four for Omaha Central. At any level of football, or sports in general, for that matter, as a team goes through a season undefeated, each game becomes more important than the last. So for two teams staying unblemished in the loss column, the season was becoming one long series of big games, one after another, each more important than the last.

4

As Good As It Gets

CHAPTER 10

IN THE DAYS FOLLOWING the scoreless tie, Frank Smagacz realized how impactful a game his team had just played. It seemed everybody he talked to asked him about the possibility of a rematch. The *Omaha World-Herald* speculated that such a game, considered impossible under the rules (although it's unclear exactly which set of rules the newspaper was referring to), would draw another large crowd.

When the *World-Herald* rankings came out on Monday, Central and Prep shared top billing, with Lincoln High trailing at third. The Links had been paced Friday night by Bobby Williams, who went wild in a 38–19 victory outstate against Grand Island. He was responsible for 326 of the team's 492 yards and scored 4 touchdowns.

While the sportswriters stopped short of treating the tie as a Central victory, at least in the eyes of those ranking the state's top teams, Central was every bit as good as Creighton Prep. The *World-Herald*'s sports staff also speculated Central's path to complete an undefeated season was tougher than Prep's, based on the strength of future opponents.

The Central coaches conducted their own postmortem on the Prep game, but the conclusions they reached only solidified what they already knew about their football team. "We were handicapped by our own stupidity—we didn't develop a passing game," Jim Karabatsos conceded. "We talked about it afterwards. And we talked about things we should have or could have done differently or better."

With all the talk about the game that just *been* played,

it would have been easy to overlook the upcoming game. Central could little afford to ease up, especially with Omaha Tech looming on the horizon, so on Tuesday after the Prep game Smagacz led his team through a hard hour-long scrimmage to make sure everyone had his mind on football. Tech had already played Creighton Prep close, and no doubt they aimed to spoil Central's run to an undefeated season.

Judging by the game's outcome, Smagacz's tactic worked. Playing at Benson Field, the Eagles were slow starters, leading just 6–0 at halftime, care of a blocked punt by Jim Brown and Malcolm Young on the Tech 35-yard line shortly before intermission. A play later Central ran 39 Pass, Gale throwing. Unsuccessful a week earlier against Prep, the play worked this time as Sayers hit wide-open Ardell Gunn on Tech's 10-yard line, from which he went in untouched for the score.

Despite trailing, Tech led Central in rushing yardage 89–33 at the half, having done admirable work containing Gale Sayers. When Tech converted a fourth-and-one on Central's 46-yard line in the third quarter, care of 283-pound tackle Ray Rivera, who slipped into the backfield to take the ball all the way down to the Central 8-yard line, it seemed almost certain the Trojans would tie or take the lead. Perhaps it was the nature of Rivera's impressive run, with would-be Central tacklers bouncing off him like pinballs, but the play lit a fire under the Central defense.

The Eagles held Tech on downs, and after a 50-yard run by Gale Sayers—supplemented by two Tech penalties—moved the Eagles down to the Trojans' 1-yard line, it seemed that Tech would crumble, but Rivera had other ideas. On the next play he used his massive frame to stop a Central ball carrier in his tracks, poke the football loose, scoop it up, and rumble 7 yards before being tackled. Rivera was proving to be more than just a big body; he was a playmaker. Tech's Jim Harbin connected with Harry Rutledge on two long passes that brought the ball all the way to the Central

40-yard line, but a fumble gave the ball right back to Central, sucking the life out of the would-be Tech rally.

Frank Smagacz didn't gamble with his good fortune and decided to put the ball in the hands of his workhorse backs. First Vernon Breakfield reeled off a 14-yard run, then Sayers carried twice to move the ball down to the Tech 4-yard line, and finally Breakfield took it in to extend the lead to 13–0. Finally, Central had some breathing room.

Down by two scores in the fourth quarter, Tech tried to pass, but a Jim Capellupo interception proved the strategy fatal. Taking over on the Tech 29-yard line, Central patiently marched the ball down the field care of its talented backfield, scoring and converting the point after with a Gunn plunge to go ahead 20–0. Central tacked on a 5-yard Breakfield touchdown later in the fourth quarter and held on to preserve a 26–0 victory, its third shutout in as many weeks. It was a decisive win that was sure to raise eyebrows.

For the game, Central's backfield triumvirate of Sayers, Breakfield, and Gunn carried the ball a combined 33 times for 252 yards, averaging 7.6 yards-per-carry and accounting for all but 12 of Central's rushing yards. Tech did little to help itself, giving the Eagles 2 interceptions and racking up a horrendous 111 penalty yards, 74 of which came in the second half as a dozen on-field fights broke out.

Battered and bruised from two weeks of physical football, and aided by a bye week before the Benson game, Frank Smagacz gave his players Monday and Tuesday off as a reward for the Tech win. The team got together anyway on Tuesday to re-hash the Tech game, and practices resumed their normal schedule on Wednesday.

When the team finally took the field again for the Benson game on Wednesday, October 26, they would face an opponent with some newfound confidence, especially after an impressive 40–0 blanking of Abraham Lincoln High School the week before. The win moved the Bunnies into fourth place in the Nebraska high school football rankings. Don Lee called quarterback Chris Beutler and the Benson team "one of the toughest hurdles along the undefeated football trail" facing Central. His assessment was spot on. Benson, a slight underdog, would be playing at home in front of a crowd of six thousand that was no doubt aflutter at the prospects of a midweek game. However, it wasn't like Central didn't have momentum of its own. The Eagles hadn't even been scored on in three games.

But the Benson game would test the Eagles' resilience. It began with Sayers, who was ill with the flu. He would play, despite the illness, and play effectively. But his performance was far from perfect. On Central's first possession, the Central backs carried the load as usual. Sayers capped off the 61-yard scoring drive with a 2-yard touchdown run. The Eagles led 7–0, but then a strange thing happened: their offense went into a stall. Fumbles on consecutive series, both recovered by Benson's John Stolly, turned into Benson touchdowns. The first Benson drive of 61 yards matched Central and culminated with tiny Ken Kortright, all of 5'4" tall, evading would-be tackles from Johnny Bruce and Jim Capellupo, and running into the end zone. The second fumble belonged to Sayers and started a Benson drive near midfield. Kortright, camouflaged by his slight frame, again scored the touchdown to give Benson the lead, which was 13–7 after a missed conversion. That remained the halftime score. Benson showed no signs of being intimidated by the Eagles, and their defensive play had proven it. Central fans in the crowd were shocked as the Eagles, slowed by the Bunnies and their own fumbles, retreated into halftime.

Central finally found an offensive spark in the third quarter, and it began with an Ardell Gunn punt return to the Benson 41. Now it was time to play. Sayers found his pulse, first with a 33-yard cutback run, then on a 4-yard score. With the game tied 13–13, Benson's Beutler committed a costly fumble on the Central 29-yard line. Steve Cenk recovered the ball, and the Eagles' offense cut loose, driving more than 70 yards en route to a short touchdown run by Jim Capellupo. The score was 19–13 Central, and it was up to their defense to protect the lead.

A good kick return started Benson at its own 40-yard line. Time was winding down, and Benson began a promising drive, led by Beutler and Dick McGuire. It had to make Central fans nervous. With two minutes left, Beutler had marched the Bunnies down to the Eagles' 20-yard line. Then Central dug in. The first big stop came courtesy of Maris Vinovskis and Steve Cenk, who tackled Beutler for a 1-yard loss. Then Gale Sayers, Don Fiedler, and others stuffed Ken Kortright for a 5-yard loss that clinched the game. Central got the ball back and, with time in its favor, ran out the clock and Benson's dreams of an upset. Final score: Central 19, Benson 13. In its toughest test since the Creighton Prep game, Central had found victory in perilous circumstances.

As the season entered the month of November and Central eyed the Westside game the following Friday, another drama left to unfold was Gale Sayers's assault on the intercity league scoring record. Sayers came into the Westside game having scored 88 points during intercity games on the season. The record was held by Omaha North's Virgil Williams, who had scored 102 intercity points in 1956. Those who gave Westside little or no chance of staging an upset at Municipal Stadium were mostly right. Central won the game with relative ease, 32–9, and Sayers stole the show.

The first of Gale's 3 touchdowns came from 12 yards out with five minutes and fifty-nine seconds remaining in the first quarter. His second was more dynamic—he intercepted a pass from the hands of Westside's Terry Rusthoven and sprinted 29 yards along the sideline and into the end zone for the touchdown. And his third was truly a play to behold. It came on a double reverse, Gale taking a handoff from Vernon Breakfield at midfield, sidestepping two Westside players, and running 50 yards behind a lead block from Ardell Gunn and into the end zone. Central led 20–0 at halftime and 26–0 at one point early in the third quarter, and they never looked back on the way to an easy victory. Gale's 20 points gave him the intercity league scoring record, surpassing Williams's mark by 6 points (108–102).

Frank Smagacz's team, with a record of 7 wins, 0 defeats, and 1 tie, now had just one game left to complete an undefeated season.

Don Leahy had never been shut out before. In fifteen years of playing and coaching football at Creighton Prep and Marquette University, no Leahy team had ever been blanked. As Don Lee noted in the newspaper, not even "Wisconsin of the Big Ten Conference" had kept a Leahy team from scoring, a reference to his college playing career at Marquette. Omaha Central changed that, and as Prep looked to its next game the following Thursday at Municipal Stadium, Leahy desperately wanted to score some points. He also wanted his team to get back to its winning ways. During a seventeen-year coaching career for the Junior Jays, Leahy would compile a remarkable 118-25-7 record, but he couldn't help it if his most recent tie was nagging at him. Now, more than ever, it was important to finish strong.

"We decided we were going to finish out the rest of the season undefeated," Leahy said. "So there was no letdown after that huge effort. If you look at the scores, Central realized, and we realized, that we had done something great. So we said, 'Let's finish it off in style.'"

Prep's next chance to win came against Abraham Lincoln High School, who, Leahy remembers, usually didn't field strong teams in those days. A.L. would be without its best running back, Gary Gilman, who had torn ligaments in his knee the previous week in the Cathedral game. Prep had its own injury concerns: John Corrigan was still ailing with a hip injury, Mike Wiley was out with a neck injury, and quarterback Mike McKim was still recovering from his concussion and wouldn't play against the Lynx. Illness had also beset the team. John Bozak was out with the flu, and Bill Heaston was nursing a touch of it also, but after agonizing all week about his costly penalty in the Central game, he was determined to play. Heaston had struggled through the week's practices and Leahy noticed his extra effort along with his mistakes. After an error-prone stretch during Monday's practice, Leahy shouted, "What class you in, Heaston?"

"A class," Heaston shot back.

Then Leahy came over and put his arm around Heaston. "Are you not feeling too well?" he asked.

"I'm not. I've been sick all week."

Rich Vomacka couldn't resist poking fun at his friend.

"Oh, teacher's pet, huh?" Vomacka taunted. "Are you *sick*, Billy?"

Heaston felt too ill to even dignify Vomacka's jab. He just thought about getting back onto the field Thursday night. He would get plenty of chances to make an impact. Don Leahy decided to stay with the 4-3 defense that had worked so well against Central, and Heaston was one of the starting front four, along with Vomacka, Fred Hoefer, and Walt Kazlauskas. In fact, Leahy was so happy with the 4-3 that it became a Prep staple from that point forward.

Against Abraham Lincoln, Don Lee likened the Prep offense to a time bomb, ticking toward explosion. Prep "sputtered" in the first half against "a surprisingly stubborn foe" before the bomb was dropped. The score was 6–0 Prep, care of a 53-yard pass from John Bjelland to Vic Meyers, until A.L. tied the game midway through the third quarter. At that point, "the second half appeared disastrous," according to a Prep yearbook writer.

The A.L. touchdown seemed to light the Prep fuse. Spenceri hit Meyers on a 29-yard touchdown pass late in the quarter, and a Dave Bouda extra point made it 13–6 Creighton Prep. An A.L. drive then stalled, and Robert Clover came on to punt the ball back to Prep. Clover never even got the punt off. Rich Vomacka plowed through the Lynx line so fast he was waiting to steal the ball straight out of Clover's hands before he could even attempt the kick. Vomacka sprinted 27 yards with the ball into the end zone for another Prep touchdown, which made the score 19–6. Student Manager Jim Phillips called Vomacka's touchdown "one of the most fantastic plays" he had ever seen on a football field.

Prep now had all the momentum, and the points kept coming. Spenceri scored on a 7-yard run; Meyers scored—again—on a 63-yard punt return after a handoff from Tom Heim; and Tom Emery caught a 6-yard touchdown pass from Bjelland on the last play of the game. When the scores were tallied, Prep had defeated A.L. 38–6, scoring most of their points in the game's final fifteen minutes. Prep had torched the Lynx for 388 total yards, including 287 passing yards on 13 of 21 attempts. All things considered, it was a fine offensive output for the Junior Jays, in spite of Mike McKim's absence.

Perhaps as a reward for their fine play, some members of the Prep team that weekend drove to Lincoln to watch the Nebraska game against Army. Nebraska won, 14–9.

Mike McKim would be back in uniform for the Junior Jays the following Friday at Municipal Stadium. Officially, McKim's head injury was deemed a "slight concussion." Prep's opponent would be Omaha North, the only team to defeat them the year before (20–19). Early in the season, the North Vikings and their young roster had struck little fear in the hearts of their opponents, but they had improved as the season went on, and Prep could little afford to take them lightly. North was coming off an upset of fourth-ranked

Benson, 20–19, and for the first time all season they made an appearance in Gregg McBride's top ten rankings at no. 8.

Joining McKim in his return to the lineup were John Bozak and Mike Wiley. However, Prep would still miss John Corrigan, thanks to his lingering hip bruise, and Tom Heim, who had hurt his knee. Omaha North struck first following a Prep interception. North sophomore Danny Miller scored on a run from inside the 1-yard line, and the North rooting section was roused by the fast start.

Prep countered in the second quarter. Faced with fourth down at the Vikings' 10-yard line, McKim authoritatively announced his return to the lineup. He scrambled out of the pocket on a designed pass and looked toward the end zone. Nobody was open, so McKim took off on foot. Right at the goal line he met North's Roger Meisenbach, a 163-pound senior. McKim tucked his head, barreled into Meisenbach, and crashed across the end zone stripe head first. It was a gutsy play, eerily similar to McKim's ill-fated scramble that had knocked him out of the Central game. McKim maintained possession as he hit the ground, and the officials signaled touchdown.

McKim stood up and trotted off the field, where he was met by Don Leahy on the Prep sideline. Leahy grabbed McKim by the shoulder pads and held up two fingers. "How many fingers?" he asked his quarterback. "You seeing double again?"

"Two." McKim said.

That was good enough for Leahy, and McKim stayed in the game. It's a good thing he did, because he cemented what was likely his best game to date in a Prep uniform over the game's subsequent drives. The next time Prep had the ball, McKim missed a long would-be touchdown pass, but he connected with John Bozak two plays later on the first phase of a hook-and-lateral, which Bozak pitched to Rich Cacioppo, who completed the 56-yard gadget by running into the end zone. One writer called it "the prettiest play of the game." McKim found Bozak again the following series on a 49-yard touchdown pass that put Prep ahead 20–7 at halftime. He started out hot in the third quarter, finding Chuck Beda on a 59-yard touchdown completion that put the game out of reach. For the game, McKim overwhelmed North with 181 passing yards, completing 6 of 16 throws. Final score: Creighton Prep 40, Omaha North 7.

A week later, players and coaches from Creighton Prep found themselves back at Municipal Stadium with a chance to make football history. They were gunning for their third consecutive state championship. A photo of five proud, mostly smiling seniors—Vomacka, Jaworski, Kazlauskas, Bozak, and Cacioppo—covered three columns on the day's sports page. All had been members of the '58 and '59 Prep title teams. Also at stake that Friday was a third undefeated season for Don Leahy in his six years at the helm of the Prep program.

Prep's opponent was Omaha Bishop Ryan High School. Nobody expected the young Ryan team to seriously challenge the veteran Prep squad, especially with a state title hanging in the balance, and any Ryan pipe dreams were squashed shortly after the 7:30 kickoff when Rich Vomacka dropped a Ryan runner for a 7-yard loss on the first play from scrimmage. Dubbed "Professor Vomacka" by the *World-Herald* sports staff, Vomacka stuffed another attempted punt by storming through the line of scrimmage and ransacking the Ryan kicker before he ever got the ball airborne. The feat was now becoming Vomacka's signature maneuver. Four plays later, Prep went in for an easy score to take the lead.

Prep led 14–0 after the first quarter, 21–0 at halftime, 28–0 at the end of the third quarter, and 35–0 when the final buzzer sounded. The game turned into a championship coronation. The Prep defense, impervious all season long, pitched its most perfect game in its final time out.

Ryan managed just 5 first downs and 128 total yards for the game. Playing from behind and forced to pass, Ryan completed just 6 of 22 attempts.

Don Leahy, the football prophet, had delivered on his promise to the Prep student body. "Third Straight State," the team's motto all season long, was now a reality. The only question remaining, it seemed, was whether the Junior Jays would be solo champions or joint champions with Omaha Central. They would have to wait two weeks, until the Eagles' November 11 finale, to find out.

As Frank Smagacz followed his team into the locker room at halftime, he was none too pleased. His team led Lincoln Northeast 14–7, but it didn't feel that way. Not to Smagacz, and not to his players, especially after giving up a 27-yard touchdown pass in the second quarter. In fact, many on the Central team mistakenly remember trailing the Rockets at halftime. The box score proves otherwise, but their memories help tell a story. With football glory in plain sight—a chance to finish undefeated and clinch a share of a state championship—Central was stinking up the joint. They call it "playing flat" in football parlance, and on this day the Eagles were a case study in the phenomenon.

Things started out well enough for the Eagles that day at Magee-Wesleyan stadium in Lincoln. Jim Capellupo intercepted a pass on the game's opening series, but Central gave it up with a fumble on the very first play. The sequence exemplified the sort of game that was in store.

At halftime, Smagacz had a few short moments to whip his team into shape, and he had to decide what approach to take. Twenty-four minutes of football stood between Central High and an undefeated season. Those same twenty-four minutes could also end in bitter disappointment. To read his players the riot act would have been a mistake, especially with a 7-point lead. To coddle them for their poor effort would also have missed the mark. There wasn't a Gipper to win one for—perhaps the ill Tim Dempsey, but that would be a stretch, especially after the telegram gag during the Prep game—so Smagacz quelled his inner Knute Rockne and opted to challenge his team with a more cerebral appeal.

"Nothing much was happening," said center Tim Nelson. "Then he just walked in at halftime and stood there in the middle of the locker room and looked around and said, 'I *thought* you guys were football players.'"

"You guys are too good. There's nothing you can't do," Smagacz told his team.

With that, he and Jim Karabatsos turned and walked out of the locker room, leaving it to the players to decide their fate.

"It was one of those moments where you're going, 'What did he just say to us?' Nelson said. "Nothing much was said. But we came out and played very well in the second half. Those are the little things that Smagacz did."

"Their plan woke a lot of guys up," said quarterback Jim Capellupo. "We talked among ourselves about what we needed to do in the second half to win, then went out and did it."

Smagacz thought nothing special of his halftime tactic. But he was experienced enough to know that such a performance could only work once a season, and no more, or else the players would see through the ruse. Jim Karabatsos could even recall a particular game during another season when the coaches never even entered the locker room at halftime. The players became upset and started throwing chairs around before coming out for the second half.

The second half started out ominously for Central. Northeast kicked off to start the half and recovered the kick, essentially a turnover in their favor. The Central defense dug in; first, Gale Sayers and Vernon Breakfield drove a Northeast runner out of bounds, and on the next play Breakfield broke up a pass attempt. When Central got the ball back, Frank Smagacz decided to lean on Gale Sayers, who, despite the team's lackluster first half, had been a bright spot, scoring 2 touchdowns. Smagacz rolled the dice on fourth-and-five, deep in Northeast territory. Sayers took a handoff around the end and picked up the first down, making it all the way to the Rockets' 2-yard line. He then "bulled his way" into the end zone from 2 yards out to keep Central ahead in the third quarter. There were more Sayers heroics, namely a 45-yard touchdown run, but a penalty negated the score.

With the Eagles leading 20–13 late in the final quarter, the game was headed for a dramatic finish. Northeast refused to wilt. First, they recovered another Central fumble. Amid a 30-yard drive with time winding down, Northeast had the ball down on the Central 6-yard line. Facing a fourth-down-and-two, the Rockets had no choice but to go for it. They chose a straight-ahead run. Central stopped the runner cold, a yard short of the first-down mark. It was a goal-line stop that championship teams make. Smagacz had the Central quarterbacks take turns running the clock out, and it was over. Final score: Omaha Central 20, Lincoln Northeast 13.

CHAPTER 11

NINE ONE-THOUSANDTHS OF A percentage point were all that separated Omaha Central and Creighton Prep in the final intercity league football rankings. Central, with an intercity record of 7-0-1 (.938), was declared league champion ahead of Prep, who finished 6-0-1 (.929) in league play. The champion, according to the *Omaha World-Herald*, was determined by winning percentage, and the result seemed to be a source of little dispute among those involved. Columnist Wally Provost noted that it was Central's first undisputed intercity crown since 1938.

The Nebraska state championship was a different story. It seemed everybody had an opinion as to whom should be crowned champion, and at least one Omaha sportswriter obliged his readers by sharing a few. Many people, likely Central fans, believed the Eagles were more deserving of an outright title because they had played nine games while Creighton Prep had played just eight. In his column on Friday, November 4, Gregg McBride shared the thoughts of Omahan David Ferguson, who had written McBride with his take on the dispute. "Awarding championships on the most number of wins seems to me the only way," Ferguson wrote.

McBride let Ferguson's bait dangle. He believed that in the case of two superior teams, the head-to-head result was of greatest importance. In this case, let the tie stand and split the championship. McBride wrote that Ferguson could award Central the "Ferguson State championship" if he wanted, but he wasn't about to pick a winner strictly on the basis of playing more games. Had Prep tied another team on its schedule, their title claim would have been in doubt, McBride asserted, but championships are not awarded based on hypothetical scenarios. As the two-time defending state champion, Creighton Prep's merit to a share of the title was not in question. As the old boxing adage stated, "To beat the champion, you've got to knock him out."

On November 14, McBride and the *World-Herald* formally declared Omaha Central and Creighton Prep co–state champions for 1960. Each team received a commemorative plaque from the newspaper. Lincoln High finished third and Omaha Benson fourth. McCook, ranked fifth, was the leading team from out-state Nebraska. The final top ten were ranked as follows:

> T1. Creighton Prep
> T1. Omaha Central
> 3. Lincoln High
> 4. Omaha Benson
> 5. McCook
> 6. Lincoln Northeast
> 7. Omaha Tech
> 8. Omaha South
> 9. Omaha North
> 10. Hastings

Then came the much-deserved spoils of victory. A few weeks after the announcement of the split state title, Creighton Prep held a banquet at the Omaha Livestock Exchange Building to honor its third straight state championship team. Endless rows of banquet tables were filled with Prep players and their families, and Don Leahy was the evening's featured speaker. The Central PTA held a similar banquet to honor the co-champion Eagles. In early January, in the press box of the Rose Bowl in Pasadena, California, the National

FIG. 25. Endless rows of Creighton Prep supporters gathered to celebrate another state championship. Reprinted with permission of the 1961 *Jay Junior*.

Sports News Service announced its top twenty high school football teams nationwide. Miami, Florida, came in first. Creighton Prep made the cut, finishing twentieth.

Individual accolades also followed. The 1960 Nebraska all-state football team was then thought to have the most speed ever in Nebraska high school history. It included five players from Omaha. Four of them were from Omaha Central or Creighton Prep: Gale Sayers, Don Fiedler, Rich Vomacka, and Walt Kazlauskas. The fifth Omahan was Paul Meckna from Benson. The all-intercity team was also littered with players from Prep and Central, including Sayers, the only unanimous choice for the second consecutive year; Fiedler; Breakfield; Vomacka; Kazlauskas; and Cacioppo. Sayers was declared team captain. Other players who had been under strong consideration for the award were John Bruce, Dennis Tiedemann, Maris Vinovskis, Mac Young, Ardell Gunn, Howard Fouts, Vic Meyers, Chuck Van Vliet, Fred Hoefer, Bob Marasco, Frank Spenceri, and John Bozak.

Teen magazine recognized Gale Sayers for his spectacular season, and Rich Vomacka made *Teen*'s Midwest honorable mention. Sayers's final statistics were dazzling. He had scored 20 touchdowns and 7 extra points for the season. The rest of the Central Eagles scored 17 touchdowns combined, including 4 apiece from Breakfield and Gunn. "Gale's headlines, of course, were harvested mostly from slashing, high-stepping, long-striding, hard-hitting, high-scoring runs," wrote Don Lee. Considering the shutout on October 7, his records look even more impressive. The 0–0 game also showed Omaha sports fans how dominant the Creighton Prep defense was, in light of Sayers's fantastic play against other teams. For the season, the Junior Jays' defense gave up just 4.1 points per game.

Knights of Columbus Council 652 (Boys Town) in May named Frank Smagacz Omaha Catholic Coach of the Year, an honor his counterpart Don Leahy had shared the year before with Cletus Fischer from Omaha South. Smagacz received the honor at a breakfast at the downtown Sheraton-Fontenelle Hotel. After another successful track season that spring, the award was no surprise. Leahy was honored too, as National Catholic Coach of the Year.

Soon the weather would turn cold. The trees would lose their leaves, mothers would dig out heavy winter coats for their children, and car owners would put chains on their tires. The long Nebraska winter would grab hold of Omaha and not let go until it was good and ready. In January, the country would welcome a new president into office—John Kennedy, who emerged victorious on the second Tuesday in November in the closest presidential election in more than forty years. Those oddsmakers in Las Vegas, it turned out, knew how to pick a winner, even in politics. Their counterparts in Omaha, who so astutely set the line for the Prep-Central game, knew how to spot a dead heat when they saw one. As the saying goes, "It's not gambling if you know you're going to win."

The Gale Sayers recruiting sweepstakes began heating up

in late January. On a trip to the Iowa State University campus in Ames, Iowa, Sayers and Vernon Breakfield, teammates since the fourth grade, liked what they saw. They liked it enough to tell Cyclone Coach Clay Stapleton that they were ready to commit to the program. According to the *Omaha World-Herald*, the Central backs would receive full scholarships, consisting of tuition, room and board, books, and fifteen dollars per month.

However, things were not as they seemed. "Though they have decided on Iowa State, the likable Negroes have an opportunity to visit Notre Dame February 6," the paper reported.

The pair took the Notre Dame trip in early February, but South Bend, Indiana, was not in either player's destiny. The University of Nebraska jumped back into the mix, and on June 10, at his Central High commencement, Sayers said he would attend Nebraska in the fall. He said proximity to home and Nebraska's offensive system were factors in the decision. Coach Bill Jennings confirmed the story, telling the newspaper that Gale had accepted the Cornhuskers' offer. Within days, rumors began to swirl. Kansas was still a possibility, and the Sayers recruitment truly became a rancorous affair. In August, Sayers visited the KU campus in Lawrence, Kansas. Coach Jack Mitchell even came to Omaha to see Gale personally. University of Omaha officials alleged that Kansas was tampering with the recruitment by using Roger Sayers as bait, supposedly enticing him to transfer to Kansas to make the school more attractive to Gale. Letters were exchanged between the two schools to air grievances on the subject.

Later in August, Gale starred for the South squad of the Nebraska Shrine Bowl in a dominant victory over Frank Spenceri and the North team of All-Stars. Sayers's South team won 32–0, paced by Gale's 4 touchdowns (two running, two receiving) on a hot day in front of a record Shrine

Bowl crowd at Memorial Stadium in Lincoln. He shone on both offense and defense, even drawing the attention of Bill Jennings, who was in attendance. "I like the way he went up there on defense and hit a few people," Jennings told Don Lee. For Gale, the game was as much a personal challenge as a team competition. Kent McCloughan of Broken Bow had been named the *World-Herald* Athlete of the Year, and Sayers wanted to prove he was every bit the player McCloughan was. There was no doubting Sayers on this day, particularly after a hard hit he delivered to McCloughan in the third quarter that knocked the out-state star out of the game.

Publicly, Gale became wishy-washy about his college destination. In early September, he told the *World-Herald* that his choice came down to Kansas or Nebraska. "I'm still going to Nebraska as far as I'm concerned . . . but I might go to KU," he told the paper. Behind the scenes, Gale was losing patience with fans and boosters from his home state. Nebraskans seemed unable to stand the thought of him playing elsewhere, and the pressure to stay close to home seemed to overwhelm him. When it seemed almost certain that Sayers would wind up playing somewhere other than Nebraska, an underground group of Cornhusker alumni supposedly resorted to dirty pool. "If he wasn't going to Nebraska, we had it arranged to route him to Iowa University," a Nebraska alumnus told sportswriter Wally Provost. "That way, it we couldn't have him, at least he wouldn't be playing against us."

This nasty element wouldn't get its way. Sayers finally decided on Kansas. He fancied the school's social life, the potential of the football team, and the opportunity to study in the school's business administration program. That balanced line of thinking indicates he had at least a mild interest in his career plans after football. Bill Jennings openly conceded the loss of the state's best player, telling the *World-Herald* that the school had tried as hard as it could but Gale was destined for someplace else and he wished him the best.

The peculiar obsession many Nebraskans had with Sayers would die a slow death, or perhaps never even die at all. Gale would be a three-year fixture on the Nebraska schedule, and fans could only bemoan his absence and root against him. Or they could change course and herald him as a native son, now on to bigger things. The choice was theirs.

Somewhat fittingly, Jennings wound up coaching Sayers after all. After Nebraska parted ways with the coach following a 3-6-1 record in 1961 to make way for Bob Devaney, Jennings took a job on Jack Mitchell's staff at Kansas. The Jayhawks, in the same calendar year, had poached Nebraska's prized recruit and its head coach. Nebraskans would quickly forget about the coach after Devaney's 9-2 inaugural season and Gotham Bowl victory. But Sayers they wouldn't forget. Now, it seemed the annual contest with Kansas had a cause célèbre, noted Wally Provost. "It's ironic if not amusin'."

Rich Vomacka was hanging around his locker one day after the football season when Walt Kazlauskas tapped him on the shoulder and said, "Well, we better go down to Hauff's and get our all-state stars."

"Let's go," Vomacka said.

That afternoon, the pair jumped into Kazlauskas's car with their letter sweaters and made the trip to Hauff's. For such decorated high school athletes, there was nothing matter-of-fact about it.

"We made a special trip," Vomacka said. "That was a big deal for both of us. You want to put that gold star and white star on there for all-city and all-state. There's not too many guys who get to do that, man. When you go into any high school and you're a sophomore or junior, you look up to the guys who made it to the top. I remember at one of our dances, a kid who was a couple years behind me at Holy Cross came up and said, 'Gosh, would you let me wear your letter sweater, just for a couple minutes?'

"I didn't let him. I can't even remember his name. But that's something kind of different."

One day after the spring semester ended and Creighton Prep was closed for the summer, Frank Spenceri called up Bill Heaston. Frank loved all sports. He played baseball for Prep during the academic year and for other teams during the summer. For years after high school, he played second base for one of Omaha's semiprofessional teams. He even got to face legendary pitcher Bob Gibson, who then was playing basketball for the Harlem Globetrotters but had returned to pitch a few games for his brother Josh's baseball team. Spenceri came up to bat, and Gibson was on the mound. Two pitches were thrown, both called strikes.

Spenceri turned to the umpire and said, "They *both* sounded high and outside."

Frank was determined not to watch a third strike go whizzing by his nose, so he attempted a drag bunt that didn't even graze his bat then walked straight to the dugout with his head down.

On this day, however, he was calling Heaston to recruit him for the summer Legion team. "We need bodies" was his sales pitch.

Heaston didn't play much baseball but decided to give it a try. Don Leahy coached the team and kept him on the roster. As Heaston remembers, he rode the bench for much of the summer. John Bjelland was one of the outfielders on the team, and it seemed his strong arm had gotten even stronger over the summer. Leahy would hit pop flies out to him in left field and Bjelland would rifle the ball on a line to home plate, hardly ever touching the ground. All summer long he kept asking Leahy to let him pitch. Leahy kept telling him no, but Bjelland kept asking. Finally Leahy told him, "Look, I know you've got a great arm, but you don't know where it's going. And I don't want to be responsible for you killing somebody."

After that, Bjelland quit asking to pitch.

During his junior year at Creighton Prep, Bjelland also made one of the toughest decisions of his young life—giving up football. He had his heart set on going to medical school and made every effort necessary to have a pristine academic record as he got ready to apply to colleges. He needed the extra time, he figured, to study. Football had to stop, so he gave it up. His discernment took such a toll that he and Leahy never even had a discussion about it.

"I wasn't real happy when I quit," Bjelland said. "That's a tough choice to make when you're a junior. Mickey Mantle made $100,000 a year. Most doctors I knew made a lot more than that, so I was motivated to see if I could become a doctor. We were kind of poor, and that influenced my decision. But Don Leahy was the epitome of a role model. He could organize his thoughts and communicate them to you. He told you what you needed to do, and you got the idea there was exigency involved. We just admired the hell out of the guy."

For Bjelland, who became a radiologist, the decision paid off.

Later that summer, Frank Spenceri was at home when Walt Kazlauskas and his father pulled up to his house. They came bearing a present, Walt's 1952 Ford. The following week, the John Wayne of the Creighton Prep football team was headed to Annapolis, Maryland, and the United States Naval Academy, and he decided his friend could make better use of the car. Spenceri joked that he got the car only because Mr. Kazlauskas had always liked him.

"Were we close on that team?" Spenceri said, his voice cracking. "Yeah, awfully close team."

EPILOGUE

On friday, october 8, 2010, Omaha Central and Creighton Prep met again on the football field. The venue was the same but its name had changed, from Municipal Stadium to Rosenblatt Stadium in honor of Omaha mayor Johnny Rosenblatt. The stadium's appearance had changed too, having undergone significant upgrades and renovations to keep pace with the ever-changing nature of athletics. A video replay board, a giant electronic scoreboard, and expanded outfield seating were just a few of the changes that had taken place since the 1960s. That entire time Rosenblatt had served as the home of the College World Series, an event that had grown in popularity like its host city. Rosenblatt in 2010 also was home to the Omaha Nighthawks, who were in the midst of a 3-5 inaugural season in the United Football League (UFL).

Over the years, Omaha-area high schools had invested significantly in football facilities, making Rosenblatt a nearly irrelevant venue for high school football. It was both a sign of the times and the growing popularity of football in the United States. Although the ballpark had served honorably as the host site for the cws, change was looming. A new stadium, TD Ameritrade Park in north downtown, would open in early 2011 and would serve as the home of the College World Series. Rosenblatt, it was announced, was scheduled for demolition.

And so, in a stroke of marketing genius, officials from Omaha Central and Creighton Prep decided one more tus-

Fig. 26. Prep and Central met at Rosenblatt Stadium one last time in 2010. Photo courtesy of Creighton Preparatory School.

sle at the charmed old stadium on the hill would be a great way to close the place down—and pay homage to participants of the 1960 game. The weekend coincided with "100 Yards of Glory," an exhibition of Omaha football history at the downtown Durham Museum that paid tribute to the scoreless 1960 game.

True to form, the 2010 game failed to disappoint. Creighton Prep, under the direction of Head Coach Tom Jaworski—in his final season at Prep—narrowly emerged victorious, 30–25. For Jaworski, the game and the season capped a successful coaching career that he was simply grateful to have had. It had all begun when Tom Brosnihan asked him to help coach freshman football. That earned him a promotion to wrestling coach, and he was on his way. "To this day, I think it's a miracle that I was a head coach," Jaworski said. "Don Leahy had great loyalty."

The announced crowd of 12,121 was the largest to see a Nebraska high school football game since 1989, when the same two schools had played in front of 12,500 people at Omaha Burke Stadium. The game began with a welcome

FIG. 27. Tom Jaworski decided 2010 would be his final season coaching football at Creighton Prep. Photo courtesy of Creighton Preparatory School.

and coin flip on the large video replay board, and at half-time spectators were treated to a five-minute commemorative video featuring interviews from players on both teams. Then the 1960 teams were introduced on the field, a contingent of roughly sixty combined players, coaches and trainers who made the trip to Rosenblatt that night. Eye black and shoulder pads had been replaced by wedding rings and reading glasses. Wearing throwback jerseys, they took the field again, not as competitors but as friends. This place, once their playground, was now a relic. And these men were part of its history.

Don Leahy, eighty-one years old, was there. So was his quarterback, Mike McKim, who on this night was simply glad to leave the stadium under his own power instead of in an ambulance. Prep assistant coach Jack Jackson also made

Fig. 28. Participants from the 1960 game met again in 2010. Photo courtesy of Nate Driml and Creighton Preparatory School.

it to the game, and he charmed players from both teams by recounting his near-tragic slide down the stadium grandstand. Some had never heard the story. Others from Prep recalled the tragic final days of their teammate Bill Pycha. Many had forgotten that he had lost his battle with leukemia just days before the game, but none had forgotten Bill's indomitable spirit.

Many from Central were there, too, including Gayle Carey, Tim Dempsey, and Fred Scarpello, who had lost much of his eyesight to diabetes. Among many topics, they discussed Gale Sayers's amazing college and professional football career and his career in business after his football days were finished. A few reopened the case of the much-disputed forward lateral penalty that cost Central a touchdown, and both sides stated their case. As one might expect, the play had been a frequent lunch topic whenever players from the two teams got together over the decades. Fifty years later, the penalty stood.

Absent that night was Frank Smagacz, who had died of heart problems in 1997 at age eighty-two. Twenty years earlier, Smagacz had been honored for his twenty-seven years of service to Omaha Central at a banquet at Peony Park. He had retired from coaching a decade before but stayed on to teach driver's ed. He also dabbled in coaching by helping teach sports to grade school girls, starting with his daughter Rose's fourth-grade softball and basketball teams.

"Back then, it was unheard of to have girls' sports," said Rose. "So for him to see that we female athletes needed to play made him a pioneer there, too. Nobody else took that on."

Jim Karabatsos was at Smagacz's retirement party that night in 1977. Smagacz sought out his old coaching buddy, who by then was teaching English at Creighton University, having also left coaching. "Jim, I could never have done anything without you," Smagacz told him. The comment nearly moved Karabatsos to tears.

"I thought that was about as high a compliment as anyone could ever pay to some little flunky like me," he recalled.

His own retirement was filled with lots of golf, and he kept a close eye on high school athletics. Karabatsos lived to see the reunion but died of heart disease in 2013 at age eighty-six. He was the subject of a moving tribute days later in the *Omaha World-Herald*. Writer Sue Story Truax called him a man who "appreciated fine writing and the turn of a good phrase" as much as a "well-turned double play."

Also absent at the 2010 reunion was former Creighton Prep co-captain Walt Kazlauskas, who had died suddenly that summer, just a few months before he was scheduled to reunite with his Prep classmates. Prior to his own death, Walt had been in Omaha to attend a wake service held for his mother. At the service he visited with Bill Heaston and Rich Vomacka. "I'm really looking forward to this reunion," Walt told his friends. His life had changed dramatically after high school when he enrolled at the Naval Academy.

"That year was the best year of my life."

Walt probably knew it, but that year ranked high on the list of most everyone involved.

At approximately 10 a.m. on Wednesday, July 25, 2012, as a few dozen interested spectators gathered behind a temporary perimeter fence in the old ballpark's former parking lot, demolition of Rosenblatt Stadium began. In a strange way, the scene seemed a mismatch, the huge stadium still capable of dwarfing the wrecking equipment that was moments away from crippling its façade.

Interested onlookers took photos while others—some with children and grandchildren—shared their earliest memories of entering the gates of the famous stadium on 13th Street. There was much to reminisce about: professional football exhibitions, barnstorming baseball games, and classic College World Series championships. The demolition of Rosenblatt had been a controversial topic in Omaha, and the stadium's fate was still a fresh reality. It's likely someone

Fig. 29. Gone but not forgotten—the demolition of Rosenblatt Stadium began on July 25, 2012. Photo courtesy of John Dechant.

in the crowd that morning had been among the 14,500 people who crammed inside the stadium on October 8, 1960, to watch what many consider the greatest high school football game in Nebraska history.

Local television crews were on site to capture footage for the evening news. So was a photographer from the *Omaha World-Herald*. More than a year of inactivity and particularly hot and dry summer weather had left the field barely recognizable to anyone aware of how it once looked. Bleachers and other adornments had been removed, too, and the quiet crowd outside the stadium that hot summer morning watched solemnly as the defenseless structure sustained the first body blows of the months-long demolition that would leave only a small replica of the infield in the parking lot of the nearby Henry Doorly Zoo.

The demolition was a reminder that stadiums, even the great ones, don't last forever. But the memories they helped create certainly do.

ACKNOWLEDGMENTS

MY RELATIONSHIP WITH THE story of the 1960 Prep-Central game began over lunch one day with my business partner Jim Fogarty. "What's the greatest game you've ever witnessed in person?" was the question on the table, and when Jim's turn to answer came, he told me about a memorable fall night in 1960 when he and some friends watched Creighton Prep hold the great Gale Sayers and Omaha Central scoreless. The romantic notion of a scoreless tie and a split state championship sounded cool. A few months went by, and then I read about the 2010 Prep-Central game at Rosenblatt Stadium. Honoring the 1960 participants that night was a nice touch, and it occurred to me that others might share Mr. Fogarty's opinion of the game.

Roughly two years went by while the idea to write about the game took shape in my mind. I needed to make sense of the idea, and eventually I realized that I couldn't fully make sense of it without knowing the whole story, or at least a more complete version than what I had. I called Nate Driml, Creighton Prep's capable alumni director, and told him about my idea. Nate and I met face-to-face at Creighton Prep, he shared some research materials with me, along with the Prep alumni directory, and I was on my way. Throughout my work on the book, Nate was supportive and resourceful and always eager for an update on my progress. Creighton Prep is lucky to have such a capable man on staff.

My journey researching and writing this book took me three full years from that first meeting with Nate. I spent countless hours in the basement of the University of Nebraska at Omaha library, scrolling through *Omaha World-Herald* slides from 1960; I turned the pages of (and mouse clicked through) so many Prep and Central yearbooks and student newspapers that I eventually lost count; I spent time at the Central High Foundation's archives looking through boxes of photographs and old news clippings; I was introduced to an unmarked room in the bowels of Creighton Prep (that some Jesuit probably once called "home") that housed a treasure trove of Prep artifacts; and I spent hundreds of hours interviewing people who could help me reconstruct the story of the 1960 season. My interviews took place in homes, coffee shops, restaurants over lunch (and sometimes dinner), my own office, and of course over the phone.

Persons interviewed during my research were Dudley Allen, Bernie Berigan, John Bjelland, Dave Bouda, John Bozak, James Brown, Sandy Buda, Gayle Carey, Henry Cordes, Tim Dempsey, Mike Fitzgerald, James Fogarty, Howard Fouts, John Hartigan, Bill Heaston, Tom Heim, Jack Jackson, Tom Jaworski, Jim Karabatsos, Roy Katskee, Tom Kearney, Don Leahy, Bob Marasco, Gary Marasco, Tom Marfisi, Mike McKim, Terry Mollner, Don Moray, Tim Nelson, Rose Parfitt, Richard Pedersen, Jim Phillips, Steve Pivovar, Larry Porter, John Prescott, Roger Sayers, Barb Scarpello, Fred Scarpello, Mike Smagacz, Frank Spenceri, Mike Spinharney, Terry Stickels, Charles Van Vliet, Maris Vinovskis, and Rich Vomacka.

Newspapers and archival sources that I accessed during my research included the *Omaha World-Herald*, the *Omaha Sun*, the *Central High Register*, the 1961 *Jay Junior*, the 1961 *O-Book*, the *Creighton Prep*, the 1999 Creighton Prep alumni directory, the *Benson High News*, Marquette University's *Hilltop*, the *Milwaukee Journal*, the *Milwaukee Sentinel*, *Life* magazine, *Holiday* magazine, and various issues of *Creighton Prep Alumni News*.

Books consulted were *Father Flanagan of Boys Town: A Man of Vision*, by Hugh Reilly and Kevin Warneke (Boys Town Press, 2008); *My Kansas-Nebraska Acts* by Gabe Parks (Gabe Parks, 2005); *Rosenblatt Stadium: Omaha's Diamond on the Hill*, by Steven Pivovar (Omaha World-Herald, 2010); *I Am Third*, by Gale Sayers with Al Silverman (Viking Press, 1970); *Football Scouting Methods*, by Steve Belichick (Snowball Publishing, 2014); *The Eternal Summer*, by Curt Sampson (Villard Books, 1992); *Truman*, by David McCullough (Simon & Schuster, 1992); *The History of Creighton University: 1878–2003*, by Dennis Mihelich (Creighton University Press, 2006); and *Upstream Metropolis: An Urban Biography of Omaha and Council Bluffs*, by Lawrence Larsen, Barbara Cottrell, Harl Dalstrom, and Kay Calame Dalstrom (University of Nebraska Press, 2007).

One academic paper was used: "From Riga to Ann Arbor," by Maris Vinovskis, which appeared in *Leaders in the Historical Study of American Education* (Sense Publishers, 2011).

My challenges were many, but perhaps none concerned me more than writing about an era of which I had no memory. The game took place more than two decades before my birth, so I strived at every turn to properly capture the spirit of 1960. I hope I've succeeded.

Charles Kelly of Phoenix, Arizona, was a great help to me throughout this project. We had numerous conversations about the book over the phone, never directly talking about football or 1960 but always discussing the writing process. For his help I am grateful.

One of the early conversations I had about the story was with John Bjelland. John is not only a character in the book but has been a champion of my project from the beginning, guiding me to sources and encouraging me along the way. Howard Fouts and Tim Dempsey performed a similar function, connecting me with important people from Omaha Central.

My world changed a lot during the years I worked on *Scoreless*. I got married and became a father, for starters. And time marched on, taking me farther away from 1960. But I kept working. I wrote my first passages of the book on December 20, 2012, and on that date two years later, for the first time, I knew I would finish. I just had to keep working.

My business partners—Dave Harding, Bob Mundy, and the aforementioned Mr. Fogarty—were supportive of me throughout this process, even when it distracted from my daily workload. For your faith in me, I thank you.

Omaha author Richard Dooling took an interest in my project early on, and I was smart enough to listen when he offered guidance on publishing.

Janet Tilden was a great resource as I neared completion. She evaluated my manuscript and gave me suggestions that I couldn't imagine doing without.

My agent, Jody Kahn of Brandt and Hochman, was a trustworthy guide in formalizing the publishing agreement, and she helped me better understand the business side of publishing.

Special thanks are also due to Rob Taylor, my editor at the University of Nebraska Press. Rob saw a vision for my story, guided me through the publishing process, and helped improve the structure of my story along the way.

Finally, I must thank the coaches and players who participated in the scoreless game of 1960. Without your willingness to open up your memories, this project would never have happened. My hope is that I can take you back to your youth, at least for a couple hundred pages.

BIBLIOGRAPHIC ESSAY

Prologue

THROUGHOUT MY RESEARCH, NUMEROUS former players of both teams told me Prep and Central played to a 6–6 tie as freshmen at Creighton Stadium, but I struggled to validate the result and the circumstances with published historical records. That was until one day in 2014 when I found two short articles in the *Central High Register*, one from the September 20, 1957, edition and the other from October 4, 1957, that previewed and recapped the game.

Frank Spenceri's memories of that day were largely responsible for inspiring my description of Tom Brosnihan's actions and the mood of the Jesuits who were unhappy he decided to play the game. A story in the September 21, 1957, edition of the *Omaha World-Herald* provided me with details of the varsity game and the other game in town that was cancelled.

Every player who remembered the game seemed to recall the awful weather. Most described it as a driving rainstorm, but historic weather records indicate it was a steady drizzle that began at midday. Central quarterback Howard Fouts recalled that day well, and he supplied me with the anecdote about teammate Richard Lloyd, who covered his helmet in white shoe polish.

Chapter 1

The opening scene of part 1 was jointly told to me by Gayle Carey, Howard Fouts, Fred Scarpello, and Tim Dempsey over lunch in October 2012. The information about Omaha Central and its many academic programs and extracurricular activities was found in the Omaha Central 1961 *O-Book* and the fall 1960 editions of the *Central High Register*. Central graduate and former senior class vice president Maris Vinovskis guided me through the connection between the Sputnik launch and its effect on academia. Other details about J. Arthur Nelson were supplemented through a personal interview with Central graduate and former television news producer John Prescott.

Multiple interviews with Jim Karabatsos gave me a deeper understanding of the athletic programs at Central and the type of students who went to school there. My interview with Roger Sayers was helpful in learning about Gale's early athletic aspirations and his own athletic career. A brief November 2012 interview with Don Moray, a former teammate of Roger's at the University of Nebraska at Omaha, also helped me better understand his tremendous athletic gifts.

Howard Fouts, interviewed separately from the aforementioned lunch, helped me visualize the limited athletic facilities at Central High. Almost all the former Central players I interviewed had strong memories of their tiny practice field, and Wally Provost's description of the field was printed in his August 6, 1963, column in the *Omaha World-Herald*.

Additional source material about players' heights and weights and academic years was compiled through research at the Central High Foundation archives in downtown Omaha. One particular file, donated by the Smagacz family, contained game programs that filled in these critical details.

Former Central coach Jim Karabatsos described to me how mediocre the school's football program was before Frank Smagacz became head coach. The team's win-loss record, which I found in the 1950 *O-Book*, confirmed his recollections, as did Wally Provost's description of the one-sidedness of the Lincoln High series in his August 6, 1963, *Omaha World-Herald* column.

A large portion of my portrait of Frank Smagacz's youth in Columbus, Nebraska, and the surrounding area was based on my phone interviews with his son Mike. I also relied heavily on various sports columns written throughout Smagacz's career, including Paul Ernst's April 16, 1979, column in the *Columbus Telegram* and a November 23, 1978, story about Smagacz and his sons by *Omaha World-Herald* staff writer Jerry Fricke. Mike Smagacz told me about his father's exploits in the Elkhorn Valley League, the Pioneer Night League, and his brief stint in semiprofessional baseball. A brief profile of Smagacz appeared in the *Omaha World-Herald* on June 13, 1938, during Frank's time with the Fremont team of the Elkhorn Valley League. The Ernst column detailed Smagacz's job moves as he went from Silver Creek to Arlington to Tekamah, as well as the financial terms of his job agreements; it also illuminated Smagacz's time coaching the University of Nebraska baseball team after his military service.

My interviews with Mike Smagacz also yielded important information about Frank and Fran's courtship, their early days of marriage, and their time in Fort Pierce, Florida, during World War II.

The circumstances surrounding Smagacz's hiring at Omaha Central and the family's relocation to Omaha were told to me by Mike Smagacz and his sister Rose Parfitt. Both Mike and Rose shared with me stories about growing up in such a large family. A February 23, 1951, article in the *Central High Register* provided me the anecdote about Frank falling asleep during Jean's birth, and I found the 1950 Central football team photo and details of the standout play of Mel Hansen and others in the 1951 *O-Book*.

Jim Karabatsos graciously shared with me the story of his upbringing in Omaha during the Depression, his home life in South Omaha, his years of military experience during World War II, and his eventual hiring at Omaha Central. Jim helped me better understand how high school football was played in the 1950s and 1960s, and he shared with me the methods he and Smagacz used to run the Central program during their years coaching. Jim was especially proud as he retold the anecdote about the signed Bob Devaney letter, which he kept in his possession the rest of his life.

Chapter 2

A series of interviews with colleague and former Omaha news reporter Jim Fogarty helped me understand Don Leahy's enormous presence at Creighton Prep during the 1950s and '6os. Jim also recalled the day Leahy stood in front of the student body at a pep rally and proclaimed the motto "Third Straight State." During interviews, Leahy himself described his role as a teacher and coach, including his personal appearance. Other Prep graduates added to the character portrait.

Almost every former Prep student I interviewed for this book had strong memories of Father Shinners and his role as assistant principal at Prep. Most confessed they feared him, at least a little. One notable exception was Chuck Van Vliet, who got along well with Shinners.

Don Leahy told me about the success of the 1958 and '59 Prep football teams, as did an article from the *Omaha World-Herald* that previewed the 1960 season. I found information about Creighton Prep's many football state championships on the school's website, dating back to its first, in 1932.

My interviews with Bill Heaston, Jim Fogarty, Sandy Buda, and Don Leahy helped me understand how isolated Creighton Prep was in 1960, when Omaha essentially turned to countryside west of 72nd Street. Information about the history of Creighton Prep and Creighton University, including the acquisition of land, was found in the 1999 Creighton Prep alumni directory (Holiday FL: Alumni Research Inc., 1999), which included a helpful history section. Bernie Berigan told me about his father's role in helping secure the land for the new school from Matt Scanlon.

Information about the Creighton Prep Jesuit priests, including Father John J. Foley, S.J., was found in the 1961 *Jay Junior* yearbook. The yearbook also profiled international students Francisco Cifuentes and Wilfried Arzt, who are mentioned in this section.

As with Father Shinners, most Prep graduates I interviewed had something to say about JUG, including Tom Kearney, Mike Fitzgerald, and Jim Fogarty. In Bill Heaston's personal collection of Prep memorabilia, I found an original demerit card. Sandy Buda, Jim Fogarty, Bill Heaston, Chuck Van Vliet, and Richard Pedersen all recalled their experience with the Creighton Prep entrance exam and the school's ranking system.

I was privileged to interview Creighton Prep coach Don Leahy on more than one occasion, and these interviews framed much of this discussion, including his upbringing near Peru, his parents' divorce, and his years as a student and athlete at Creighton Prep. He also shared stories about his college years at Marquette University and the other football coaches who influenced him. Other details about Leahy's playing and coaching career were available on the Creighton Prep website, to which I was directed by Prep alumni director Nate Driml, and in the Marquette *Hilltop*, the school's annual yearbook, which I accessed electronically.

A *Milwaukee Journal* article titled "Like Peas in a Pod Are These Hilltoppers," which appeared in the paper September 12, 1948, revealed much about Leahy's early career at Marquette and his friendship with Jim Green. Leahy described for me his first taste of college football action against the University of Iowa and the subsequent injury that ended his season. As an aside, Leahy posits that facemasks have much to do with the spike in football head injuries in recent years. Before facemasks, he claims, players had nothing to protect their faces from serious injury and thus were more reluctant to lead into tackles with their heads.

Leahy also told me about the career choices that faced him after college and the events that led him to return to Creighton Prep. A simple question about his favorite offensive and defensive schemes prompted him to share with me the plan he and L. G. Friedrichs put in place for success at Prep. There was no shortage of information about Mike Dugan's career as a Junior Jay, mostly from Leahy and *Omaha World-Herald* articles published on November 3, 1954; February 7, 1955; May 20, 1956; and June 7, 1955.

Rumors of Leahy leaving Creighton Prep for Iowa State were first published by the *Omaha World-Herald* on December 15, 1956. The *World-Herald* also documented Leahy's promotion to head coach on February 25, 1955. Other than Tom Brosnihan, who was deceased at the time of my writing, I was fortunate to interview Don Leahy's assistant coaches— Dudley Allen, Bernie Berigan, and Jack Jackson—and they each shared with me stories of their coaching and teaching backgrounds. Leahy told me about the time he left Prep for the University of California, and Bernie Berigan told me about his role in helping Leahy return to Omaha. The ordeal was also followed closely by Don Lee at the *Omaha World-Herald*, most notably in articles on April 3, 1957, and April 21, 1957.

Chapter 3

Jim Karabatsos, Don Leahy, and Dudley Allen all shared with me their personal memories of the annual Russell Sporting Goods coaches' party. All three provided useful information about the life of a high school coach and his family in 1960.

Bill Heaston from Creighton Prep provided me a large stack of personal memorabilia from his high school days, and the stack included a receipt from 1959, when he purchased his varsity letter. On that receipt I found information about the Russell store's satellite locations and its main Omaha branch. I also used the receipt to learn the cost of a letter sweater and chevrons. Bill told me about the Russell operation and that of its competitor, Hauff's. I found a McDonald's advertisement in a 1960 *Omaha World-Herald*, and there I learned the cost of an All-American Meal.

Gregg McBride's September 8, 1960, column in the *Omaha World-Herald* was one of the most valuable pieces of research I found in writing this section. His perspective added context to the high school football scene in Omaha and gave me a better understanding of the lifestyles of coaches in those days. I relied on a similar McBride column, also published that September, later in the chapter while explaining the findings of the National Football Federation and the growth of the sport nationwide. In *Father Flanagan of Boys Town* (Boys Town NE: Boys Town Press, 2008), written by Hugh Reilly and Kevin Warneke, I came to better understand how Father Edward Flanagan used football to help showcase the great work of Boys Town. James Fogarty of Omaha illuminated that research by sharing with me his memories of Skip Palrang.

Dudley Allen was the first person who told me the tale of Tom Brosnihan's plunge into a ditch surrounding Carter Lake, and I subsequently heard similar or different versions of the story from others associated with Creighton Prep. Then in 2015 I interviewed Gary Marasco, a 1963 graduate of Creighton Prep, who willingly shared with me his version of the incident, which I found particularly helpful because he was the driver at the wheel when the car veered off the road.

The stories of coaches searching for fields to play and practice on were told to me by Don Leahy and Jim Karabatsos, who both went through the exercise. They both shared with me how thankless the life of a coach's wife can sometimes be. Former Prep student manager Mike Fitzgerald shared the anecdote about washing uniforms at the Leahy household after games and practices.

The speculative chatter from the Russell Sporting Goods party was inspired mostly through sports articles in the *Omaha World-Herald* from the fall of 1960, including the recap of Cassius Clay's first professional fight (October 30) and the United States' gold medal–winning basketball team (September 4, 11, 19). I had the opportunity to interview Omahan Bob Boozer many times before his death, and Bob graciously shared stories from his college, Olympic, and professional basketball experience.

I relied on the memories of longtime Nebraska sportswriter Larry Porter and Omaha newsmen James Fogarty and Henry Cordes to write my portrait of Gregg McBride. All three also gave me tremendous insight about Don Lee.

The closing paragraphs of this chapter about the sports fervor in Omaha were based on my own experience living in the city and the memories of Terry Stickels, a former Omahan, who now lives in the Dallas area.

Chapter 4

This chapter of part 2 relies heavily on three key sources: my personal interviews with Roger Sayers, news articles from the *Omaha World-Herald*, and Gale Sayers's 1970 autobiography, *I Am Third* (New York: Viking Press, 1970).

The opening description was composed by combining the memories of Sayers's teammate Tim Nelson, Creighton Prep alumnus John Hartigan, and former Omahan Terry Stickels. I found a thorough profile of running backs Sayers, Breakfield, and Gunn in the April 21, 1961, edition of the *Central High Register*, and it included the anecdote about Sayers getting stopped by police on the way home from a track meet. I referenced this article frequently as I composed paragraphs on the three running backs. *Register* sportswriter Jeff Wohlner, in his article "Eagle's Clause," published on October 7, 1960, referred to the Central backfield as the fastest in intercity history.

Had I given him the opportunity, Sayers's former coach Jim Karabatsos probably could have discussed the Sayers brothers with me for days on end, but eventually we had to end our interviews. It was clear to me how privileged he felt to coach such a talented athlete. He also shared stories about other players on the 1960 Central team, including quarterbacks Jim Capellupo and Howard Fouts and linemen James Brown and Don Fiedler.

The story of Nebraska's woes trying to recruit Sayers started with an October 25, 1960, article in the *Omaha World-Herald* titled "'Soft-Sell' Defended by Husker Coach." Sayers gives his own version of these events in *I Am Third*, and Don Lee's reporting in early 1961 chronicled the various recruiting trips Sayers took to other schools and the path that led him to the University of Kansas. Most of Sayers's teammates remembered the Pookie Snack'n Burger promotion, and Sayers told the story in *I Am Third*. Creighton Prep lineman Bill Heaston, who once worked at Otoe's, described to me the magnitude of the hamburger.

Roger Sayers graciously opened up to me about the struggles his family had during his childhood. Gale's own writing in *I Am Third* helps support those memories.

Former Creighton Prep assistant coach Jack Jackson told me about the street slang term used to describe the Central-Tech game in the days before racial awareness had begun to take hold in the white population.

One of my great pleasures in researching this portion of the book was interviewing Maris Vinovskis by phone. Now a history professor at the University of Michigan, he offered a unique perspective on Omaha Central and the city in general from his days there as a youth. He also provided me "From Riga to Ann Arbor," an article about his unique background that he wrote, which was published in *Leaders in the Historical Study of American Education*.

Bill Heaston and James Fogarty, who both attended Creighton Prep, shared stories about Don Fiedler's career as an attorney, including the story of the doctored package of cigarettes.

Twice I interviewed Fred Scarpello, including once by phone, along with his wife, Barb. Together they told me their story and the difficulties Fred had in giving up football due to diabetes.

Chapter 5

I interviewed Mike McKim by phone and email three times in June and July 2012. Mike's memories of 1960 and his time at Creighton Prep were the most vivid of any player or coach I interviewed for this project; ironically, he had virtually no memories of the game against Omaha Central, at least from the first quarter on, because he was knocked out of the game with a concussion. I supplemented those conversations with news articles I found about his father and grandfather in the *Omaha World-Herald*. Those articles were published on July 7, 1943, August 17, 1944, December 11, 1948, and December 26, 1969. In Gabe Parks's memoir, *My Kansas-Nebraska Acts* (Omaha NE: Gabe Parks, 2005), I found information about some of Harry Truman's visits to Omaha. I completed my portrait of McKim's grandfather Edward by accessing the magnificent scholarship of David McCullough in *Truman* (New York: Simon & Schuster, 1992), his landmark biography of the president.

I interviewed McKim's former teammate Chuck Van Vliet by phone, and he corroborated McKim's stories of the hot summer job at Flinn Paving.

Frank Spenceri, McKim's quarterback tutor at Creighton

Prep, told me about learning the position from Don Leahy and competing with McKim for the job. So did Tom Heim, who charmed me by recounting the story of his broken ischium. Every former player from Creighton Prep that I interviewed told me about the significance of Don Leahy's trap pass and its effectiveness. I received my most helpful descriptions of the play from Sandy Buda, Frank Spenceri, and Don Leahy.

When I asked their teammates to name the toughest members of the Creighton Prep football team, the names Rich Vomacka and Walt Kazlauskas always came up. I interviewed Rich, but sadly I never had to opportunity to talk to Walt. The anecdote about Kazlauskas as a freshman in Dudley Allen's classroom came from Father George Sullivan, who retold the story at a Creighton Prep alumni luncheon.

Bill Heaston spent more than half a day with me recounting his Creighton Prep experience and sharing football stories. He also brought along a sizable collection of memorabilia that included an actual Creighton Prep demerit card. Also included were game programs from his football days; they were inscribed with handwritten notes from his aunt Sophia Rauber, who attended most of her nephew's games. Heaston was one of my best sources on Prep lineman Bill Pycha, and he told me about their time together working on the county road repair crew. Mike McKim aided in the profile and called him a "big roly-poly" kid. The 1961 *Jay Junior* published limited but valuable information on Pycha, too.

Chuck Van Vliet and Don Leahy told me about the captains' practices that took place at the University of Omaha before the start of the season and their importance in building team spirit.

Chapter 6

This chapter, along with other sections of part 2, relies heavily on the reporting of Don Lee and Gregg McBride of the

Omaha World-Herald. McBride and Lee both published previews of the Prep versus South game on Friday, September 9, 1960, and another article, titled "South Outlook Brighter for Applebee's 2d Year," published on September 7, provided background on the Omaha South lineup. Lee's recap of the game on September 10 was equally valuable in recreating the game.

I relied on the *Omaha World-Herald*'s 2010 book *Rosenblatt Stadium: Omaha's Diamond on the Hill* (Omaha NE: Omaha World-Herald, 2010), written by Steven Pivovar, for background information on the legendary ballpark and the men who ran it. Don Leahy, Bernie Berigan, and James Fogarty provided additional background on Charlie Mancuso and his longtime involvement in city sports. Jim Karabatsos shared his story of playing at Municipal Stadium on opening day in 1948, and I found the *World-Herald*'s coverage of the event in the following day's paper.

During a 2015 interview with John Bjelland, he told me about his first meeting with Bob Gaeta. He also shared notes from a condolence letter he wrote to Bob's widow shortly after Bob's death.

Dave Bouda gave me his personal history during our 2014 interview, including the story of his sudden rise to varsity football. Sandy Buda told me about his days playing at Creighton Prep, and he shared stories about his father Carl's playing days and experiences as a bar owner in Omaha. Buda and Bill Heaston described for me what Don Leahy's Saturday practices were like, including mandatory mass.

Steve Costello was one of the more interesting characters I learned about in writing this book. I first learned his name from Frank Spenceri, and then others, mostly former coaches such as Leahy, Allen, and Berigan, added more to his character profile. To learn more about scouting football, I read Steve Belichick's 1962 book *Football Scouting Methods* (1962; repr. Snowball Publishing, 2014).

The death of Nebraska governor Ralph Brooks was front-page news in 1960, and thus I deemed it worthy of inclusion into this section, relying on the *Omaha World-Herald*'s coverage of the event from the September, 10, 1960, edition of the paper. The following day's paper had equally comprehensive coverage of the Central game against Lincoln High and Bobby Williams. The September 26, 1960, edition of the *Central High Register* also published a recap of the game.

The discussion of the track and field battles between Gale Sayers and Bobby Williams draws from Sayers's own writings in *I Am Third*. When Williams died in 2012, Stu Pospisil wrote a lengthy piece about Williams's career for the *Omaha World-Herald*, which I also used to help write his profile. Larry Porter recapped it all in 1978 in an article titled "Sayers' Leap Still Incredible," published by the *Omaha World-Herald*.

Former Central running back and cornerback Gayle Carey had great memories of the Lincoln High game, in particular the moments when the momentum swung in Central's favor after a series of Lincoln High turnovers. Jim Karabatsos also remembered the game well and considered it a landmark moment in the Central season.

The details of Frank Smagacz's public relations maneuvers with Omaha sportswriters were told to me by Mike Smagacz. Mike and his sister Rose Parfitt also told me about the Wonder Bread award the family received. Smagacz's smooth relationship with the media was evident in reading between the lines of numerous columns published during his career, most of them complimentary of his dealings with sportswriters. Perhaps nowhere was this more evident than in Wally Provost's August 6, 1963, column about the beloved Central coach.

Longtime Omaha journalists Henry Cordes and James Fogarty vouched for Don Lee's sports reporting. So did retired journalist Larry Porter.

In my interviews with Jim Karabatsos, he explained how the

Central coaches divided the coaching responsibilities, including scouting, which he handled. Gayle Carey, Howard Fouts, and Maris Vinovskis helped compare and contrast Karabatsos and Frank Smagacz. Many former Central players remembered Smagacz's imitable speech patterns, including Howard Fouts and Tim Nelson. Nelson told me the story about Smagacz's practice of huddling on defense to keep warm.

Mike Smagacz and Rose Parfitt told me about Frank Smagacz's second job with the post office. Most former players recalled how hard Smagacz worked, including Roger Sayers, who found it fascinating how Smagacz still found time to coach at Central.

This section relies on recaps of the Creighton Prep versus Benson game from the *Omaha World Herald*, which was published on September 17, 1960, and the 1961 *Jay Junior*. I also studied Don Lee's preview of the Prep-Benson game in the *World-Herald* from September 16, 1960.

Former Prep lineman Bill Heaston shared what it was like playing against Benson quarterback and future Lincoln mayor Chris Beutler. My attempts to interview Beutler fell through. I came across an advertisement for "Coffee with Dick and Pat" Nixon in the September 13, 1960, edition of the *Omaha World-Herald*.

Heaston remembered the Benson game vividly, including the play where Bobby Gaeta scooped up Chris Beutler's fumble and ran it in for a touchdown, flanked by Walt Kazlauskas. Heaston's aunt Sophia Rauber kept handwritten notes of the game on a program, which Bill passed on to me for my research. Gaeta's Star-of-the-Week award was revealed in the *Omaha World-Herald* on September 21, the Wednesday after the game.

The sports reporting in the *Omaha World-Herald*, published September 17, 1960, guided me as I wrote about the Central-

South game. Student reporter Jeff Wohlner also had a fine recap of the game in the *Central High Register*, which was published on September 26, 1960.

On September 19, 1960, Gregg McBride published his first prep football rankings for the season in the *Omaha World-Herald*. These were both informative and insightful, as I learned from his writing the sort of criteria he used to rank the state's best teams.

I located the Central injury report in the September 22, 1960, *Omaha World-Herald* sports section. This complemented my interviews with Tim Dempsey, who told me about his mononucleosis and the lengthy recovery ahead of him. Dempsey also recalled his father's career at Central as the school's head engineer and his dad's close relationship with Frank Smagacz.

Chapter 7

For sources on Omaha history, I relied heavily on my personal interviews with former newsmen James Fogarty and John Prescott, who provided a great perspective on life in the city as a teenager in the 1950s and '60s.

The portions of the chapter about John Rosenblatt and the Omaha Plan draw from *Upstream Metropolis: An Urban Biography of Omaha and Council Bluffs* (Lincoln NE: University of Nebraska Press, 2007), written by Lawrence Larsen, Barbara Cottrell, Harl Dalstrom, and Kay Calame Dalstrom. I learned more about Rosenblatt in *Rosenblatt Stadium: Omaha's Diamond on the Hill*, by Steven Pivovar.

Upstream Metropolis contained helpful information about the origins of the Omaha Airport Authority and the new passenger terminal. I learned of its completion in the *Omaha World-Herald* in an article from October 4, 1960, titled "Air Terminal 30 Pct. Done."

I was able to access information about Omaha's population from the U.S. Census Bureau's website, and *Upstream*

Metropolis helped me reconcile the population changes with evolutions in city dynamics.

James Fogarty and John Prescott helped me understand the great significance of the stockyards' presence in Omaha during the middle of the twentieth century. Two magazine articles I located also assisted writing this section: "An American City's Dream," published in *Life* magazine on July 7, 1947, and "Nebraska," by Nebraska novelist Mari Sandoz, which was published in *Holiday* magazine in May 1956. The *Life* story gave a helpful perspective on the origins of the Omaha Plan.

Fogarty and Prescott also described for me the diversification of Omaha as a city and the distinctions among old Omaha, new Omaha, and South Omaha. I learned of the unfortunate fate of South Omaha mayor C. P. Miller in a *Sun* newspaper (of Omaha) retrospective that was published on April 13, 1957.

For the paragraph about Dwight Eisenhower and his obsession with golf, I drew from Curt Sampson's *The Eternal Summer* (1992; repr. New York: Villard Books, 2000). I found a small news item in the October 4, 1960, *Omaha World-Herald* about Eisenhower becoming the oldest man to occupy the White House.

I found movie advertisements for *Psycho* and *Ocean's 11* in the September 5, 1960, edition of the *Omaha World-Herald*. I accessed online a February 20, 2014, story about Omaha's famous steakhouses, titled "Omaha's Storied Steakhouses: The Closed, the Closing and the Final 5." I searched online for images of old steakhouse menus to locate prices of meat, and I found an old Angelo's menu from the era.

On Friday, October 7, 1960, the *Central High Register* ran a story about skirts and slacks, which I employed for the discussion of teenage fashion trends. The story also mentioned the new Brandeis store opening at Crossroads Shopping Center.

The section about the Ak-Sar-Ben racetrack was a product of years of listening to Omahans tell stories about the track's glory days. Readers will have to trust that I acquired a decent sense of the racing scene in those days. James Fogarty, who uncovered Omaha's bookmaking operations in a series of articles in the *Omaha World-Herald* that were published between 1973 and 1977, told me how the bookies would hide out to avoid being seen by police surrounding the track. Fogarty's stories won him statewide recognition from the Associated Press. I tracked down an Associated Press story online titled "Whereabouts Remain a Mystery" that I drew from to write about the vanishing remains of the racehorse Omaha. Again, I employed Mari Sandoz's "Nebraska" feature to describe the Ak-Sar-Ben coronation ball.

I relied heavily on Don Lee's article in the *Omaha World-Herald* following the Prep versus Westside game from September 24, 1960. The paper also published a helpful preview of the game on September 22, which I drew from. The latter article was the first time the story of Bill Pycha's illness surfaced in the news.

Numerous interviews helped me understand Bill Pycha and his battle with leukemia, including those with Don Leahy, Jack Jackson, Thomas Kearney, Mike Spinharney, Bill Heaston, Mike McKim, and Jim Phillips. I did some research online to learn about the history of treating children with leukemia in the 1960s. I found helpful information on the website of Leukemia and Lymphoma Research, a charity dedicated to improving the lives of those stricken with the illness. I also located an article from National Public Radio titled "How 2 Children with Leukemia Helped Transform Its Treatment," written by Amanda Aronczyk, published on March 24, 2015. One of Pycha's former teammates, John Bjelland, a physician, was another helpful source as I wrote about the situation.

When discussing game action from the Prep-Westside contest, I relied on interviews with Frank Spenceri, Mike McKim, and Don Leahy, who recalled the game well and explained Leahy's philosophy on playcalling. The 1961 *Jay Junior* provided me with the "sad day in Mudville" anecdote.

The rankings referenced in the opening paragraph of this section appeared in the *Omaha World-Herald* on September 26, 1960. In that same edition of the paper I found the news item about Tom Osborne's pro debut.

I was unable to identify the reason for the Central versus North game being postponed and moved to Benson, but some former players suspected it may have been the result of being without a field to play on.

The following day's newspaper contained a detailed write-up on the Central-North game, which I relied on for much of the recap. John Bozak, who attended the game, provided a spectator's perspective. I found a recap of the Central versus Abraham Lincoln game in the October 1, 1960, *Omaha World-Herald*. The catchy headline in anticipation of the Creighton Prep game I referenced ran atop page 3 of the *Central High Register* on October 7, 1960.

The recap of the Creighton Prep versus Omaha Tech game that begins the final section of part 2 relies on a news story about the game from the 1961 *Jay Junior* and an October 2, 1960, story from the *Omaha World-Herald*.

Creighton Prep quarterbacks Mike McKim and Frank Spenceri both explained to me the reason for the lineup switch in the Tech game; both indicated that Don Leahy made the move with an eye toward the upcoming game against Omaha Central.

The scene inside the Prep locker room at halftime was inspired by a photo published on page 54 of the 1961 *Jay Junior*. The expressions on the faces of those in the locker room tell a story; clearly, nobody on the Prep side felt comfortable with a tie score at intermission.

Many of the same sources I interviewed about Bill Pycha's illness two sections previous assisted with writing about his death, namely Thomas Kearney and Bill Heaston. Pycha's obituary made the *Omaha World-Herald* on Wednesday, October 5, 1960. Information about the student-led rosary and funeral was available in the 1961 *Jay Junior*. John Bjelland assisted me by confirming the date of Pycha's death and funeral with Blessed Sacrament parish in Omaha.

The quotes at the close of this section essentially speak for themselves, and I'm grateful for those who shared their feelings about Pycha's death with me, including Jack Jackson, Mike McKim, Mike Spinharney, and Don Leahy.

Chapter 8

The opening paragraphs of this chapter, about Don Leahy's precision as a football coach, were inspired by my interviews with Leahy's former players and colleagues, who attested to his attention to detail. Sandy Buda, Mike McKim, and Mike Fitzgerald were especially helpful in framing this description of the man. Leahy himself willingly divulged the extent of his preparation during our interviews.

I came across Don Lee's coverage of Leahy's speech to the Creighton Prep Mothers' Club in the October 6, 1960, *Omaha World-Herald*. I found it noteworthy that Leahy kept such a commitment during an otherwise busy and taxing week.

During our interviews, Leahy shared with me his game plan for playing Omaha Central, which included his strategy of assigning all three linebackers to Gale Sayers. Former players Dave Bouda and John Bjelland added detail to Leahy's recollections, and Bjelland provided the memory of the chalkboard in the Prep locker room with the week's game plan written on it.

This section begins with a hypothetical conversation that could have taken place between Frank Smagacz and Don Lee. Based on the frequency of their communications, I find the potential for the phone call and the subject matter—the upcoming football game—reasonable assumptions.

My description of other coaches preparing for Creighton Prep's trap pass was inspired by my interviews with Central assistant coach Jim Karabatsos, former Central player Tim Dempsey, and former Creighton Prep players Frank Spenceri, Mike McKim, and Sandy Buda.

Jim Karabatsos and Howard Fouts shared the story behind developing the halfback pass for Gale Sayers. I found other hints about Smagacz's game plan in an article from the *Omaha World-Herald* written by Steve Pivovar on September 23, 1981, titled "Prep-Eagle Tilt Friday Won't Equal '60 Gate." In our interviews, Karabatsos described the hype during game week and how he and Smagacz tried to insulate the team from it.

Jim Phillips, a former student manager at Creighton Prep, shared with me the story about running into the group of Central players at the Golden Spur one night during game week.

Don Leahy and Bernie Berigan provided background information on the series between Creighton Prep and Omaha Central, but neither could pinpoint the reason for the long gap in the series. Berigan shared with me a spiral-bound, privately published document titled "Creighton Prep 1955 Football," which contained scores from games in the Prep-Central series and a recap of the 1955 game where Frank Smagacz was penalized.

Terry Mollner, a member of the 1960 Creighton Prep football team, and Tom Marfisi, a Mollner contemporary at Prep, explained the bookmaking operations that went on throughout the city, including the South Omaha grocery store mentioned in this part of the text. James Fogarty's stories published in the 1970s also aided this background.

This section, which was the first part of the book I wrote, relies heavily on my interviews with former Creighton Prep players Mike McKim, Frank Spenceri, and John Bozak and Student Manager Jim Phillips. Others provided certain details; for instance, Bill Heaston described the moment when Don Leahy pulled him aside to watch the trainers apply tape to Fred Hoefer's leg. Dave Bouda recalled the silence of the bus ride.

Former players from Omaha Central have less vivid memories of their pregame routine; perhaps Frank Smagacz's laid-back personality had something to do with it. So, I had to mine elsewhere for information about the day's activities at Central. I found a short news item in the October 7, 1960, *Central High Register* about the student council selling beanies to promote school spirit.

Tim Dempsey told me the story of the telegram gag his father and Frank Smagacz concocted to help motivate the team.

The material about the presidential debate between Richard Nixon and John Kennedy began as a nice aside, but once I finished writing it I felt there was more to it. This was a case of one noteworthy event in American history (the series of first televised presidential debates) intersecting with a landmark event in Omaha history (the Prep-Central game). I remembered discussing the importance of these debates from my time as a journalism student, but I decided to go beyond my own experience and instead rely on news coverage of the debates in the *Omaha World-Herald* to frame the discussion. The paper had stories about the debates on October 6–8, 1960. Nearly a month before, on September 11, 1960, the paper ran "Title-less Nebraskan a Top Kennedy Aid," a lengthy profile of Ted Sorensen, written by Darwin Olofson. This was helpful in connecting Kennedy's appeal to Nebraskans. I kept tracking the race throughout the fall 1960 editions of the *Omaha World-Herald* and found other helpful news items along the way, including an October 16 story about Kennedy kissing his first baby on the campaign trail and two October 17 stories about Kennedy's rising momentum. The presidential sidebar seemed to tie together when I found an article in the *Central High Register* from November 18, 1960, about the Central straw poll. When I read that Frank Smagacz received one vote in the poll, I suddenly had a way of connecting the material to Central High and its football program.

Chapter 9

Throughout my work on this book, I kept hearing from former players and coaches that game film from the 1960 Creighton Prep versus Omaha Central game existed, yet nobody could account for its whereabouts. Some even confessed that they had seen it over the years. At one point I was unsure how I could ever write a believable description of the game without seeing the film, but as I continued interviewing its participants, I realized I had plenty of material to support a descriptive account of the game. Eventually I quit worrying about what I was missing and instead focused on what I had.

Don Lee's coverage of the game merited the bulk of the front page in the sports section of the October 8, 1960, *Omaha World-Herald*, and this lengthy story—and its sidebars—gave me great direction during my writing. It included anecdotes, such as the unknown man who called up to Central Police Station looking for Municipal Stadium and the good-luck llama, that I included in the chapter.

The rest of the chapter relied heavily on personal interviews. The list of those who contributed material for this chapter is lengthy: Don Leahy, Jim Karabatsos, Jack Jackson, James Fogarty, Fred Scarpello, Barb Scarpello, Mike Smagacz, Bill Heaston, Rich Vomacka, Frank Spenceri, Mike

McKim, John Bozak, John Bjelland, Tom Heim, Howard Fouts, Gayle Carey, Tim Nelson, Maris Vinovskis, Dave Bouda, Jim Phillips, Sandy Buda, Bob Marasco, Tom Jaworski, and Chuck Van Vliet.

Prior to starting my own research, Nate Driml, Creighton Prep's alumni director, furnished me with a copy of "The Greatest Game in Nebraska High School History," a story about the game written by Bill Pserros, which appeared in 1981 in serialized form in the now-defunct *Nebraska Sportsworld* magazine. While I was intent to conduct my own, original scholarship for this book, the Pserros article was a helpful background tool in understanding this story.

While I was fortunate to interview Gayle Carey in person for this book, his quotes about the hard hitting and pads popping came from a commemorative video produced by Creighton Prep in anticipation of the game's fiftieth anniversary.

The halftime scene in the Creighton Prep locker room was based on John Bozak's recollections; the Central halftime scene came from the collective memories of Jim Karabatsos, Gayle Carey, and Howard Fouts.

The story about the fan at the World Series game who nearly tumbled over the Forbes Field grandstand chasing after a foul ball was something I found on the front page of the October 7, 1960, *Omaha World-Herald*. The photo in the paper coincided perfectly with Jack Jackson's nearly suffering a tragic fall from the grandstands. The 1960 World Series was won by the Pittsburgh Pirates in seven games. Considering that in games two and six, both played at Pittsburgh's Forbes Field, the Yankees thumped the Pirates by a combined score of 28–3, and that for the series the Bronx Bombers doubled up Pittsburgh's total run output (55–27), the victory was as improbable as it was shocking. The staggering statistics are as much a tribute to Mickey Mantle and the Yankees' prodigious hitting talent as they are to the Pirates resolve.

Other helpful sources in writing this chapter were the 1961 *Jay Junior*, the 1961 *O-Book*, and the October 21, 1960, edition of the *Central High Register*.

My personal interviews with Bill Heaston inspired the first few scenes of this section, which includes the moments in the locker room after the game, at Gorat's Steakhouse that night, and at the homecoming dance.

The discussion of the bus ride back to Creighton Prep relied on my interviews with Heaston, Mike Fitzgerald, Don Leahy, and Frank Spenceri.

The 1961 *Jay Junior* published a helpful summary of the Prep homecoming activities, including the dance, which I used in writing that part of the story. Others interviewed who shared their feelings about that night were Rich Vomacka, Frank Spenceri, Howard Fouts, and Tim Dempsey. Dempsey told me about his recovery from mononucleosis and the fundraising campaign Gale Sayers started to help pay for his hospital bill. I validated the fundraising story by locating mentions of the "Tim Dempsey Fund" in the October 21, 1960, *Central High Register*.

This section relies strictly on interviews with John Bjelland and Mike McKim, who both shared their memories of the day after the game. In the final paragraph of this chapter, I took my own liberties—based mostly on my own experiences in athletics—as I wrote about the importance of upcoming games as each team moved through the season undefeated.

Chapter 10

After the scoreless tie, the *Omaha World-Herald* sports department gave its full attention to Central and Prep; write-ups that previewed each team's remaining games were published on October 10 and 12, the latter detailing Frank Smagacz's interactions with fans in the community.

Jim Karabatsos told me about the team's approach immediately following the game and Frank Smagacz's desire to keep the team focused.

I relied on the *Omaha World-Herald* (October 16) and the *Central High Register* (October 21) for summaries of the Central versus Tech game. On October 19, the *World-Herald* ran a short news item written by Don Lee titled "Vacation to End" that provided details about Central's practice schedule and the two-day break from practice Frank Smagacz gave his team. On October 27, Don Lee recapped the 19–13 Central victory over Benson in the *World-Herald*.

As part of a lengthy season-long recap in the November 18, 1960, edition of the *Central High Register*, student sportswriter Steve Gould wrote about the Central victory over Westside and Gale Sayers's pursuit of the intercity league scoring record. The *Omaha World-Herald* did the same on November 3 and 5, and both sources helped me write the passage about the Westside game.

For the opening paragraph of this section, I relied on Don Lee's postgame story in the *Omaha World-Herald* from October 8, 1960. It included the statistic about the game being the only time a Don Leahy team was held scoreless. I located Leahy's career record on the Creighton Prep website. During my interviews with Leahy, he told me how important he and his team felt it was to finish out the season undefeated.

A preview of Prep's game with Abraham Lincoln ran in the *World-Herald* on October 12, and a recap appeared on October 14. Both were helpful in writing about this game.

My interviews with Bill Heaston provided information I used to describe his illness—and overall mood—between games.

I relied on Mike McKim's memories of the Omaha North game, his first game back after his concussion, to write the Prep-North recap. The *Omaha World-Herald*'s coverage of the game on October 22 also helped me write this section; so did the 1961 *Jay Junior.*

Don Leahy recounted the Prep finale against Bishop Ryan. Considering the stakes, he and his team played it cool; they had little fear of Ryan. The *Omaha World-Herald* previewed the game on October 28 and recapped the outcome a day later; these stories, along with a write-up in the 1961 *Jay Junior,* were useful in writing this part of the chapter.

While newspaper and yearbook accounts of Central's final game provide important details, they didn't tell as complete of a story as the former players I interviewed. Howard Fouts, Gayle Carey, and Tim Nelson all recalled the team feeling almost embarrassed by their first-half effort against Lincoln Northeast. Nelson shared the story of Frank Smagacz's halftime speech, and former coach Jim Karabatsos gave me some insight into how he and Smagacz approached situations when the team needed motivation.

Additional insight into the Northeast game and the halftime situation came from Henry Cordes's story "'60 Gridders Remembered," which was published on November 21, 1980, in the *Central High Register.* There I found quarterback Jim Capellupo's quote about the halftime speech. I also relied on the *Omaha World-Herald*'s coverage of the game from the November 5, 1960, edition of the paper.

Chapter 11

Sportswriter Gregg McBride released his final statewide football rankings in the November 14, 1960, *Omaha World-Herald,* although the paper had already declared Omaha Central the intercity league champion four days earlier. McBride's column in the *World-Herald* on November 4, 1960, was a great inspiration to this section of part 4. In it, he addresses the issue of comparing records of teams who have played an uneven number of games, and he shares with readers the insights of David Ferguson, who's mentioned here, too.

The boxing adage I referred to comes from my own memory; I trust readers of this book will have heard it also. The same is true of another adage about gambling later in this section.

For the lengthy lists of postseason awards mentioned in this section, I relied on continuing coverage of the prep football season in the *Omaha World-Herald*, the season-end write-ups in the 1961 *Jay Junior* and *Central O-Book*, and a year-end story about the football team in the *Central High Register* that was published on November 18, 1960.

The discussion of Gale Sayers's college recruitment was based on Sayers's own writings in his autobiography, *I Am Third*, and the *Omaha World-Herald*'s coverage of the saga in late 1960 and early 1961, particularly stories published on January 27, 1961; August 20, 1961; September 3, 1961; September 9, 1961; and November 3, 1961.

I relied extensively on personal interviews to learn about the rest of the school year at Creighton Prep. Rich Vomacka shared the story about going out to get his all-state star with Walt Kazlauskas. Frank Spenceri and Bill Heaston told me tales from Legion baseball, and John Bjelland told me his reasons for giving up football to prepare for medical school.

Epilogue

Much of the background for the epilogue comes from my own memory, particularly as I followed the 2010 reunion of the 1960 Prep versus Central players. Other pieces of Omaha history mentioned come from my own memory and knowledge of the city's sports community. The *Omaha World-Herald*'s coverage of the 2010 events was also helpful.

My discussions with Creighton Prep alumni director Nate

Driml added background to my understanding of the events of that week.

Finally, my interviews with players and coaches who were there that night helped me complete the profile.

The demolition of Rosenblatt, which ends the book, was an event I witnessed personally—at least the first stages of it that July morning in 2012. At that point I had begun my work on this project and thought there could be tremendous value in seeing the event in person. Little did I know the scene would inspire the closing passage of my book.